STOP, POLICE!

Surviving an extraordinary police career and a lifesaving operation

By Richard Foster

Copyright

Paperback ISBN-13: 978-1-0682924-0-8

Editing by David Meikle
(Clever Writing) in Winchester. www.cleverwriting.co.uk

Book Cover by Chris Stone
(Stone Creative Graphic Design)
contact email: info@stone-creative.com

Book Title: STOP, POLICE!

Publisher: Moorhill Publishing

Edition: 1st Edition

Website: www.richard-foster.net
For more details from the author, news, updates and photos.

STOP, POLICE!

Trigger warning – Reader discretion advised

The events I have witnessed and are contained in this book include detailed anecdotes of real-life crimes, including topics such as domestics, violence, death, murder, sexual offences, suicide and other potentially disturbing content such as medical emergencies or mental health. While presented in a respectful and storytelling format, the subject matter may be upsetting to some readers.

Reader discretion is advised.

Table of Contents

Introduction

Everything in this book is totally true to the best of my recollection. I have decided to refer to people by first names or nicknames to help provide some anonymity. This is my life story, and not everyone may want to appear in it.

Those people who do feature in the book will hopefully recognise themselves and I thank each and every one for enriching my life. If you failed to appear, it is not because you were not important to me, but in writing an autobiography it would be impossible for me to recall and give accounts of each and every interaction I have had in my life.

I still love you all, and thanks for buying the book and taking the time to read it. If you feel you have missed out starring in this account of my life, please drop me an email with your recollection of the interaction we had together.

Firstly, it would be great hearing from you, and secondly it will be great to jog my memories. Thirdly, I might just write another book (if people want it?) and I would love to add you to it!

Almost on the wrong side of the law

My eyes hurt from the bright lights, so I blinked a couple of times. As my vision cleared, I could see clearly that I was smack bang in the middle of what looked like a TV cop show. I was sitting in the passenger seat of a sporty Vauxhall Nova SRi. My mate Brad was in the driving seat, gripping the top of the steering wheel with both hands. I could smell the 4-star petrol and hot brake pads.

He had borrowed his mum's car so that we could go to the cinema. The cinema, near Bury, Lancashire, was a recently opened American-style multiplex.

An '80s soft rock anthem was pumping out from the top-of-the-range 'Pioneer' cassette player. What had just happened? Were we in big trouble?

I looked out of the windscreen through the slight blue haze of cigarette smoke. It was about midnight and dark, but the car was stopped in the road at the entrance to a large roundabout outside the library, in the northern working class town of Rochdale, Greater Manchester, England.

We were overlooked by its imposing sandstone block Grade 1 listed, Gothic revival style Victorian-built Town Hall, as if being judged.

I rubbed my eyes as the strobing effect of the flashing lights on the marked police traffic car made my eyes glaze a little.

The actual flashing lights on the police car were nothing like modern police cars' highly visible strobing LEDs. This was the late '80s and the vehicle was a 'jam butty', as my brother used to say, with a red stripe down the middle of the car, sandwiched between the white paint. The car had two single blue lights positioned on each end of a roof bar.

Those revolving lights contained a single, stationary bulb around which a curved mirror revolved in a blue plastic dome. However, in the darkness it gave off an impressive light.

This police car had screeched across our path, blocking the road and our access to the roundabout. The sound of persistent sirens still filled the night air with a musical 'nee nah, nee nah'.

A police van had now stopped directly behind us, blocking us in and preventing our car from reversing. A sign reading 'Police' backwards was proudly illuminated on the front of the van.

A small panda car with a single blue light had pulled up alongside, in case we had any ideas about trying to leave by any other route. Brad switched off the engine as yet another traffic car arrived at the roundabout.

'Fuck,' Brad cursed under his breath.

'We're in the shit,' I added, stating the obvious.

I had a tight knot in my stomach and a sense of impending doom. Had the coppers mistaken us for someone else? Were they going to arrest us?

'I bet it was the police van we passed in Heywood,' I muttered.

'I didn't see one,' Brad replied, sounding surprised. 'What, a Bedford van?'

'Yeah,' I said, wondering how he hadn't spotted the van that had got us into this mess.

Heywood was made up of a couple of main roads, a few shops, lots of terraced housing and some cobbled streets. I had noticed the police van approaching the main road, from one of those streets in Heywood about 15 minutes ago, as we sped along, eager to get home from the cinema. I had glanced at its headlights as we drove by.

'Oh, yeah, I remember, there was a shitty clapped-out van behind us, I think. That'll be it.'

We could see the van was old, dented and scratched with some rust appearing on the wheel arches. Heywood was about four miles away, and it dawned on us that we had just been involved in our first police pursuit…being the ones pursued!

Little did I know at the time that I would be involved in many more high-speed police pursuits in the future.

A tall and imposing policeman, a traffic sergeant, emerged from the darkness and walked over to our car. He was joined by the driver of the Bedford van, a woman police constable.

Brad wound down the driver's window fully, so the sergeant could speak to him. In a serious and authoritative voice, the sergeant said, 'This officer has been following you since Heywood. What's the hurry?'

As Brad answered, I was thinking that surely the police had a faster van than that old piece of crap. Brad explained he had not seen the police van. This encouraged the sergeant to lead Brad down a long line of questioning, getting him to unwittingly admit to 'driving without due care and attention'.

The WPC was visibly shaking from the adrenaline coursing through her; being the end of the 1980s, car crime was rife with vehicles being nicked all the time. 'Joyriding' was all the rage.

She must have seen two 18-year-old lads in a fast hot hatch car, that we could never have afforded ourselves, driving too fast on the empty night-time road. She would have assumed the car was stolen. Unable to keep up with us, she had radioed the control room and called it in as a suspected stolen car being pursued.

'Is this your car?' the sergeant asked, peering at us as the blue lights flickered all around.

At the same time, the WPC was on her radio conducting a PNC (Police National Computer) check on the car registration to see if it was reported stolen. Luckily for us, we were in the clear.

'No, it's my mum's car,' Brad answered as the nervous female officer fed more details about us over the radio.

As the checks continued, he gave his mum's name, home phone number and address. Of course there were no mobile phones back then, so a call from the police would have woken up the entire household.

We waited anxiously. I wondered if Brad was insured? What about the MOT? Surely his mum would not have been driving around in a stolen motor.

Then my heart sank. My eyes had been taking in the scene during the police investigations on their radios. I looked around the car's interior and noticed something ominous in the centre console beside the gear stick. I had a horrible feeling in my gut.

Next to a packet of white Silk Cut cigarettes, I made out a small brown 'pebble' that I recognised instantly as a small lump of 'draw'. Oh my God, I thought. I am sitting in a car, surrounded by excited police officers hoping to arrest us, and I can see their opportunity straight in front of me.

To be fair, the amount of cannabis resin was tiny, but would that stop the cops from arresting us? What should I do? If I reached for the brown lump and hid it, the police might see it and arrest me. I did not fancy a night in the police cells. I dreaded a call home to my parents from the police; they would have gone berserk.

We were just two clueless 18-year-olds who had not been in trouble with the law before. I just sat there, trying not to look at the brown lump.

Luckily, the cops did not seem too bothered about me or in searching the car. They had their hearts set on arresting some 'joyriders' and recovering a stolen car. That wasn't going to be us, thankfully.

The sergeant returned to the driver's side and spoke to Brad.

'You are two very lucky boys. The car isn't stolen and if that van had been fitted with a calibrated speedo, we would have been prosecuting you for speeding.'

We looked over again at the dilapidated Bedford. What were they doing, driving around in such a dented, scratched old heap? Not a good look.

'Pay more bloody attention to the road,' the sergeant said sternly. 'Now get off home!'

'Yes, officer,' Brad replied in a relieved, squeaky voice.

We took this as our cue to leave. As soon as the traffic car moved out of the way, Brad drove off slowly.

Why did that sergeant let us go? Too much paperwork? Or was it that he could see we were two adventurous teenagers and not real criminals? I, for one, am grateful that he used his discretion that night. My life could have been so different if he had not sent us on our way.

On the drive home I laughed with Brad about the cannabis. He had also not noticed that the drug was on full view. But we were both aware that we had come close to a very different outcome, with lady luck on our side.

As my mind processed the events of that night, looking back, I think that a small seed had been planted: 'Bloody hell. The police. That looks like an exciting job!'

Surrounded by poverty

Context is important in decision-making and trying to understand people. I have always found listening to people's lives and stories interesting, and suspect that using my listening skills has helped me greatly as a police officer. It meant that I avoided jumping in at the deep end, making decisions without a full understanding of the situation or of the person I was interacting with.

To bring a little bit of context about me, and so you can understand who I am, it is important to tell you about my childhood, background, growing up, family and friends. Also, you will find out about my involvement in so many situations and incidents.

My parents connected back in 1959. They met in a pub, then went off to a dance. Dad was keen on Mum, and said he would take her out a week or so later. However, he didn't arrive to pick her up and the relationship looked to be a non-starter.

Well, a few days later, Mum went looking for my future father and found him in the same pub. In those days, ladies didn't go into bars on their own. Dad was taken aback to find her in there.

'I'm really sorry that I didn't take you out,' he apologised. 'I didn't have enough money.'

My mum gave him the benefit of the doubt as she liked him, so they started dating. Dad wanted to get married straight away, but Mum was more cautious. She was also juggling between jobs and, at the end of the day, she was only 18 years old. They kept in contact, all went well, and married in Bury a couple of years later.

I believe most people are a creation of the many outside influences that they encounter. We all make mistakes, and hopefully we all learn from them.

I believe this continued learning stays with us our whole life, forming and moulding us into who we are today. The next chapters will be a selection of some of the influences that have made me who I am.

My earliest childhood memory was from the time I was in the South of France with my parents, aged two or three years old. My parents had been on a long, extended holiday and were considering living in France permanently. It was very hot and sunny, and I remember my parents being happy; I was just enjoying their love and being in their presence.

I recall sitting on an old military cannon on the wall of a French fortification, looking out to sea. I was dressed in a summery T-shirt and shorts, with the sun beating down and a massive, wide smile across my face. As for me, I was king of the castle!

My childhood was really happy, not wanting for anything or having the feeling that I was missing anything. I felt loved by my parents and siblings, and was well provided for. That is not to say that my parents were well off or rich, because they were not.

My dad had been in the army and would often tell exciting stories at the dinner table of some of his adventures abroad. After leaving the army, he became a long-distance lorry driver and would be away for weeks at a time, as he drove and transported goods in HGVs all over Europe. This was all part of a normal life to me, having to get used to him being away from home, but also this created a strong bond between me and my mum. She was left looking after my brothers, sister and me.

As for my dad, he was a tall, big, strong friendly character, or so I thought. In my early teenage years, friends would call around to see if I wanted to go out. But most of them were a little scared to knock on the door, due to his presence and deep voice. This made me smile, as I knew there was nothing to be scared of, really.

By this time, my dad had finished working as a lorry driver, and my parents had a business running a fish and chip shop.

My mum and dad ran a few chip shops in their time. They had one in Whitworth near Rochdale; in Sandy Lane on the Greave Estate near Rochdale Football Club; and another at the top of Yorkshire Street, where I worked as a teenager.

At the Greave Estate 'chippy' I learned to ride a bike, aged about six or seven.

The back garden had a large grassed area. Down the middle there was a path, leading to a back gate. My brother Geoff taught me how to ride a bike there.

At first, I rode along with stabilisers. One day, without me knowing, my brother took off one of the stabilisers. The idea was that I would cycle along the path, gain confidence and then he would take off both stabilisers.

So I cycled like mad, not knowing the stabiliser had been taken off, and sure enough I started to wobble and veer, fell off and grazed my knees.

My brother actually did me a favour, to be fair. I learned very quickly that, if you fall off your bike, you get straight up and you just go again. That is what I did.

It was such an important lesson. You need to grow up with a bit of resilience and just get on with it.

In the police, as you'll discover later, they took my stabilisers off in the end!

The Greave Estate building was a takeaway fish and chop shop in a row of other shops. My parents had saved up £500 to buy the lease, and that was a lot of money back in the '60s and '70s. Their bank manager provided the other £500 needed to secure the deal.

The chip shop environment was a big part of my childhood. After all, I was born in a fish and chip shop! Customers from all walks of life, many working in local factories, would come to buy their evening meal. We opened at 11am, through lunchtime, then a break for a couple of hours, followed by the teatime and evening sessions.

The chip shop business came about because Dad would often visit cafés while he was driving lorries. One day, he stopped at a café in Dorset and saw that someone had dropped a fried egg on the floor. A few days later, on his return journey, the egg was still there. He thought, if someone can make a living when they are totally useless, he should have no problems.

The Greave Estate chippie was basic, to say the least, with an outside toilet. We were the only people who lived and worked in a shop there! I slept in my parents' bedroom. I was the third child to come along, as Mum and Dad already had my sister Susan and my brother Geoff. I wasn't too popular in my early years, as my dad had freshly decorated the bedroom, but I obviously didn't like the smell of the wallpaper. I just tugged at the newly decorated wall and pulled the wallpaper off around my cot!

Many people didn't have proper cooking facilities in their homes, so they came in for their takeaway meals. My parents got to know everyone on the estate and, for the large part, most were great people living in difficult circumstances.

As an example, every Friday, one family would always buy their 'tea' as we called it 'up north'. The family only appeared to own one bowl, as the father would arrive first and order his chips and gravy. After paying and receiving his food, he would go home to eat it. The bowl would go backwards and forwards as other people in the family had their chips.

Another family came in with a green plastic container. The hard-working tub made several appearances during the evening, being filled with chips for various members of the family.

Some of our customers wanted what was called 'pea wet', the liquid surrounding mushy peas. My parents poured that over their chips and added some fish scraps. Local people couldn't afford the peas or the fish, so Mum and Dad added those bits and bobs and just charged for the chips.

For those with some more money, we provided takeaway sandwiches with fillings including bacon and egg. That was an unusual service in those days.

I would like to point out that we did serve our takeaway food in cartons and paper, but some people preferred the meals served straight into their own plates, bowls and pots.

The Yorkshire Street shop was broken into a few times. Thieves would try to steal anything of value, but were also after cooking equipment, especially a large, expensive commercial microwave. Dad managed to divert interest away from the microwave by putting a notice on the door saying it was out of order. A brilliant bit of social engineering that worked a treat.

I had an early experience of violent crime in my local area, with a stabbing just along from our chip shop. A newsagent, Alan Chadwick, stabbed two robbers as they tried to raid his premises. His family were also in the shop at the time.

Alan was standing at the counter when two men in their 20s came in, demanded money, and started to beat him up.

Well, he grabbed a flick knife, kept behind the counter for opening bundles of newspapers, and stabbed the two men. One of the robbers collapsed and died at the scene and the other was seriously injured.

You can imagine the fury in the local community when Mr Chadwick was charged with murder and attempted murder. He was kept in custody for 10 days. There was even a petition with nearly 8,000 signatures, calling for his release.

I remember the celebrations, even in the chip shop, when it was announced that the prosecution charges had been dropped.

My first real memories of home were growing up in deprived areas of Rochdale. I was exposed to poverty and all the social problems associated with these types of large estates including crime, substance abuse, violence and general misery. However, I was only about five to 10 years old at this time, so none the wiser and this was my 'normal'. I just got on with it and did not consider where I lived to being any different to anybody else.

Eventually, we moved out of chippy accommodation and into a semi-detached house in the village of Norden, outside Rochdale. We had a car port down the side of the house and a drive leading down to a garage with a large wooden door.

If I close my eyes and think back to that time, I can still smell the inside of the garage, with paint and turpentine used for painting the fence. There were also lots of mysterious cardboard boxes stored up on high shelves.

As an inquisitive boy, I explored the garage to uncover what was stored in those boxes alongside the bikes, skateboard and lawnmower. Strangely, most of the boxes were full of products such as washing up liquid bottles and other household consumables.

To be frank, we had about 60 bottles of washing up liquid, which would have been more than enough to keep a restaurant's pots and pans clean for years. What the hell did we have so much of this for? I noticed a couple of the boxes had slight damage to the corners, with some of the product leaking out.

When I asked my parents about the unusual goods in the garage, it was explained to me as items that had 'fallen from the back of the lorry'.

I knew, at an early age, that this meant 'stolen'. However, these had literally fallen from the back of my dad's lorry and were now not wanted, or so I was told!

The start of my learning curve

I started school when I was five years old, close to Norden, a couple of miles from Rochdale. It was a C of E school in a relatively nice area. My mum worked in the kitchens in the Catholic school opposite, preparing school dinners. For some reason I arrived a week or so after the term had started.

I recall being walked into the classroom, not knowing anybody and feeling a little bit wary and worried. But the teacher held my hand and showed me around, making me feel at home.

She introduced me to someone who was playing in a sandpit. This person was called Jon or sometimes Jonny, and he became a lifelong friend. Sometimes you meet someone in your very early years and they can become friends for your whole life, as with Jon.

Jon lived in a two-up two-down terraced house with a small yard out the back. If you can imagine Coronation Street, it was in the same style as that.

When you walked through the front door, you went straight into the living room. Immediately the smell of the open fire hit you. Jon's mum put a newspaper up against the fireplace to light the fire, and I remember seeing a fireball of flames shooting up the chimney. Also, there was the strong aroma of pipe and cigarette smoke. Jon's grandfather lived with the family at the time; in the late '70s and early '80s, most adults seemed to smoke.

School was definitely different from what education is like today. I never really enjoyed school and, looking back, it was probably down to my kinetic learning style or the teachers I had. School was one of those places I had to go to; there was no way of escaping from that environment.

I got on with the subjects that I liked, not messing about. I enjoyed making friends and really valued those acquaintances. My only complaint was that we couldn't chat in the classroom!

I tried my best to get out of subjects that I didn't like such as French, PE or Religious Education. Our term was to 'wag it', which meant bunking off and missing a lesson. This was when the school day became exciting.

At Oulder Hill, my senior school, the building backed onto a golf course. We could sneak onto the course and hide in bushes close to one of the greens. We saw golfers coming out of the clubhouse and preparing to tee off. Some of them had caddies, advising them on how to play their shots.

And so we lay in wait. As soon as balls landed around the green, we made our move. We dashed out to collect as many balls as we could and then shot off back into the bushes with our trophies. Our ears were ringing with the yells from the golfers who had played impressive shots, only for their balls to disappear. They were waving their clubs at us, furiously.

With the balls safely in our schoolbags, we would run off to another part of the course to avoid capture and inflict more damage. Another group of angry golfers and more balls for our expanding collection. Much better than enduring some boring lessons!

Being entrepreneurial, on other days we would to go to the clubhouse and offer our services as caddies. Most of the players didn't have a caddy, so they liked the idea of someone looking after their clubs and giving advice. It made them look more professional.

Of course, we had no idea what we were doing but we were quick learners and went out with the real amateurs. We would select a club for them and suggest how to hit the shot. It made them feel really special. If we charged £5 for a round, often that would become £10 with the tip: a massive amount of pocket money in those days.

Our 'scams', if you like, were far from over. To add insult to injury, we sold the balls that we had nicked from the course. That meant we had the caddy fee, the tips, plus cash for the nearly new balls acquired by devious means.

If we were challenged by the school about non-attendance, we had standard excuses. For example, we could say we fell over in the mud playing football and had to go home to get changed. The checks on attendance were nothing like they are now. As far as I am aware even my parents had no idea that we were skipping lessons to take part in our various dodgy schemes.

As a kid, I learned quickly to keep my head down. I recall one boy who had been naughty. The teacher was going crazy at this child, shouting and screaming over something that had been so minor.

The male teacher picked up the child by the scruff of his jumper and lifted him off the floor with one arm. He held the front of the jumper near his neck, until this boy's head hit the false ceiling and was pushed up through the large white ceiling tiles.

Punishments at school were different back in the 1970s, and I remember thinking: I do not want that to be me.

At senior school, or 'upper school' as we called it, punishments were particularly severe. I always thought of myself as a fairly good kid, but I failed to escape the wrath of one teacher.

In the winter, there was a rule. If it had been snowing, we were allowed to play outside. However, we were not allowed to throw snowballs at the front of the school. Even to this day, I can't understand the difference between throwing a snowball at the front of a school or at the rear of a school.

On one wintry day, it had been snowing heavily overnight and the ground was a blanket of frozen, crisp snow. It was fantastic and the walk to school had been so much fun with my friends, playing in the white paradise.

However, my geography teacher, during the lunch break, had seen me throwing a snowball somewhere at the front of the school. That afternoon I went into my geography lesson and sat down. Each of the classroom tables sat two pupils to each, and I had just placed my bag and coat on the back of the plastic chair. My geography teacher called out, 'Richard, come to the front of the class.'

I dutifully stood up and walked to the front of the class, not knowing I was going to be made an example of. With a vindictive smile on his face, he said, 'What are the rules about throwing snowballs at school, Richard?'

I replied sheepishly, 'Err, I'm not sure, sir.'

'You cannot throw them at the front of the school. Everyone knows that! So why did I see you throwing snowballs, this lunchtime, at the front of the school?'

My mind was racing to find the correct answer. This was now damage limitation time.

I replied, 'I dunno, sir?'

I know, I know. This was not my finest hour in testing my speed of thought. In some sadistic, sick power trip, the teacher picked up a metal waste paper bin and put it down by my feet at the front of the class. Everyone looked on in silence. I stood there with my head bowed down in a submissive stance.

'Go on. STAND IN THE BIN, BOTH FEET,' he shouted.

Looking down, I could see about 20 sticky balls of used chewing gum, of different colours, some white, grey and some pink, that had been discarded by pupils caught with gum in previous lessons. I carefully stood in the bin, which was, quite frankly difficult, with my size 14 feet. I had to stand like a kind of uncomfortable, lanky ballerina on the balls of my feet, as I felt my weight squash down on the gum underneath me.

Without warning, the teacher turned his body quickly, punching me in the stomach with all his might. His clenched fist struck me with so much force that I was knocked back immediately, winded in the stomach. However, I had no time to worry about that, as I was now like a felled tree that had just been chopped down, and was slowly falling to the ground. My body crashed to the floor with a loud thud.

'Bastard,' I thought as I stood up. I brushed myself down and was told to sit at my desk.

It was that particular teacher's method of humiliating someone. If OFSTED had been in existence back then, I'm not sure what they would have made of the justice system at the school. I very much doubt they would have awarded the school an 'outstanding' grade.

I may not have been the most academic kid, but made up for this by having lots of friends and great friendships. That was the joy of school for me; not the academic part, but learning the art of communication, friendships, negotiation and dealing with conflicts and dramas. I loved meeting new people and still do.

School is so much more than the actual academic learning. With the freedom I had, I was pushing boundaries to see how far I could go, and what advantage I could gain. On occasion this got me into a few scrapes, rather than real trouble.

As the youngest child in the house, I was able to subconsciously learn from the mistakes that my sister and two older brothers had made. I was making continuous mental notes to avoid making the same mistakes…in getting caught, at least.

This provided me with a childhood that prevented me from getting into any real, serious trouble.

Why did everything happen to me?

My gangling, ungainly frame has encountered quite a few calamities throughout my life, as you will discover later. My first real injury as a child came when I was running home one day to the chippy aged about five years old. My mum and I had just got off the bus from visiting the town centre, and I had been bought a fairly large, colourful, plastic trumpet.

I was so excited about this new toy. I was blowing into the trumpet mouthpiece, arms outstretched to the side, and making an awful loud racket. It was great fun! Being so excited, I was trying to run home while holding the trumpet with one hand and blowing into it.

This was really difficult, running and playing an instrument. Everyone knows that some men are not good at multi-tasking. I decided to put the whole mouthpiece of the trumpet into my mouth as I ran, so that I could swing my arms to help balance and run quickly down a short hill.

Suddenly I felt myself falling forward and could only guess I had stumbled over my own feet. My face slapped down on the concrete pavement, pushing the trumpet mouthpiece deep into my throat, cutting open the inside of the back of my mouth.

Stunned, I looked down at my hands and knees to see that they were all grazed and bleeding. I was in tears. Suddenly, from total joy and happiness, I was completely distraught!

Yes, it was still the '70s, so I was wearing short trousers, as all children seemed to back then. Normally and very fashionably made of brown corduroy, as I recall.

In shock and a little pain and unable to speak properly, my mum stood me up and brushed me down. After a quick triage assessment of my condition, looking me up and down, and with a quick wipe of a handkerchief, she announced that 'You'll be all right', and we carried on walking home. No trip to a hospital, no accident and emergency department.

What was called for was the best medicine, comprising a large bowl of cooling ice cream for my throat. This was the best treatment ever.

Now, you might think that not taking me to an A&E department was irresponsible. In my opinion, it was not. I could clearly still talk and eat, and nothing had snapped off in my throat. I'm sure that a looming evening shift at the chippy for my mother had nothing to do with it.

What it did teach me was another lesson in resilience. Sometimes you just had to brush yourself down, put on a smile and get on with life. This was an important lesson for me to learn at such a young age.

My first exposure to real sport came at middle school. I was tall for my age and the expectation was that I would be good at sport, which I was not; maybe average at best. When I took part in sports like basketball, which everyone felt I should 'ace' due to my size, I found I was all gangly arms and legs, and not very co-ordinated.

I tried out other sports such as sprinting and rugby, but again failed to impress the teachers or myself for that matter, with my lack of skill or speed.

One of the sports lessons most of the kids feared was cross-country running. For me, this was something I found I could tackle fairly well and actually enjoyed. The cross-country course ran for more than two miles over a number of Pennine hills behind the school, down a quiet country lane, and finally back onto the tarmac for the final stretch of road towards the school.

This was great fun, as on the whole we were left unsupervised to make our own way around the course which was marked out. Cross-country running was never really carried out during the summer months and was always in the cold and wet weather of winter.

My arms and legs would turn a shade of pale white and pucker up like chicken skin as it was often so cold. This was a great motivator to get moving, as the running really warmed you up.

I often saw some of the kids stopping and crouching to shield themselves from the weather behind high dry-stone walls, used to separate the sheep and cows in the farmers' fields. An occasional puff of cigarette smoke would rise up like an angry dragon from the huddle, and I would realise they had just taken this sports lesson as an opportunity for a quick 'fag break'. I had no interest in this, and would pound along like an odd-looking gazelle.

Legend has it that two girls once got a lift in a taxi at the top of the road near the start of the course and were dropped off near the finish to avoid running the whole route. That is how much this lesson was hated by some.

On one particular run, the weather had created a scene like something from the classic 1981 horror film, *An American Werewolf in London.* It was bitterly cold and damp, but the air was fairly still.

A thick fog had rolled in and engulfed the surrounding hills and all the cross-country course. I could not see a thing in front of me; it was a real 'pea souper'. I would have even been happy to take shelter in the pub in that film, *The Slaughtered Lamb,* it was that bad.

Having run the route many times before, I was happy and confident that I could find my way around the course and get back to the school. On this occasion I was making good time and tackling the final 'off-road' stage, running down a steep grassy hill with two other competitors by my side.

My mind began to drift off and I started to imagine myself as one of the iconic runners from the 1981 film, *Chariots of*

Fire. Why the heck not? I was dressed the same as the athletes in the scene as they ran across the beach in training.

I was dressed in my school PE kit which comprised white shorts, a white T-shirt and white plimsolls. As my mind drifted, and I was starting to hum the theme tune of the film, disaster struck.

While running down the hill, I was abruptly brought back to my senses. I found myself flying through the air, head first, doing a rather poor impression of *Superman*.

A pain was running through my body, but my brain could not quite understand what had happened. My flying motion stopped suddenly as I was pulled back by my feet.

My brain kicked in and I realised what was happening. The fog had reduced visibility, and I was running fast downhill without paying attention. I had run straight into an electric fence, which had not only shocked me, but lifted me clean off my enormous feet.

The wire was now tangled on my feet and pulling me backwards like a really rubbish bungee jump on wet grass. The wire was making a loud 'cracking' noise against my skin, and I was break-dancing on the ground because of the continuous electric shocks. I could hear a loud cheer and catcalls from other students who had witnessed me running into the electric fence.

Yes, that is the great thing about British social culture. If anyone drops an item, falls over or does something embarrassing, before someone comes to your aid and helps you, expect them to take the piss out of you by cheering first!

I find this quite amusing and one of the great things about living in Great Britain.

Unperturbed by my predicament, I got up and dusted myself down. I took a bow and carried on running to the end, ignoring my pain and minor grazes. At least the werewolf never caught me.

Oulder Hill was a massive school, as I recall, with well over 1,000 pupils from 11 to 16 years old. It was also a large community school, which meant it had a giant swimming pool and substantial leisure complex including a theatre named after Rochdale icon Gracie Fields. Towards the front of the building there was a nursery with its own private outside space. This was surrounded by a six-foot high brick wall.

The outside space was the size of a basketball court, but more circular. When the toddlers weren't around, we invented a game called 'death square'. This was a game of danger and daring, holding your nerve and displaying lots of skill. It involved a tennis ball or football being dropped into the enclosed area.

One person would start off the fun, with everyone else also in the square. This person would kick the ball and see if they could hit anyone else who was running around. If the ball made contact with someone, the ball kicker and everyone else would chase the victim who had just been hit. He had to get out of the square, desperately clambering at the walls to escape, with the other boys in hot pursuit.

The unfortunate victim could be kicked as hard and as many times as the pursuers wanted. If the victim managed to scramble to safety, he joined up again with the others and became an attacker. And so the game went on until there was just one of us standing.

As you can imagine, this game was not sanctioned or authorised by the school in any way. It was quite normal for someone to be dragged off the wall by their feet, landing face first on the ground, to be then kicked repeatedly.

Some might call it violent. Some might call it dangerous. Some might call it downright stupid. We just saw it as character building.

One day, walking home from secondary school, I clutched an envelope containing my school report. I was going to give it to my mum. I had no concerns about the content of the report. I had been working hard, not bunking off or anything at this stage, and keen to find out what the teachers really thought of me.

So I met Mum at the Co-op store in the village of Norden. She would do the family shopping every other day and we would walk home, a mile or so, carrying the packed disposable bags. I remember vividly the plastic cutting into my fingers, carrying those heavy bags.

Mum wondered why I was looking battered and bruised. I confessed to a fight with a local lad, who was well known as a bully. He had been picking on me repeatedly during the day. This had culminated in a bit of a fracas outside the school with him name-calling and pushing me until I was at the end of my tether.

Although I wasn't stockily built, I was very tall. I reached out and pushed him back in front of his friends, a gathering crowd and the queue at an ice cream van. I shouted at him to leave me alone. He fell backwards, really embarrassed, making him even more angry.

Suddenly he came at me with his right fist, punching me in the right eye. My head was stunned and I felt immediate pain as my eye started to swell. I couldn't see clearly as the eye started to glaze over. The pain was intense.

This was probably the first real fight I'd had, apart from with my siblings. I felt a real sense of anger and a red mist came over me. I dropped my schoolbag and puffed out my chest, clenching my fist.

I span round and hit him clean in the face, connecting really well and feeling the pain in my knuckles as he stumbled backwards. He wasn't expecting any sort of retaliation. I'm not really a fighter, but I've always believed in standing up for myself.

I took this opportunity to 'leg it'. I snatched my bag and ran as quickly as I could along the road to Norden and the Co-op. I needn't have worried as he didn't chase after me. On reaching my mum, the eye had blackened completely and there was a swollen bubble underneath. I could barely see out of it. Mum said I should dust myself down and not worry. Because I had fought back, she said, it wouldn't happen again.

When we arrived back with the shopping, I emptied out the bags and laid a packet of butter on the table. You had to make it last. To make things fair, the butter was divided up amongst the family at the start of the week.

Everyone seemed to like butter, and it became a mode of currency as the week went on. Gradually, the portions diminished, being used for toast or baked potatoes. You could trade a portion of butter for favours, household chores or other treats such as sweets and desserts.

On this occasion, before the butter was divided equally, Mum opened the envelope with my school report. She started laughing and I was concerned. Why was she laughing so much?

The teacher had kindly written in the report: 'Richard has been an absolute pleasure to teach this year, always giving 100% effort with a challenging task or helping a classmate who is struggling. He approaches every situation with enthusiasm and determination. What truly sets him apart is his kindness and consideration towards others. He is never involved in any conflicts and offers a helping hand when needed. He is a credit to both his family and the school, and I have no doubt that he will continue to shine.'

Mum looked at the gigantic shiner on my face and smiled again!

In my previous schools, I had always enjoyed a good school dinner. When I moved up to senior school, I was given £1 a day to purchase my lunch from the canteen. I wanted to save this money, although it was difficult to get through a whole school day without feeling hungry.

We would often go off to the local supermarket and purchase a basic packet of custard creams for about 30p, thus saving 70p a day to be spent on other things. Not the healthiest of choices, I know!

Occasionally, we would go to the local chip shop, a Chinese takeaway, to buy bags of chips.

Every time we went in, the lady serving us asked if we wanted a fork with our chips. Like some *Carry On* film from the seventies, she asked if we would like a fork, in a strong Chinese accent.

We stood there giggling, as she said the same thing every time and we gave the same answer. She must have experienced this about 1,000 times, but she always smiled politely while we fell about laughing.

The money we were saving mounted up, and we pooled our cash together. On the odd occasion, when we were bunking off school, we would look to buy some booze. Now aged 14 or 15, this was the hobby of choice for our friendship group. As I was the tallest, everyone assumed that I looked the oldest, which I did not. I have always been blessed with a rather young-looking face, not even shaving for a while in my younger years!

So the group of friends decided that I should go to the off-licence and purchase some alcohol. They were all older than me, by about a year, so they held the power and my complaints fell on deaf ears. To me, it seemed like a stupid idea to send the youngest person in to buy the booze.

Next, they came up with an idea to dress me up and make me look older. One of my pals took me to his house where he borrowed his dad's long trench coat and flat cap. I looked ridiculous, more like something out of *Inspector Gadget*.

Anyway, feeling totally out of place, I strolled up to the front door of the off-licence and peeped inside. I looked at the shelves, probably resembling a worried shoplifter as I glanced around. I was feeling anxious and self-conscious, while at the same time trying to play it cool.

I tried my best to appear as if I was meant to be there; a middle-aged man buying booze during the day. I selected a two-litre bottle of strong white cider. This was the type that, if spilled on a varnished work surface, would take the veneer straight off.

I placed the bottle on the counter and fumbled in my pocket for the coins. I counted out the 10ps and 20ps that we had saved up. It was as if I had just broken into a piggy bank. As I carefully placed the coins on the counter, the shopkeeper looked at me with total lack of interest. He picked up the coins, put them in the till and allowed me to walk off on my merry way.

All my mates were ecstatic. We spent the rest of the afternoon at a friend's house, watching poor quality videos and getting slightly tipsy. Most of the Betamax videos were 'knock off' copies of films from the time, like *Rambo*.

However, we were more interested in one particular video that appeared to come from a home movie camera; not many people had those in the eighties. As soon as this unmarked video started to play, a grainy static and unprofessional interference appeared on the screen.

The mate who lived there quickly jumped up, appearing to recognise the video. All we could see was a wall and the edge of a bed. He dashed across urgently to reach the video player and ejected the tape before we could see what was on it.

As you can imagine, this led to much ribbing and mickey-taking. Was it a video of his parents being naughty? We never found out.

Danger, danger, danger!

When we had time in the evenings or weekends during the long school holidays, Jon and I went off out to explore the countryside. One of the best bits about kicking around with Jon was that we could go on adventures and explore the environment around us. Jon lived just outside Rochdale, on the edge of magnificent countryside surrounded by the Pennines, loads of fields, dells and reservoirs. Such a treat for young explorers.

Locally there were old mills and lots of other interesting places to capture our attention. One particular mill, heading up from Norden on the way to Greenbooth reservoir, was dwarfed by a massive chimney. This red brick building was completely derelict.

The building seemed totally out of place within a dell, surrounded by trees and bushes, not roped or fenced off. We were free to explore wherever we wanted. We spotted a tunnel near the chimney and decided to have a look. We went inside, struggling to see anything in the eerie darkness.

We crawled along, me crouching right down because of my height, and kept going until we reached the foot of the chimney stack. Back in the open air, after about 50 yards, we looked up and saw the top of the majestic chimney with birds fluttering around up there. It was such an adventure, like being in a foreign country.

There was no Health and Safety back then! Jon and I were trying to be adventurous, in the way we had seen on television and in films, particularly war movies. We found a manhole cover and a set of metal steps that went down to goodness knows where. It seemed strange to see all of this in the countryside.

We clambered down the steps, 20 feet or so, to find a sewer system. The air was dank and wet. The smell wasn't particularly bad, surprisingly. It seemed to be more of a storm-type drain.

As we delved deeper and deeper into this subterranean world, we were questioning if this was a safe thing to do. Were there hidden fumes that we couldn't see or smell? Would we collapse, struggling for air? What would happen if one of us slipped and broke a leg? Who would come to rescue us?

As a result, we scared ourselves half to death and decided this wasn't our greatest of moments. We headed back the way we had come, through the tunnel and out into the open air again. Safe and sound, ready to tell this story of daring and adventure to our friends!

I mentioned Greenbooth Reservoir just now. It really was a special place for us. Nowadays in that area, you can look towards the top of the rolling hills and see giant wind turbines slowly turning their massive blades, generating electricity. Back then, there was no sign of that.

All you could see was the Victorian-built dam that made up the reservoir. We headed up to the reservoir and went swimming, often jumping off the high sides. What made this more exciting than anything else, other than having fun with your friends in freezing cold water, was a massive hole like a drain. It was about 10 metres in circumference, like a huge bath being emptied.

The sense of danger, being able to swim close to this hazard, but not too close, was vast. There were large signs warning us not to swim which we heeded to a certain degree; none of us felt brave enough to dice with certain death by being sucked into the plughole. The reservoir itself was split into a number of smaller reservoirs, with the last one built in the 1950s when a village called Greenbooth existed. The valley was flooded, consigning the village to history.

Legend has it that, on a hot summer's day when the water is low, you can see the top of the church spire. Many a person claimed they had witnessed this phenomenon. However, that is utter nonsense, because there was never a church in the village. But when did the truth ever get in the way of a good story?!

I can recall another incident involving Jon. Close to his house there was a building site, again with no Health & Safety or any precautions. There was no metal fencing to keep people out. As far as we were concerned, it was our playground.

We could explore partially-built houses, climbing ladders onto the various floors. There were no windows, with walls missing. What an amazing experience for seven and eight-year-olds to burn off energy and try out new skills…like learning to drive.

On this particular building site, we spotted a dumper truck. We climbed on board, unlike nowadays where there would be a number of crime prevention measures in place and anti-theft devices. There was nothing of the sort back then.

There was just a keyhole on this particular dumper truck to switch on the ignition. It was a simple, basic machine with a steering wheel, pedal and brake. A gearstick made it go backwards and forwards.

There were no keys to be seen. We imagined what it would be like to drive this giant yellow beast. We were both in the Cubs and Scouts and always told to have a 10p piece in our pockets in case of emergency. There were no mobile phones back then. The idea was that you could go to a phone box, on most street corners, call back home and ask for help. That was before the pips started and you ran out of time.

We studied our 10p piece. It looked similar in shape and size to the slot where the key went on the dumper truck. We turned the coin and, bingo, the engine fired up! What a basic design, for a coin to work in the ignition!

The engine roared and thick black diesel smoke billowed from the exhaust pipe, sticking up into the air behind us. We both sat there, impressed with our efforts. Slowly and gingerly, I pressed the accelerator pedal. Sure enough, the dumper lurched forward. I pressed the brake and it came shuddering to a halt.

Slowly building our confidence, within a few minutes we were happily driving the vehicle around the site, pretending we were taking part in a Lombard RAC Rally, much to our delight.

The building site wasn't overlooked, so no one could see what we were up to. To be fair, even though technically we had taken the dumper truck without consent, we had no intention of stealing it or causing damage. We were just playing a real-life construction game as far as we were concerned.

There was much debate about who was the better driver. I claimed I had the upper hand although I suspect, in reality, Jon took the honours. He was slightly older and had the edge.

Little did I know it, but starting vehicles using implements other than the key would come in useful when I became a police officer later in life. I would be dealing with the epidemic of stolen vehicles that was engulfing the country in the '90s.

Near Jon's house, a large field ran along the side of a hill as far as the eye could see. A small brook trickled alongside, dotted with the occasional tree on the banks.

One autumn day we were by the side of the brook and could see a load of leaves around us. We thought it would be a good idea to build a large pile of leaves into a den and hide underneath. One person would be the enemy and the other the Allied forces.

We constructed a massive den at the base of a tree; so far, so good, and we were pleased with our efforts. As the day wore on, it began to get cold. We decided that we needed a fire to help us warm up.

Off we went to collect more leaves, twigs and bigger sticks. We created a firepit and surrounded it with stones. As we happened to have a box of matches with us, starting the fire was easy.

We were mesmerised by the flames, flickering and dancing. We added more twigs to the fire and scoured round to get bigger and bigger pieces of wood. Hunting around, we were only vaguely aware that the wind was getting up, stronger and stronger. We looked back to see sparks shooting out of the fire in all directions. Our combustible war bunker was now a lethal hazard.

Flames were leaping around the side of the tree. They were licking up, 15 feet or more, and the foolhardiness of our actions began to dawn on us. To make matters worse, the bushes around the tree also caught fire and we were faced with an inferno. We just looked at each other, confused.

Crazy as it seems, we collected handfuls of water and threw them onto the flames. The miniscule amounts had no effect whatsoever. We decided just to 'leg it' as quickly as we could away from the scene of the crime.

Back in the direction of Jon's house, then, feeling really guilty as we heard the sound of fire engines in the distance. As we looked back, we could see a large fire in the middle of the field, resembling something of Biblical proportions.

Personally, I felt terrible. We had burned down a whole, healthy tree. About 10 years later, though, my conscience was totally cleared when an entire housing estate was built on the field. Now, there is nothing but concrete. The beautiful tree would have had a few more years of life, although cut short by our childhood adventures.

Another day, we decided to make candles by melting down some wax. What could possibly go wrong? We had no real artistic flair and were not following any sort of plan. It just seemed like a good idea at the time, to make some unusual shapes for a bit of fun.

We found lots of used candle ends and melted them down on an old tin tray in the oven. Due to the energy crisis of the seventies, every household had burnt ends of candles; this had been the only real form of light during the many power cuts.

To start with, all was going to plan, although a mess did start to develop in the kitchen. Jon's parents were in the other room, and we felt confident in our abilities, with the intention of cleaning up afterwards.

We placed the hot wax, close to boiling point, on a metal tray in the middle of the kitchen table. Absolute chaos ensued. In an instant, the whole tray caught fire. Flames shot up into the air, catching us by surprise.

No need to worry, everything was under control as far as we were concerned. We had no need to call for any sort of parental 'back up' or fire brigade. After all, we were Boy Scouts and had loads of experience around fires. If we put it out quickly, it would not burn or scorch the wooden kitchen table and Jon's parents would be none the wiser.

Jon quickly jumped up to the rescue and proceeded to fill a large jug of cold water to extinguish the flames. As he returned to the table with his arm outstretched, jug of water held tightly in his hand out in front of him, I leaned back in my chair to avoid being splashed.

Jon poured the contents of the jug onto the baking tray of hot and fiery wax. I can only describe the next few seconds as terrifying. There was an enormous whooshing sound as oxygen seemed to be sucked into the room to feed a massive fireball.

Jon had magically conjured up what appeared to be an evil spirit of fire and hot, spitting wax. The giant ball of fire was the size of a large beach ball that grew and rose quickly into the air. I could now smell the strong scent of burnt human hair, as we realised the fireball had vaporised the hair on our arms, eyebrows and eyelashes. Somehow, we had avoided the hair on our heads being set on fire.

'Shit, shit,' we both cried out as the fireball hit the ceiling, scorching and melting some of the polystyrene ceiling tiles.

The fireball vanished just as quickly as it had appeared. Jon had killed the evil spirit. The tray and part of the table were still covered with molten wax, and flames shooting out. The fire was brought quickly under control with a wet tea towel, but we were both shaken up.

Fortunately, we did not cause too much damage and our hair grew back. We accepted our mild ticking off.

Looking back now, I realise our injuries could have been much more serious. It could have been an absolute disaster.

Another of my school friends, Matty, was a real character. His dad was a successful businessman who owned a garage in Rochdale. Matty got into trouble when he 'borrowed' a car from the forecourt to see a Rochdale girl who was on a college field trip in the Lake District.

Off we went in a classy Volvo 480, which drew admiring comments from Lake District tourists, as it was the latest sporty model. The girl was staying in a converted manor house. We climbed up to the girl's bedroom window and clambered in to see her. We headed back home on the same day, chuffed to bits with our adventures.

No insurance for our trip, but no accidents, and we escaped with a telling off from Matty's dad.

Another time, when Matty's family were away on holiday, we discovered a large collection of investment wine in the house. We just thought it was cheap plonk. The wine was worth about £200 a bottle back then; we knocked back a whole case of the stuff over a weekend.

Again, a lecture from Matty's dad, with sincere apologies, and we were more or less off the hook. We were really getting away with it…

My explosive younger years

Bonfire nights up north are brilliant. They are celebrated with great vigour. That is surprising to me because 5th November, Guy Fawkes night, is an event with its roots firmly down south in London, remembering the plot to destroy Parliament. A fight between Protestants and Catholics. Nowadays I'm not sure if many people realise why they are letting off fireworks.

Back in the '70s and '80s, as a kid, you spent the whole week building the biggest bonfire possible.

Close to us, there was a pub that had a giant bonfire in the middle of their car park. They would happily allow us to add wood to the pile from wherever we could find it. We were preparing a towering inferno; a monolithic structure, ready for Guy Fawkes to be placed on top.

Being enterprising, we would use old clothes and trousers to form a scarecrow character. We always made this a week early, drew a face on it and placed a hat on top. Then, looking like very young 'Big Issue' sellers, we would sit next to a local shop and put a hat out shouting 'penny for the Guy', hoping passers-by would throw us money for our efforts.

To be fair, it was quite a money-spinner for us at the time. Our 'Guy' helped with a few pennies for the cause, then we concentrated on making the bonfire with masses of piles of wood. We discovered large pallets at the back of businesses and industrial estates, dragging them across the neighbourhood.

Anticipation began to build for the bonfire feast. We looked forward to parkin: traditional ginger cake with syrup, brown sugar, oatmeal and spices. This delicacy was cut into small squares. This, to me tasted even better than Christmas cake. On a cold November night, as a child, it would really warm you up.

If you were still cold, you could try the black peas. These were as hot as lava and served in a polystyrene cup. I remember they were soaked overnight with lashings of vinegar and a pinch of salt. They were purple-podded peas, not now so readily available.

When the bonfire was lit, you didn't need a cup of black peas to warm you up as the heat from the fire would be as intense as a towering inferno. Woe betide you if you tried to throw an empty polystyrene cup or paper plate on the fire, once lit. You couldn't get close enough, not even within 10 feet, because the heat would burn off your eyebrows and hair from your arms!

The final treat on bonfire night was treacle toffee. Again, home-made and produced especially for the occasion. It would be made of black treacle. This was a really sweet, hard toffee. When you bit into the toffee, the stuff moulded around your teeth. Anyone with fillings on their teeth would lose them rapidly. It felt as if your jaw was welded together with the sticky toffee.

We let off fireworks in various places after buying them in the local shops. Most shopkeepers at that time didn't check if you were old enough to buy them. They more or less let us get on with it. The fireworks were relatively cheap, too.

The standard way of doing things could become quite boring. We wanted to see what would happen if we lined up rockets in bottles and fired them across the street. We watched the rockets shoot off and bounce around. No harm was done; we weren't aiming them at people or vehicles.

To me, Catherine wheels were a little bit dull. All they did was spin round in a circle, firing off sparks. I much preferred bangers, as they would explode with an almighty bang. And I loved the mighty 'air bomb repeater' which was the crème de la crème of fireworks. This 'bad boy' was a long hollow tube, filled with gunpowder and eight small individual 'charges' that, once lit, would fire about 100 feet into the air. They would each explode with a massive bang. They were ace!

It felt like that, at times, we were mini scientists, wanting to explore different experiments, in particular with the use of fireworks. Jon and I would go over to his grandad's house which was no longer lived in full-time. We would select items as experiments to use with the fireworks.

Our first plan was to see what would happen if we dropped a banger inside a tub of talcum powder. Rummaging through the bathroom cupboard, we found a cardboard tube of Hai Karate talc and eagerly took it into the back yard.

We pushed the banger inside, digging it deep into the powder. Leaving the lid off, we lit the fuse of the firework and ran back to a safe location, looking on in awe behind the relative safety of the back door to the house. We felt like those scientists, watching the atomic bomb explosions in the Pacific.

We waited and saw the fuse fizzing down. A few sparks, a small puff of smoke, then nothing. So what to do next? We both remembered watching those government TV adverts warning children never to return to a firework. Neither of us, quite frankly, wanted to be burned, lose a hand or a digit to an unexploded firework.

We glanced at each other, waiting, both thinking the same thing. Then, to our utter amazement and joy, the firework exploded. Just like those scientists monitoring the atom bomb testing, we witnessed a massive white mushroom cloud. It engulfed the whole of the back yard. Quite frankly, ours was better. It smelt wonderful.

But, damn it, there was only one bottle of Hai Karate in the cupboard. We had to now adapt and think, what else what we could we experiment with?

We spent the next hour dissecting our favourite firework, the air bomb repeater…that long tube with eight single charges hidden inside. These were much louder and more dangerous than the standard bangers. This made them a real prize.

We set about cutting the firework with our penknife and emptying out the gunpower, carefully removing the fuses. We were left with our plastic tub containing the gunpower and eight separate cardboard charges with a small fuse coming out of each one. We also had a long length of fuse that we could adapt and tie as needed.

We decided it would be fun to recreate a car chase from a film or TV sequence like *The A-team* or *Starsky and Hutch* with one of the cars spinning off a toy car track and then exploding. We did not have mobile phones or a camcorder to record this 'stunt' in those days. This was going to be done all in one take, and we would be the only witnesses to our own Hollywood blockbuster.

Jon had set up an amazing Scalextric racing car set. Scalextric was a brand of slot car racing sets, with the ability to race two or more cars against each other. I could not afford a proper set, but Jon had a superb version of the game, with lengths of tracks twisting around the living room floor.

He had Formula One cars, Lombard RAC rally cars, like the Ford Escorts of the day, and he also had Minis like you would see in the film, *The Italian Job*. We thought it would be an idea to place an explosive charge in one of the cars as it drove around the living room. We could then recreate a scene from a film and the car would hopefully blow off the track.

The one dangerous part was that we had to be relatively close to the Scalextric set because the controllers were attached to the vehicles with leads.

Everything was set and we lit the fuse; the race was on. The cars raced around the track. Suddenly there was an almighty bang. The firework was inside such an enclosed space of the plastic car; it seemed to amplify the effect of the firework.

The car was blown to smithereens. Jon and I ducked and dived to avoid the flying fragments of shrapnel and plastic being projected all over the living room. We looked at each other and fell about laughing.

The afternoon had been a great success as far as we were concerned. It was, however, ruined a little bit when we noticed a pile of silk linen had become a victim of the explosion. A large hole had been burned in the fabric.

It wasn't some cheap towel. This was expensive bedding fabric that had been placed in a neat pile. We did what any self-respecting kids would do. We grabbed the pile and turned it over, hoping no one would notice.

I vaguely recall that Jon received a bollocking from his parents at a later stage, as his neighbours had complained. Once more, I was not present for that dressing-down and avoided any blame!

Jon's house had an inside toilet, but also still had the original brick-built toilet block outside in the back yard. A close neighbour kept a ferret in their outside toilet. That ferret absolutely stank, much worse than anything you might normally find in a toilet.

Jon's family were all so friendly. Well, maybe not so much the dog called 'Scamper'. He was a small white poodle with an angry personality. Given any chance he would snarl and try to nip or, should I say, bite. Eventually, a truce was negotiated. We left each other alone to keep the peace.

Jon had a 'landline' phone in his house. When we got bored watching just the three TV channels available to us at that time, we decided to amuse ourselves with this magical piece of technology by the front window in the living room.

Before the internet, to make a phone call, you had to share your phone number with the friends and family you wanted to keep in touch with. If you did not know the number, you had the option of looking it up in a telephone directory.

Telephone directories at the time consisted of two books, one called Yellow Pages, which contained a list of businesses in alphabetical order according to the business or service you required. The second was another thick paper book with residential phone numbers listed against the name of the subscriber.

Each book covered a geographical area, and these books were delivered to your house once a year for free. Each book contained hundreds of pages. Many celebrity 'strong men' of that era would take on the challenge to rip a phone book in half with just their bare hands!

We had no intention of trying to rip this phone book up. Instead, we would look up what we considered to be funny names, such as A. CRAP or BEN DOVER. We would then proceed to call the numbers and ask questions such as, 'Are you having A CRAP today?' while trying to stifle our laughter, then hang up.

We didn't stop at residential numbers, but would call local funeral directors from the Yellow Pages, asking, 'Is it dead there today?' Again, we found this highly amusing at the time. I realise now that this behaviour was not appropriate and childish, and I take this opportunity to apologise and confess to my sins. However, all those antics still make me smile today!

Growing up in Norden near Rochdale could be quite boring as a kid. We would go to the youth club at the local school to play table tennis. Also, the scout group in Norden was really good fun. We would go camping and learn to light fires, tie knots, go orienteering and all the usual stuff.

We roamed the streets until darkness fell. One evening, we thought it would be fun to see if we could make a tower out of milk bottles. We patrolled the neighbourhood and collected the empty bottles from doorsteps. We were careful not to make any clinking sounds and alert the residents.

We found a patch of waste ground where we were able to build a tower about four to five bottles high. This pyramid structure was quite a feat, showing off our early engineering skills. Unfortunately, when we tried to make the tower taller, everything came crashing down with broken glass everywhere.

We all looked at each other and decided to have another attempt. Off we went, collecting more bottles from doorsteps. We selected a house where we knew a boy from school lived. He happened to be picked on a lot, because his dad was a policeman. What an opportunity to play a prank.

We crept down the path to the front door, imitating the moves made by SAS soldiers on some sort of covert mission. We stacked about 20 bottles against the front door. As a finishing touch, we placed a milk bottle on the door handle, knocked on the door and ran off as fast as our little legs would carry us.

We knew that, as soon as the door opened, the bottle would drop onto the pile, with everything smashing on the doorstep.

Sure enough, as we ran down the street, we could hear the crash of breaking glass behind us. We all burst out laughing and ran off into nearby woods. It was just one of those stupid things we did as kids.

In our early teens, Jon and I would take the bus from Norden into Rochdale, onwards into Manchester. It was a good service, with little buses called 'Ribble Riders', relating to the Ribble Valley.

The larger double-decker buses had seats made of Formica and velour with a metal bar across the back. As it rained a lot, there would often be condensation and damp within the bus itself. Sometimes the windows became totally drenched. It was also a time when everyone smoked, and there would be a blue haze throughout the bus as people puffed away on cigarettes and pipes.

To pass the time on the journey, just before we got off, we would make small bangers to scare people on the bus. These were made using a chocolate bar and a box of matches. First, we took a match out the box and stuck the wooden end in between the Formica and the top rail of the seat in front.

Opening the chocolate, there used to be fine tin foil wrapped around the bar. We would tightly tie a length of the foil around the end of the match head. We sometimes also scraped off some extra sulphur from another match to achieve a bigger bang.

Just before getting off, we lit another match and set fire to the wooden part of the match in foil, halfway down. This slowly burned towards the end which was covered in foil.

This would produce a loud bang and make people jump. We never considered the dangers, including causing a small fire in the bus. As far as we were concerned, it was all just for laughs.

Of course, had our pranks backfired, it would have been no laughing matter!

My overseas adventures

My learning curve took an upward turn when I decided that I needed to move on. The sense of adventure burning inside meant that Rochdale, for all its positive influences, had to be left behind…

I was only 15 when I left school. I had no intention of going on to university; I just wanted to get into the world of work and have some money in my pocket.

Before I thought about anything else, in 1988, I decided I needed a holiday with my mates. I headed straight down to the local travel agent and booked two weeks in Majorca. My friends were amused when, at still only 15, I was able to secure my holiday at a child's price.

Also, while in the Venture Scouts, we enjoyed a trip to Switzerland. We stayed in a small hamlet close to the prestigious area of Gstaad. I remember being on the cross-channel ferry and a very long coach trip of about 24 hours driving through France, Germany and Luxembourg into Switzerland.

It was not your typical scouting jamboree-type camp. Everyone including the leaders – who were relatively young– were all of the mindset that we were going to have a decent holiday.

We went down to the supermarket and bought several cases of lager. It became more of an extended drinking session than a scouting holiday. We did one hike, five miles up to the top of a mountain. We had a few pints at the top and hiked back down again. That was the extent of our scouting abilities in Switzerland.

One day we visited a famous old hotel which looked like a castle. It was an amazing building and location. Unfortunately for the residents paying premium prices, we all rocked up with our shorts and towels, and bought day tickets to use their pool and diving board.

Our rowdy behaviour was probably more akin to an 18-30 holiday with us shouting, playing music from ghetto blasters, divebombing in the pool and drinking. We had a right laugh, but fortunately didn't receive any complaints from residents or staff.

On one occasion the rep turned up at our accommodation, a chalet-type building, on a small 50cc moped. While he was in the building talking with the leaders, we decided that we might borrow the moped. We managed to get it started, using the same method used to start the dumper truck many years beforehand.

The bike spluttered into life and then we rode along the street for the next 10 or 15 minutes, laughing and joking. It didn't cross our minds that we had no insurance or driving licences. I was later to learn that this would have been classed as taking a motor vehicle without consent. To us, at the time, it was just a bit of a laugh, as with our previous escapades. Luckily no one was injured with no harm done.

Later on, the rep came out and laughed and joked about our misdemeanour. This incident could have had a totally different outcome!

Another adventure in Switzerland involved Girl Guides and Rangers, who were a bit older. They were staying in a building next to us, so you can imagine that there was a lot of fraternisation with the opposite sex. Their leadership was more robust than what we were used to!

We would often chat to the girls as they left for or came back from their activities. A plan to see the young ladies was hatched...

After people had gone to sleep in our chalet, a group of us slipped out of the accommodation. We walked around the back of their large wooden building. In the storage area we saw a wooden ladder, hooked against the side of the wall. Quietly, we lifted the ladder off its hook and carried it around the building to where we knew older Ranger girls were staying, five to a room.

We raised the ladder up to their window ledge. We climbed up, one by one, and gently tapped on the window. The girls found this thoroughly amusing and invited us in without their leaders knowing a thing.

We had brought drinks with us, of course, and partied on into the night! We returned home, faced with the issues of smuggling some cheap Chinese firecrackers, cigars and butterfly knives back through Border Control. We had purchased these on our travels, not paying enough attention to the possible fall-out.

The dodgy items were hidden in our main cases in the hold of the coach. We had a moment of fear as the customs and immigration officers boarded the coach at the French ferry terminal in Calais. Luckily, they just wanted to inspect our passports and did not check our bags. After all, we were just 'innocent Scouts' to them.

At the next Venture Scout meeting we attended on our return, we did get a proper bollocking. The guides leader from London had written a complaint to The Scout Association about our behaviour. The head district scout leader in the North West gave us the bad news.

It didn't matter, nobody got thrown out, we'd had the best holiday ever and it was well worth it!

Working in 'The Black Box'

It was 1986. Thatcher was in Number 10, Top Gun was in the cinemas, (I loved that film!) and I was fresh out of school with a haircut that owed more to optimism than it did to style.

The '80s were full of unique trends and bold statements, and the flat top for guys was no exception. It was distinguished by its sharp angles, high, flat crown, and distinct patterns shaved into the sides. It quickly picked up momentum at the early onset of the '80s and proved to be a cultural phenomenon.

The flat top symbolised confidence and individuality. I blame my haircut on *'David's Barbers'* in Spotland Road, Rochdale. My dad had taken me there for years, then I used to go independently as I got older. The trouble was, David the barber had a new toy. A special plastic comb that helped create that unique flat top style and he wanted to use it. I joked with my mates that it didn't matter what style of cut you went in and asked for – you always came out with a flat top! That barber's shop is long gone and is now the site of a Lidl supermarket.

I digress. I had just left school and my immediate future, I was told, involved getting a proper, full-time job. This was easier said than done. Unemployment was stubbornly high, which meant regular pilgrimages to the Jobcentre in Yorkshire Street.

The place smelt of nylon carpet and body odour. It was a sea of little index cards pinned to cork boards and plastic display racks, each one a tiny portal to a potential future. I remember standing there, bewildered by the sheer number of vacancies on display. If there were so many jobs, why was everyone always going on about unemployment? I came to the rather uncharitable conclusion that perhaps some people just preferred the leisurely pursuit of not working.

Among the cards, two caught my eye. They were for a Youth Training Scheme, or YTS, the government's grand plan to stop teenagers like me from immediately becoming a drain on the state. Both were for the glamorous, futuristic role of computer programmer. Now, my experience in this field was, shall we say, niche. I owned an Acorn Electron home computer, The smaller and cheaper version of the BBC Microcomputer.

The Acorn was a magnificent beige beast on which I'd spent countless hours. Most of this time was dedicated to playing games, normally loaded by playing a cassette tape with a high-pitched sound squealing away or typing in the programme by hand from a computer magazine. I had also dabbled in a bit of programming myself, mastering the art of making swear words scroll elegantly across the screen. My crowning achievement was sneaking into Tandy and Dixons to type these profane little masterpieces onto their display models, before scarpering, giggling like an idiot.

To my utter astonishment, after a couple of aptitude tests, I was offered both positions. The pay was a princely £30 a week. This was a time before the internet was in everyone's homes, before the dotcom boom made millionaires out of people who knew how to build a website. I was about to make a decision that would steer my life in a completely different direction. I turned both jobs down.

Why would any sane teenager reject the chance to be at the cutting edge of technology? The answer, my friends, is simple. Rochdale Borough Council was offering £60 a week. Double the money. My brain, which operated on a sophisticated algorithm of calculating potential beer funds, saw this as a no brainer. More money meant more pints down the pub. The logic was flawless.

So I became an administrator in the council's 'junior pool'. The job itself was a whirlwind tour of local government bureaucracy. One month I'd be helping to pay out pensions, and the next I'd be processing forms for children with special educational needs. I even had a stint in Environmental Health, where my duties included ordering spare parts for bin lorries and ensuring the fuel reserves for the road sweepers were properly audited. It sounds about as thrilling as watching paint dry, but honestly, I loved it. I was indoors and dry, the money was good, and the work was steady.

Plus, for most of my time with the council I was based in the 'Black Box'. This was a six-storey office block named Telegraph House, and was located opposite the bus station and multi-storey car park. Officially opened in May 1978, the offices were ready for use the following year, and became the municipal administration hub for Rochdale Borough Council.

The building was futuristic looking, made of glass that appeared black from the outside. Within the footprint there were businesses including The Travellers Rest pub; a café, dry cleaners, clothing shop and a newsagent. It was also conveniently close to a new McDonald's, which became the unofficial clubhouse for me and my friends to dissect the day of work over a lukewarm coffee.

The Black Box had a bit of a reputation, mostly for something called 'sick building syndrome'. People were always off with mysterious ailments, which were usually blamed on the wheezing air conditioning system circulating germs. I never knew if that was true, or if the sheer pressure of working for the council just made people want a day off. Mental health wasn't really a 'thing' back then, so who knows.

Getting the job had been an event in itself. The interview day was like something from the early rounds of The X Factor. A huge, snaking queue of hopeful young faces, all vying for one of about 20 positions. I went through the application, the interview, the aptitude test, and somehow, I was picked. At the time, it was water off a duck's back to me. I was completely nonplussed, with no real grasp of how lucky I'd been to land the role. Hundreds of people went for that job.

The junior pool was a motley crew, but we were all in the same boat. There was a lad I knew from school whose name escapes me now, but I'll never forget his prosthetic arm. I thought it was the coolest thing I'd ever seen, like something from a James Bond film. He'd patiently show me how the claw on the end could grab and hold things, a skill he put to great use in the mail room where he worked. The truly brilliant part was an attachment he had for it: a snooker cue rest. The man was a wizard on the table. He beat me at pool every single time, without fail.

Then there were Richard, Kath and Ian. As part of our training, we had to go to night school at Hopwood Hall College to get a BTEC in Business Studies. Kath was the smart one, the academic I aspired to be, though she confessed to being utterly hopeless at maths. I, on the other hand, had scraped a CSE in the subject and could just about get my head around the concepts. During one exam, I found myself in the unfamiliar position of being the brains of the operation, subtly feeding Kath the answers I hoped were correct. We both passed with flying colours, which taught me a valuable lesson: qualifications aren't everything.

One evening after college, we were cutting through the Rochdale Shopping Centre. All the shops were closed and shuttered, but the main thoroughfare was still open as a right of way. Richard, with a mischievous glint in his eye, announced he had something to show us. He glanced around the empty, tiled concourse, then reached into his rucksack. He pulled out what looked like a black 9mm semi-automatic pistol.

Dropping to one knee, he held the gun in a two-handed grip and fired five rounds into the echoing space. The sound was deafening. BANG. BANG. BANG. The noise of each shot reverberated off the glass shopfronts. He looked up, grinning, then performed a ridiculous commando roll, scrambled to his feet, BANG, BANG and then stuffed the gun back in his bag.

'Don't worry,' he laughed as we all broke into a panicked run towards the subway exit, 'it's only a replica!' Miraculously, no security guards appeared and no police appeals were ever made. In this day and age, I suspect that little escapade would have ended very differently. For us, it was just another Tuesday.

Life in the Black Box wasn't all paper shuffling and replica firearms, though. One afternoon, a man in a suit walked onto our office floor, flanked by a uniformed police officer. My blood ran cold. This is it, I thought. They've found out about the gun incident. As they moved closer, the man in the suit pointed directly at me, and then a few other blokes in the office. The police, our manager explained, needed volunteers for an identification parade. Not realising I had a choice, and hearing the magic words 'you'll be paid', I immediately agreed.

We were marched over to Rochdale police station and lined up in a room against a wall, complete with the height chart you see in the films. A sergeant explained the procedure. The suspect would be brought in and could choose where to stand in the line. We were all to look straight ahead. No talking, no winking, no helpful nodding towards the guilty party. The suspect was brought in, a rough looking bloke about my age. Charming, I thought, I didn't realise I looked that weathered. The suspect had an earring, so to level the playing field, we were all made to wear a plaster on the same ear. We also had to wear white paper disposable overalls, like the suspect was wearing.

Then the witness, a middle-aged woman, was brought in. She walked briskly down the line and back again, a complete formality, before pointing squarely at the suspect.

'That's him,' she said with a look of rage in her face.

The bloke just smirked. We were dismissed, handed our cash, and sent on our way. Brilliant. Beer money for the night. It never even occurred to me to wonder what would have happened if she'd pointed at me. I didn't even know what the suspect was accused of!

That became the first of many ID parades I took part in. It was a great little earner, and I'd volunteer every time I saw a police officer walk through the door at work. Looking back, I suppose that's where another spark of interest in joining the force really came from. It seems my path away from computer programming had led me somewhere far more interesting, after all.

The most important lesson of my life

Growing up in Rochdale in the nineties was, for the most part, a grand old time. It's one of those northern towns that gets a bit of a bad rap, often mentioned in the same breath as 'social and economic problems', but for me and my mates, it was just home. This was a time before the ugly truth of paedophile grooming gangs came to the notice of the local police and were associated with offenders living in Rochdale.

My mates and I all had jobs, we had laughs, and we had an uncanny knack for getting into scrapes. We never set out to commit criminal acts. We were just a bit naive, a bit daft, and blessed with the kind of youthful optimism that borders on the certifiably insane.

Brad wasn't the only one to attract the attention of the local law enforcers. Take my friend Matty, for instance. One evening he called round, the proud owner of a newly acquired set of wheels and asked if I fancied a spin.

'Absolutely,' I said, hopping into the back. Earlier that day, he'd been off to take his driving test.

'Congratulations, mate!' I said, giving him a hearty slap on the back. 'Knew you'd pass.'

We picked up a few of the other lads and cruised around Norden, Bamford and Rochdale when Matty, with the sheepish air of a man about to confess a cardinal sin, admitted that he hadn't, in fact, passed his test at all. He'd failed. Utterly deflated and determined to put two fingers up to the system, he'd marched straight to a local dealer of end-of-life cars and slapped down fifty quid for what could only be described as a cow on its last legs.

A sudden, cold silence fell upon the car. There we were, rattling along in a banger with no MOT to its name, being chauffeured by a man with no licence and no insurance. To be fair to Matty, he wasn't a bad driver. After seeing his driving in action that night, I was genuinely surprised he'd failed, and we managed to spend the entire evening avoiding the attention of the local constabulary.

As the night drew to a close, however, even Matty conceded that his career as an outlaw motorist was probably short-lived. So, he decided to give the car a proper send-off. Inspired by the televisual genius of *The A-Team* or *Knight Rider*, he was going to crash it. Not in a spectacular, Hollywood-style fireball, you understand. This was a low-speed, rather pathetic crunch into a wall behind some garages on a patch of wasteland. It was just enough to wreck the car completely. We all stood around, howling with laughter, immensely grateful that our brush with the law had ended not with a bang, but with a rather sad, metallic whimper.

This flirtation with vehicular idiocy wasn't a one-off. Once we'd all passed our tests and become legitimate, road-legal citizens, our ambitions grew. Our favourite destination became 'Birch Services' on the M62. It was the perfect distance, far enough to feel like an adventure, but not so far that it bankrupted us in petrol money. Plus, it had arcade machines, hot food and coffee for those night-time adventures. The journey itself, however, was the main event, thanks to a game we invented called 'Yarman'.

The rules of Yarman were breathtakingly simple and monumentally stupid. As the car sped down the motorway, the passengers would wind down their windows, hoist themselves up to sit on the sills and, while clinging on for dear life to the grab handle inside, attempt to link hands with the person on the other side of the car over the roof. Upon successful connection, you would both triumphantly shout, 'YARMAN!' Looking back, I can see how this could have ended in multiple, gruesome tragedies. It's a miracle we all survived with our limbs intact. They say the part of the teenage brain responsible for risk assessment doesn't fully develop until you're an adult. I can personally vouch for the truth in that.

Our resourcefulness wasn't limited to automotive stunts. It also came in handy for impromptu DIY. I remember a house party at our mate Fletch's place. His parents were away, the music was pumping, and a glorious summer evening was in full swing. I suspect the neighbours weren't quite so pleased with the loud music. Then, the unthinkable happened: the booze ran out. After a quick whip-round, Fletch, our noble host, offered to make a supply run. The only problem was his decision to borrow his parents' car. The screech of metal on metal, as he scraped the entire length of the car against the garage door opening, brought the party to a dead halt.

The side of the car was a mangled mess of dented metal and flaking paint. We all stood on the driveway, staring at the unfolding nightmare. But we were a resourceful bunch. Like a montage from an episode of *The A-Team*, we sprang into action. A search of the garage unearthed rattle cans of spray paint in roughly the right colour, a tub of bodywork filler and an electric sander.

Now, there's a very good reason why the world's finest craftspeople don't tend to work after several cans of lager. Undeterred, we set about our task with gusto. We sanded, we filled, we sanded again, we masked off the area with old newspapers, and then we sprayed. I can't recall the precise quality of our workmanship, but I imagine it was utterly atrocious. I didn't stick around to witness the grand unveiling for Fletch's parents. We'd left long before they returned, our mission accomplished.

Of course, you couldn't be a teenager in the north in the nineties without being exposed to drugs. It wasn't something I was ever particularly interested in, but it was just… there. Part of the scenery. On one occasion, I was out in a car with my mates when one of the lads announced he wanted to buy some cannabis. Back then, resin was considered the good stuff. He'd been given the number of a new dealer and, after a clandestine call from a phone box, the deal was on.

We set off from Rochdale and drove to the neighbouring town of Oldham, ending up on a dodgy estate. We drove up a steep hill, turned the car around at the top, and parked outside the given address. My mate had been instructed to wait in the car. As we waited, the front door opened and a giant of a man emerged. He was well over six feet tall, with an athletic, muscular build that was frankly terrifying. His eyes were piercing, scanning the car and its occupants from a distance. I'd never been to a drug deal before and I was petrified, my mind racing with every gangster film cliché I'd ever seen.

He strode over to the car wearing a designer shell suit. The passenger window was wound down, with a handle of course. A sweet, heavy waft of cannabis smoke hit us as he leaned in.

'What you boys want?' he said, his voice a low rumble.

One of the lads ordered 'a Henry' – an eighth of an ounce. The dealer named his price which was agreed upon. The dealer, whose face was a permanent mask of suspicion, uttered the immortal words, 'Show me the money'.

A wallet was duly opened, revealing a modest clutch of £10 notes. The dealer eyed them, then us, then the general vicinity, as if expecting a SWAT team to abseil down from the lamppost. His right hand dipped into his pocket. For a heart-stopping moment, I was convinced this was it. He was going to rob us, or worse. My imagination, always a keen scriptwriter of my own demise, had already cast him in the role of a budget-version Sweeney Todd. The glint of metal confirmed my fears as he pulled out a large Stanley knife, flicking the blade open with a practised flick of the wrist.

We all recoiled in our seats as one, a synchronised gasp of pure, unadulterated terror. The dealer, however, looked utterly perplexed by our reaction. With his other hand, he reached into his jacket and produced the real object of the transaction, a hefty nine-ounce bar of cannabis resin. He plonked it on the car roof and, using the terrifying knife with the casual air of a chef chopping carrots, began to slice off our portion. No scales, of course. This was a man who measured by eye, a seasoned professional in a very unprofessional line of work. He nodded towards the window, the money was passed over, and a lump of hash was slipped into my friend's trembling hand.

Just as we were breathing a collective sigh of relief, our paranoia kicked into a higher gear. Down the hill, an estate car pulled across the road. From the top of the street, simultaneously, another car appeared, headlights blazing. They were unmarked, naturally, but in our heightened state, they screamed 'Police!' faster than a flashing blue light.

'Shit, it's the feds!' someone yelled, and that was all the encouragement our driver needed. He slammed his foot on the accelerator, hurtling away from the dealer's house and down the hill. We spotted a side road, a potential escape from the pincer movement we had so brilliantly deduced.

As we swerved into it, tyres squealing, we finally got a clear look at the masterminds behind the 'sting operation'. The driver of the estate car was an elderly resident attempting a three-point turn, and the other car was just…another car. We had managed to scare ourselves half to death over absolutely nothing. For all my terror, it turned out that buying drugs in Oldham was less like a scene from *Goodfellas* and more like a slightly dodgy takeaway order. It all seemed like an awful lot of bother for very little reward, but my brush with the world of narcotics, it turned out, was far from over.

My eighteenth birthday arrived, and with it, a rare parental concession. Having never been allowed a party, I was finally granted permission. The catch? It couldn't be in the house. It had to be in the garage. I jumped at the chance. This wasn't just a garage; this was going to be my own private pub, my Hacienda. We cleared out the lawnmower and the cobwebs, setting up a pasting table as a makeshift bar. Working in a pub had its perks. The licensee at Madison Square sold me an 88-pint keg of bitter and even threw in the gas canister and pumps to get it flowing. My very own pub, right there amongst the oil stains and rusty bicycles.

The night began beautifully. My mates came over, we were joined by my older brother, and it was all a bit of a knees-up. It was all perfectly civilised, a mere warm-up for the main event, a proper night out on the tiles in Rochdale. Dressed to the nines, I was channelling my inner Don Johnson from the TV show *Miami Vice*. I wore my white suit with green flecks over a T-shirt. In my own head, I was the epitome of 1980s cool, cruising through the neon-lit streets of Miami. In reality, I was a lad from Rochdale in a questionable suit, heading for a taxi.

Our first stop was a wine bar on Drake Street, *the* place to be. Situated nearly next to the newly opened KFC, it had a nightclub on the ground floor and a bar upstairs, thick with cigarette smoke and the scent of hairspray. Some of my mates hit the dance floor and I bagged a table by the window, feeling terribly grown-up and, finally, legally able to be there. I was soon joined by a friend from school and his uncle.

'It's my eighteenth,' I announced proudly.

The uncle smiled. 'If I'd known it was your birthday, I'd have got you a present'

He paused for dramatic effect. 'Tell you what…'

He opened a silver cigarette case. Inside were several hand-rolled cigarettes, each with a cardboard smoking tip at one end and a neat twist at the other. Joints. He passed one to me.

'Happy birthday, lad.'

I thanked him, lit it up, and sat there smoking the joint by the window, chatting away happily. Now, cannabis had never done much for me. I'd tried it a few times and couldn't really see the attraction. This, however, was different.

It started with a feeling of light-headedness. Then, the world began to slow down. The flashing lights from the dance floor below became lazy, intermittent pops, like an old-fashioned press camera. The thumping bass of the music warped into a deep, sluggish thud. People's voices melted into an indecipherable drone. I felt a strange warmth spreading through me, but my heart seemed to be beating in slow motion.

I needed the loo. Excusing myself, the words tumbled out of my mouth, thick and slurred. As I stood up to walk the short distance to the stairs, I looked down at my feet. I couldn't feel them touching the floor. The sensation was one of levitation. I was floating across the dance floor, past smiling faces with big hair and even bigger shoulder pads. It was the strangest, most disconcerting feeling I'd ever had. I glided up the stairs, feeling increasingly queasy, and stumbled towards the gents.

Slamming the cubicle door behind me, I was overcome by a wave of nausea. For the next forty minutes, I was intimately acquainted with the porcelain of that wine bar toilet, my body violently ejecting every last drop of birthday bitter until there was nothing left but bile. I have a vague, distressing memory of my white Miami Vice suit not faring too well during the ordeal.

Eventually, the heaving stopped. My head cleared. The music snapped back into focus and my vision returned to normal. I staggered back downstairs to my seat. My friend's uncle looked at me with a flicker of concern.

'You alright there, lad?'

'I don't know what draw you put in that,' I mumbled, 'but it was bloody strong.'

He just smiled. 'That'll be the opium,' he said, as casually as if he were discussing the weather. 'It's your birthday, after all. A little treat.'

He winked. 'If you ever want any more, you know where I am.'

Naively, I just nodded and thanked him, thinking no more of it. It was only the next day, recounting the story to my other mates and still not entirely sure what opium even was, that the penny dropped. I looked it up in the family encyclopaedia. The entry was brief and to the point. Opium, it turned out, is the raw material from which heroin is made.

My friend's uncle wasn't just being generous. He was a heroin dealer, and his 'birthday treat' was a recruitment drive.

First, I felt a surge of anger, then a profound sense of relief. I had been lucky. My body's violent rejection of his gift was the best thing that could have happened.

It was a close call, a very close call indeed, but from that moment on, I made a conscious decision. I was never going to touch drugs again. I'd learned the hard way that you never truly know what you're getting, and some birthday presents are best left unopened.

Living the American dream

When I was about 18, I joined a scheme to go to America, organised through Camp America. They were putting fairs on in the UK to advertise the camps. I thought it was an opportunity to do some travel and get paid for it. I had been active with Boy Scouts in the UK, so the idea appealed to me. I just thought it all sounded amazing.

You would spend three months of the year working out there at a summer camp, then you had another three months when you could travel afterwards. So I did that for two years.

We conspired to get fake IDs, pretending we were 21, allowing us to buy alcohol in America. At the time you could get an international driving licence through the AA in the UK. This was a picture of yourself, a passport photo stuck to a piece of card, and they filled in the details by hand. When it came to the date of birth, we just gave them a couple of years extra. They could see our UK paper licences, but hadn't compared the details! We thought that was excellent, because we had the opportunity to now go drinking while in America.

I was a member of camp staff, organising activities such as arts and crafts, swimming events and hiking. As I am an adventurous type, wanting to do 'other stuff', I managed to spend a couple of weekends in Boston with American and international friends I had made at camp.

During the first year, with our dodgy driving licences, we bought a car to go travelling after our three-month stints at the camps. We drove north to south, New Hampshire to Florida, and south to north. We just stopped off wherever we fancied. Sometimes we stayed in motels and other times we camped out in tents.

We spotted our mode of transport on sale at a garage for $200. It was an enormous, green Dodge Diplomat from the 1970s, like you would see the police use in films from back then. We thought the Dodge was as cool as anything and we called her 'The Green Goddess'.

People had warned us before we left for the USA that, if the police stop you, just stay sitting there. Don't try to get out of the car. If need be, the advice was, put both of your hands out of the window, so they can see you are not armed. We were told that they would have guns drawn, so you didn't want to make a sudden move and end up being shot. A lot of people over there are armed, so they just assume that everyone has a gun. The UK and America? It's like chalk and cheese.

One night we stayed in a National Park. In some of the parks, there are strict laws about drinking alcohol outdoors.

We met up with some of our friends from the UK who were also travelling round. They had bought an old car, too. We bought tins of beer and had an all-night party in the National Park, drinking heavily. We crashed out under the stars on the rough ground. We were woken in the morning by the National Parks police, gently kicking us and pointing guns at our heads.

'Are you making your own licence plates over in Pennsylvania?'

'What are you on about?' we answered, confused.

The number plate on our friends' car had either been stolen or dropped off. A handwritten cardboard one was inserted in its place.

Until we started to speak to the officers, they assumed we were criminals or, at any rate, up to no good. Once they realised we were British tourists, and telling the truth, they were absolutely fine and put the guns away. They did remind us that we weren't allowed to drink in the park, even if we were 21, but didn't follow that up.

Another night, driving through a desert, blue lights came on behind us. The officers pulled us over. We were all lined up at gunpoint. Little did we know that it was a popular drug smuggling route.

After checking us over, we were still under suspicion. Another unit arrived, along with a dog. The dog sniffed everywhere, looking for drugs, but didn't find any and so we were free to go. Again, they were okay with us when they established that we were telling the truth. Matty, one of our group, did have to walk in a straight line for one of those sobriety tests, but he passed without any problem.

On another occasion we were pulled over by the police, with Matty again driving. A patrol car was hiding behind a motorway bridge. It turned out that Matty had been speeding about 10mph over the limit. There was a lot of traffic on this four-lane freeway; Matty said, in a moment of madness, that we would try to outrun the cops. He was weaving in and out of the lanes, causing mayhem.

'Don't be stupid,' I blurted out, as the cop gave chase, with memories of Brad's much earlier misadventure flowing back.

Matty thought better of it and pulled over. Again, the cop approached us at gunpoint! As soon as he realised we were British tourists he became quite friendly. He still wrote out a speeding ticket for Matty of about $200. The fine was never paid. Even to this day, Matty wonders if he is still being pursued for the money!

The Dodge Diplomat did its job. We travelled thousands of miles in it. Eventually we just abandoned the beast in an airport car park. Job done.

Another way of travelling, after the Dodge had had its day, was to deliver cars. Say someone moved from New York to Los Angeles and needed their car delivered. Various companies had the cars delivered for a fee.

People like us would drive the car to the location. We were given a date to deliver the car and all we had to do was pay for fuel, which was very cheap over there.

We enjoyed the journey to our destination, used a car wash before dropping the car off, and continued on our travels.

Reflecting back on my life, the USA had such a strong influence on me. As a kid, I had been brought up on a diet of American films and TV shows. America was cool…and, well, New York, New York!

The Big Apple is a busy and vibrant city and, only being 18-19 years old, my visits there were incredibly exciting. I looked on in awe at everything I had seen on TV: construction road chimneys billowing steam from the street level, the constant traffic, pedestrians jostling for position on the 'sidewalks'; the honking of horns from the slow-moving traffic; the constant flow of yellow New York cabs; and the wail of police sirens in the distance.

I looked up, to see the vast skyscrapers of Manhattan towering above me. However, with the excitement came danger.

On one visit to NYC, Matty had just flown into JFK airport to join us, to travel across America at the end of the summer camp. On his arrival in the city, even before getting booked into a room, with his rucksack on his back, he saw a very American hot dog stand on the sidewalk.

An Italian American with a deep gruff voice was working at the small aluminium-sided mobile fast food stand that had wheels and could be pushed by hand. Naively, he went to buy a New York chilli dog, just like in the movies. He pulled out his money and had a $100 bill in his hand, as he had no change yet.

In a flash, a slim youth snatched the money from his hand and ran off quickly, being enveloped into the crowds of pedestrians, never to be seen again. Being traditionally British mates, we mercilessly took the piss out of Matty for getting robbed on day one of his travels. It did, however, provide us with a good reminder that we had to be careful. It could have been much worse.

Back in Rochdale, before travelling, when working at the pub 'Madisons' I had been telling a customer of my impending travels. He had suggested that, if I was in NYC, to try the following, which we did.

While in Manhattan, we jumped into the back of a yellow cab. I shouted at the driver, 'Follow that car…fast as you can' and thrust a $20 bill into the driver's hand.

'Quick as you can, he's getting away!' as we pointed to a random car in the distance.

The driver smiled back and said, 'Sure thing!'

The taxi driver stamped on the accelerator, causing the wheels to screech as they span round on the hot road surface. A plume of white smoke rose up from under the cab as it lurched forward and we were thrown back in our seats. We all had big smiles on our faces as we chased another car like a cop show through New York!

Well, $20 bucks at the time was a fair amount, and was never going to last for a long taxi ride, so after five minutes or so, we shouted for the driver to pull over and we all bailed out of the cab, laughing.

I also had the chance to drive in New York city. It nearly turned into a nightmare. I was with Matty, Obi, an Australian, and an English lad called Rick, both from camp. I was driving the Green Goddess and took a wrong turn into the Bronx. Four dumb white lads driving through a heavily black, gang-style neighbourhood.

I tried to calm the others saying, 'Don't worry. It's all cool, so long as we keep the car moving.'

We could see large groups of young black men, dressed looking like something from a Michael Jackson 'Bad' music video. All eyes were on us. It was as if they had all stopped talking and were just following us with their gaze, wondering what the hell we were doing in their neighbourhood, and were we a threat to them?

We had driven straight into a narrow dead-end street in the Bronx. On both sides, rows of older, often brick or brownstone-style apartment buildings stood close together. Leading up from the sidewalk to the main entrances of these buildings were distinct sets of concrete steps – classic stoops – creating a repeating visual rhythm down the block. Gangs sat on the steps, eyeballing us all the while. Roughly parked, old American cars lined the curbs, and the street ended abruptly, giving it a contained, we-were-in-the-shit feel.

Matty suggested we try to turn around without stopping and find a McDonalds. No one would shoot us in a McDonald's, would they? That was the theory.

A sense of fear had overcome the interior of our car. I made a wide swing out to turn the vehicle around 180 degrees in one clean movement. Unfortunately, the old Dodge had the turning circle of a bus, and I had to do a very quick three-point turn, slamming the car into reverse using the 'shift stick' gear handle.

Luckily, nobody attacked us. We drove coolly out of that street and onto a road that was situated under the subway system. We were exposed to the sights and sounds of the trains rattling overhead. It was then, we saw the 'Golden Arches' of McDonalds in the distance. We drove up, parked the 'Green Goddess' and all went inside. It felt like the music had stopped and all eyes were on us again. It seemed as if we were the only white people in the whole of the Bronx.

We all ordered burgers and asked the cashier for directions to downtown Manhattan, which she provided. This was in the days before mobile phones and Google Maps helped you out of this type of situation. The cashier was really friendly; I guess once people heard our accent, they quickly realised we were just lost tourists. We managed to escape safely!

In total, I only spent a few days in New York during the two years I visited America. On the first occasion, I met up with a woman from Rochdale, called Linzi. She had been my immediate supervisor when I worked at the council. She had also decided to travel to America, but to work as an au pair and was staying with a family in New Jersey.

We met up for a few days to take in the tourist sights. We visited the Statue of Liberty, watching a highly talented street performer. He was hustling the crowd for loose change with an acrobatic performance while we waited in a long line to get on the Staten Island ferry.

We visited all the usual landmarks including travelling to the top of the World Trade Centre. It was either that or go up the Empire State building, but I could only really afford one of the adventures. We opted for the Twin Towers and, being higher, grabbed an amazing selfie at the top with a cheap plastic 35mm camera.

It proved to be a rare opportunity, given the tragic events of a few years later.

I was asked to become a criminal!

As a teenager growing up in Rochdale in the late '80s, I was doing all the stuff teenagers were doing at the time. I would record my favourite music tracks from the Sunday night chart show, off the radio onto a cassette, while trying to avoid catching the DJ speaking between tracks.

I would play computer games like Pac-man and Elite on my BBC Acorn Electron home computer... and go out drinking underage in pubs!

The first pub my mates and I went to was up Drake Street in Rochdale. A little backstreet style boozer, with an old-fashioned landlord. It was a bit of a dive to be honest, dimly lit and smelling of stale ale, stale crisps and cigarettes. The wallpaper had yellowed after decades of exposure to cigarette smoke.

Aged 15, we coolly walked in with the confidence of youth and approached the bar. A thin old guy with a large red nose, and wearing a flat cap, sat at the end of the bar nursing a pint.

A couple of locals glanced up at us, then paid no more attention.

The landlord asked us what we wanted.

'Five pints of bitter, please,' in my deepest voice.

To my surprise, he reached down to grab some pint glasses below the bar and started pouring pints of beer. We were all obviously underage, but the landlord didn't care. He told us to sit at the back of the pub, warning us not to annoy any of the regulars. We paid for our drinks and kept out of the way of the locals. This was bloody great!

We progressed on from this pub, trying out many more boozers in the town and surrounding villages. By the age of 17, our pub of choice was definitely Madisons (aka Madison Square). Owned by the Greenall Whitley brewery, this was a modern town centre pub. The kind of place to go to on a weekend, before heading out clubbing.

Madisons was positioned at the back of Rochdale Police Station, just over the main road to Hopwood Hall College. A modern purpose-built pub, Madisons had an overhanging tiled canopy running along the front of the door. It had a raised brick flowerbed where patrons stood in queues to get in or gathered by the wooden outdoor picnic-style tables for a pint and a smoke, overlooked by the council high-rise flats known locally as the Seven Sisters.

The inside was split into three levels. The main bar area was mainly for standing. There were pillars that had small wooden standing tables to perch your pint on, with occasional bar stools.

Walking into the venue, you would have been face-to-face with the bar that ran nearly the whole length of the pub. The toilets were to the right of the bar and the food counter was off to the left. I say food counter; nearly all pubs of the time in the town centre were for drinking, not eating. Madisons could maybe knock up a cheese sandwich or some scampi and chips, but not much more.

A space to the right of the bar was used as a DJ/karaoke/dance floor area. At one end of the pub was a sunken area with seats. The other end was mirrored in the same style but raised, not sunken.

What set Madisons apart from the rest of the town centre pubs was the entertainment. Both sides of the front doors were dominated by a wall of TV screens. There were approximately 12 on each side, creating two massive screens. These were not sleek flat screen TVs, but large cathode-ray tube televisions, set into a giant frame of thick brass tubes around each screen. The frame matched the brass tubing that ran down the front of the bar.

This was one of the country's first video juke boxes. £1 got you three videos from what was available on the jukebox. We were in the middle of the MTV generation and this was in Rochdale! Madisons was definitely the place to be for a night out.

Me and the boys were all regulars, and went to the pub most nights. A pint of Festival bitter (not the cheap stuff) was only 77p a pint. This made going out drinking fairly affordable. As time went on, the landlord started employing us all to work at the pub. It made sense as we could still have a night out, see our mates, and get paid for it.

When I was asked to work behind the bar, I had to admit to only being 17 years old. The landlord told me not to worry because I could collect and wash glasses and empty ashtrays instead. Once old enough, I could work behind the bar. Result!

The uniform comprised black trousers, white baggy oversized shirts and red dickie bows. We looked 'the business'. Tony the doorman wore a suit and a dickie bow. Not very practical thinking back, but this was in the days before SIA licences. Tony was ex-military and a top boxer. Probably the toughest fella I have ever met. He normally worked alone but, if it kicked off, any of us behind the bar would help out.

Even though the police station was next door, it often took a long time to get a response from the Old Bill should a group of drunken lads cause trouble. Tony often sorted things out before the police arrived.

On one such occasion, a group of lads in the sunken seating area had been causing problems and refused to leave. Tony went to ask them to vacate the premises, but one brave drunken idiot who refused to take the hint stood up and squared up to Tony.

Tony cut any discussion dead and, without warning, hit the idiot in the face, knocking him clean out with just one punch. I can only describe the melee that followed as a scene from the Wild West. The whole group stood up and started fighting. They broke the wooden stools and used the legs as makeshift coshes. Glasses and ashtrays were being thrown at Tony, some breaking and some not.

But Tony was unfazed by the level of violence, which was extreme. Like *Robocop* from the '80s film, he locked onto each troublemaker one by one, then systematically knocked them out with one or two clinical punches. The last two lads ran as fast as they could out of the doors, not wanting to meet the same fate. We helped to drag the injured or unconscious out of the pub. The walking wounded from the group helped to pull their friends away to safety.

No police complaints and no CCTV. The group of hooligans had just been dealt with swiftly, and in a way that prevented the pub becoming a soft touch for criminal gangs and others seeking to take advantage. Tony was an excellent doorman and a really friendly bloke. He passed away many years later; RIP Tony, it was a pleasure knowing you.

It was not what I would call a dodgy pub, but working in Madisons exposed me to various levels of criminal activity before joining the police. I feel this definitely helped me in my career later on. It made me more streetwise and gave me a better understanding of people and what makes them tick. Social communication skills and reading changes in people's behaviour highlighted any risk to me or others.

As time went on, I worked at the pub not only Thursday, Friday and Saturday nights, but also some midweek and lunchtime shifts. Evenings shifts would often involve a 'lock-in', drinking after 11pm with a takeaway curry from Soloman's curry house, or going clubbing. All the city centre pubs and clubs looked out for each other, and as we were known staff from Madisons, we could get into all the clubs in Rochdale for free!

Lunchtime shifts were quieter, catering for office staff having a pint and a basket of scampi and chips. During one midweek shift, at about 2pm, a lad who was a regular came bounding in full of excitement and confidence. He asked the landlord if he could offer some goods to him, his staff and the customers for sale. The landlord agreed. The lad was weighed down with a large canvas duffle bag over his shoulder that he pulled over his head, dropping it on the floor in front of the bar.

He started his well-rehearsed patter like an experienced market trader.

'You are in luck, as this is a limited time offer! These will not be around for long.'

He unzipped the bag and started pulling out individually cellophane-wrapped designer polo shirts, dress shirts and pairs of jeans.

'I have been able to obtain a job lot of factory smoke-damaged designer clothing. Nothing snide, all kosher. Every top is a fiver, jeans are a tenner. I have even got some Levi 501s in there.'

Immediately this local had the attention of everyone in the pub, keen to purchase a bargain. They formed a small crowd as he set up his makeshift stall on the floor of the pub, laying out more and more clothes.

People started selecting items and buying them. I was curious as to why they did not smell of smoke? Then it dawned on me that he was most likely lying and they must all be nicked. Probably all shoplifted that day in town. He was flogging this nicked haul as quickly and as cheaply as he could so not to get caught with the goods.

I noticed the jeans still had ink dye tags attached. I knew they would break if removed without a special machine in the shop. I now know how the tags can be removed without the machine and preventing the dye ruining the clothing, but at the time I had no idea. I passed on the offer of the cheap clothing, but a lot of people did bag a 'bargain' that day.

One evening, I was walking to work in my Madisons uniform. I didn't own a car at that time but was enjoying the walk during a warm summer's evening. I was just entering the subway from Spotland Road, leading into the Rochdale Exchange shopping centre. This was a great short cut for my route on foot into work.

I heard a car door slam closed behind me and I glanced back over my shoulder. Four lads of Pakistani heritage, all aged in their late teens to early 20s had got out of a saloon car. They quickly followed me down into the entrance of the underpass, out of view of passing cars. I instantly felt uneasy, as if something bad was going to happen.

One of the youths grabbed me by my arm, stopping me walking and pulled me around to face the group.

He just said, 'Give us your money.'

Being 6'6" tall, I thought he was taking the piss. Was this guy for real? He was only about 5'10" and of a slim build. I glanced at each member of the group, weighing each one up, sensing this was about to get physical. I needed to work out who I may have to hit first.

'Or else?' I questioned.

With that, I spotted the main suspect now had both his hands down by his side. He suddenly dropped a two-foot length grey cut-off scaffolding pole from the inside of his shirt sleeve, catching it in his hand.

Fuck, I thought. This was going to be a very unfair fight. Totally unprovoked, he immediately swung the cosh with his right hand, hitting me in the jaw. An intense pain resonated through my skull. I could taste the bitter iron taste of my own blood in my mouth. I raised my arms to protect my head and felt him rain down further blows from the cosh. I went down, crashing to the floor like a sack of spuds. The blows were too powerful to retaliate. I was just trying to protect my head as best as I could. Once on the floor, the other lads started kicking me in the body and head. The pain was short-lived, as I was knocked unconscious.

I came round a short time later on the cold concrete floor. I was on my own now. Feeling dazed, I checked myself for any serious injuries. Nothing obvious. I steadied myself on the wall as I stood up and dusted myself down. The small amount of money I had on me was gone. My gold watch had also been ripped off my wrist. It was not really expensive, but that was not the point. I felt angry. Why would someone do that? Why me? What gave them the right to mug me? I had so many questions. I was raging inside with anger.

I walked through the shopping centre and the remaining short distance to Madisons. Bearing in mind that the police station was next door, I should have gone and reported the crime as a robbery. Instead, I was really pissed off and wanted revenge. A few of the lads were already in the pub and could see the state I was in.

Jon offered to drive around the town and find the lads who had done this. A seed was planted at that moment and we quickly pulled together a posse of about 8-10 people to dish out some summary justice. I told the landlord I would be back soon to start my shift, and we jumped into a couple of cars and started our search for the offenders.

It was probably best we never found the group of lads that evening. After an 'area search, no trace' I returned to complete my shift. The following morning, I turned up to work at the council offices, and my boss was shocked and horrified at the state of my face. I had a black swollen eye, my lip was cut and I had various bruises. I explained what had happened to her and she immediately called the police.

I spent most of the day in a CID office drinking tea, giving a statement to detectives, and looking at photos of suspects in large folders in the hope I would identify the offenders. I was, unfortunately. unable to pick anyone out. The police were brilliant and made great efforts to catch the offenders, but they were never brought to justice. I put the incident down to experience and moved on.

At weekends we were very busy and would have four or five bar staff serving drinks flat out. The bar would be five deep with customers. It was great fun, music blaring, chatting up women and ignoring idiots waving a £5 or £10 note to grab the bar staff's attention. *Yes mate, I know you are there, but these other people were in front. You can wait.*

Monday, Tuesday and Wednesday tended to be a bit quieter than the rest of the week. The landlord would put on events to fill the place up. On one occasion, he put on some cheap cocktails. Very cosmopolitan and right up the street of any northern aspiring yuppies! The trouble was, none of us knew how to make cocktails apart from a pint of Green Monster, Snakebite or a Slippery Nipple, but they did not really count.

However, the brewery did know an expert, who was sent to the pub to train us. Large rubber mats were placed behind the bar and all the staff listened to this man with excited interest. He placed a list of ingredients for the most popular cocktails behind the bar for us to refer to.

We were more interested in how to learn the skills that looked really 'showy', like throwing bottles of spirits and tossing glasses to each other, or mastering the short and long pour techniques.

We wanted to put on a performance behind the bar during service. Who better to teach us than the instructor who trained Tom Cruise for the film *Cocktail!* Well, that's what we were told at the time, as to who he was.

We all fell hook, line and sinker for this story. Looking back, I doubt some dude with a northern accent was actually John Bandy, the bartender who trained Tom Cruise. The actor's training was held at a Bartending School in Toronto, Ontario. This felt like a little too far for John, all the way from

Canada, who drove down the M62 to Rochdale just for one night.

The dude we had training us did know his stuff when it came to making cocktails. He was brilliant, starting us off on fake weighted plastic spirit bottles to throw. We soon moved onto the other skills and we quickly became pretty good at it. The rubber matting did save the occasional slip, but we could all soon toss a bottle over our shoulder or slam a Boston shaker onto the bar.

Our discounted cocktail nights went down a storm with the customers. We had other events to try to bring in the crowds like DJs, inflatables, mud wrestling and karaoke.

Karaoke was a big thing back then. Straight from Japan, it gave talented or tone-deaf singers like myself the chance to sing popular songs of the time to crowds of drunken people. The problem was that everyone was shy at the start of the night and didn't want to embarrass themselves.

The DJ hosting the karaoke night needed a willing volunteer to start off proceedings. I was quickly nominated as the one to make a fool of himself first. My opening number was always 'Unchained Melody' by the Righteous Brothers. It was a massively popular song after being used in the blockbuster film *Ghost* in 1990. My version was probably not so popular! I was able to sing slowly and with a deep voice, as the song was not too difficult.

Customers then filled out a slip of paper, with the song they wanted to sing, and the night would be off to a great start. Madisons was a great venue for karaoke. As we had the big TV screens, everyone in the pub could follow or sing along with the words to the songs if they wanted.

One regular customer, who loved the karaoke machine, was a lad who I'll call Dave, not his real name. He was in his early 20s with dark wavy hair. He visited the pub three or four nights a week.

Dave's song of choice was 'Hold the Line' by American rock band *Toto*. When he picked up the wired microphone and started singing, the pub stopped. He had a really strong voice and it sounded like *Toto* were in the pub, playing a live gig. He was very confident and talented, and Dave's performance was phenomenal. Always with money and not shy when it came to buying a round of drinks, he was the life and soul of the party.

The staff and regulars got on really well and, on occasions, met up for social trips out. One such trip on a Sunday was to Alton Towers theme park. A chance to ride rollercoasters and have a laugh. I never went, as I was working the Sunday and Monday shifts at the pub, but a group of about 10 or 12 customers had a day trip. I didn't think anything more of it, until I was working behind the bar on Sunday night.

It was really quiet and I was standing next to the end of the bar, leaning on an empty glass food cabinet. I was chatting with some of the regulars, waiting for the next customer. One of the girls said worriedly, 'Did you hear Dave never turned up to the Alton Towers trip? Nobody heard from him and he never answered his phone.'

On the face of it, this was not unusual, as we didn't have mobile phones, just house phones. She pulled out a Silk Cut cigarette, lighting it with a Zippo lighter and took a deep drag. She went on to say it was highly unusual for Dave, as he loved that sort of thing. He had paid for his ticket and everything. She had heard rumours he might have been nicked by the Old Bill, but she didn't know anything else.

The following evening, I was again behind the bar working. Being a Monday, it was quiet with only a maximum of about 15 customers spread out around the pub. Dave walked in, looking a bit glum.

'The usual?' I asked, to which he nodded and I poured him a pint. After giving him his change, he pulled up a bar stool and sat at the end of the bar.

'I heard you never made it to Alton Towers,' I said.

'Nah. I got nicked. The Rozzers raided my house,' Dave replied.

'Bloody hell,' I said slowly.

Dave leaned in slightly towards me. I sensed he wanted to speak, but out of the earshot of others in the pub. I leaned in and Dave spoke in a low tone.

'I got nicked for an armed robbery. I held up a Post Office.'

'Fucking hell,' I gasped. 'Go on.'

I was encouraging him to spill the beans and tell me more. This revelation was totally unexpected. He slowly and carefully explained what had happened. He had decided to rob a local Post Office. The plan was to wait and watch, until there were no more customers, then he would enter. He explained how he entered the Post Office wearing a full-face motorcycle helmet to hide his identity.

We were now joined by the landlord, who also listened silently with interest.

Dave continued, explaining he slipped a note to the cashier stating that this was a robbery. He had a gun that he pointed at the Post Office worker. The cashier, who would have been terrified, filled some canvas money bags with bank notes, passing them to Dave via the hatch in the counter. Dave covered up the gun and money, then walked out, so as not to attract attention. He got into his car, an Austin Mini, and made his escape.

Oh my God! I had so many questions to ask. I couldn't believe I was speaking to an actual armed robber. Looking at him and knowing him as I did, I would never have put him down as an armed robber.

I asked him, 'Why? What made you do it? It seems a little extreme!'

Dave replied, 'It wasn't really for the money, it was for the rush. Bigger and better than any drug. That adrenaline rush is out of this world!'

He continued talking about the euphoric high he had immediately during and after the robbery.

Dave said, 'I'd have probably gotten away with it if some old biddy hadn't seen me getting into my mini wearing a crash helmet. She wrote down my car reg and told the police when she heard about the robbery.'

The landlord asked, what had he done with the gun afterwards?

'I should have ditched it, but the police found it back at mine.'

I was stunned. He carried on saying the police had also found most of the money back at his home. The landlord then suggested Dave should have approached him about getting rid of the gun, as he would have had no problems doing that.

My mind was racing. The landlord was talking about dumping a gun used in crime, or knew some very heavy people. Where do I work? I only thought I worked in a town centre pub, not some meeting point for organised crime. This all felt a little bit heavy and way out of my comfort zone.

'How come you're out then, and not banged up?' asked the landlord.

Dave claimed he was one of the first people in the country to ever get bail for an armed robbery. To this day, I still don't know how he was able to be bailed for such an offence. I can only guess. The landlord went off to the cellar, which was just a refrigerated room at the back of the pub, to change a beer barrel. Dave was still eager to speak to me. He glanced around nervously.

'I know I'm gonna get banged up for a number of years. I need to make sure I've got a nest egg for when I come out. Do you want to help me? I've got it all worked out.'

I was speechless at the enormity of what was being asked of me. Dave continued speaking.

'I'm gonna do another robbery on a post office, but well away from the town. I'm looking at driving to Halifax. I'm not going to make the mistake of taking a real gun this time. I'm just going to hold up my fingers or a piece of tube in my pocket. You don't even have to come in with me. I just need somebody to act as a lookout outside, but who can run fast and drive a car.'

Dave was deadly serious. I was also feeling a rush of adrenaline now, at the prospect of being invited to take part in such a serious crime. Was I being stupid? Flattered maybe, but this wasn't me. I may have been naive and made a number of stupid mistakes growing up, but I wasn't a criminal. Definitely not an armed robber! With good reason…

I had decided that being a police officer was the career for me. It certainly didn't take a brain surgeon or rocket scientist to work out that taking part in an armed robbery would be a bad career move. I thanked Dave, but politely declined, stating I didn't have the bollocks for it.

Sure enough, a few months later, Dave was convicted of two armed robberies and jailed for seven years. Whenever I hear the song, 'Hold the Line' by *Toto*, it reminds me of Dave.

The whole incident left me thinking. Could joining the police be any more dangerous than this?

Raised in Rochdale, made in Portsmouth

When I was about 20 years old, my parents were on my back, saying that I needed to get a proper job; a career that would provide for the future and come with a pension. I looked into all sorts of different things, still with the police option on my mind.

At school we had a careers talk. We filled out a sheet and ticked off various metrics. That was sent off to a super computer somewhere. A few weeks later we received our results, suggesting our preferred professions and what we might consider as job possibilities.

My number one option, picked by the computer, was for a taxidermist. I had to look up exactly what a taxidermist did. I read all about preparing dead animals for preservation. I did laugh and then thought, no thank you. Stuff that!

There were other opportunities such an air traffic controller, the prison service and even working as a gardener.

I knuckled down at the careers office. This was before the days of the internet. You had to go to a careers office or the library and do your research. I took home the prison service details for a good look through.

When I really thought about looking after Britain's most dangerous prisoners, I changed my mind. Villains didn't want to be locked up and weren't fans of prison officers. I knew that this career was not for me. I take my hat off to anyone who does that job. I have had a brief glimpse of what it is like to be inside a jail. I must say that prison officers do an outstanding job at keeping us safe, as well as the prisoners they are looking after. I believe that, very often, it is a thankless task.

I wanted some adventure, well away from prisons, and not a desk job either. That's when I thought more seriously about a career in the police. I tried to find out about various policing roles, knowing that I would have to join as a constable. It would be a two-year probationary period and then I would be able to look at other specialised roles within the police service.

I had also been interested in joining the armed forces and considered the Military Police. I went along to the military careers office, explained my interest and took away an application form. When I started work on the form, pen and paper back then, my dad asked what jobs I was looking at. I said I was thinking about joining the Military Police. I told him I was looking at a role there, becoming a 'Red Cap'.

Without warning, he went off on one: 'You're not becoming a bloody Red Cap. They hate everyone. Everyone hates them. Doesn't matter whether you are in civilian life or in the military, nobody likes them.'

So that put a total kibosh on the idea.

It is only now as I write this, in my 50s, I realise that Dad must have had a run-in with the Military Police when he was in the British Army. Whether it was justified or not, I have no idea. That can be the only explanation for such a strong reaction against the Military Police.

I love the Royal Navy recruitment advert titled, 'Made in the Royal Navy - Born in Carlisle'. It was created as a recruitment advertisement for the Royal Navy and Royal Marines. I was raised in Rochdale, but made in Portsmouth – not by the Royal Navy, but eventually by the police. Here is how it all started…

I had a look at the police forces in my area. Could I join one of them? I contacted Greater Manchester Police and they invited me into their headquarters. I had a short interview with a sergeant there. Unfortunately, he explained that there was a recruitment freeze on, and they weren't taking on any new constables.

My hopes had been dashed. I thought I was never going to join the police. I found out more about my grandfather who had been a police officer with Lancashire Constabulary. I had never heard many stories about his antics. He was a quiet and reserved man. I learned that, at one, time, he lived in a police house.

His wife, my grandmother or 'nana' as I called her, always used to say she felt sorry for the criminals who were locked up. She sometimes looked after the people who were kept in cells for the weekend. Those were in the days before PACE, the Police and Criminal Evidence Act, brought in during 1986. The Act stipulated strict timelines that people could be held in detention before being charged or released.

That family tradition helped to drive me on.

I checked with Lancashire, the neighbouring force area to Manchester, but again I was told about the recruitment freeze. I then looked at all surrounding counties such as Yorkshire and Cheshire, but all had a recruitment freeze on except for Merseyside. Now there has always been a lot of banter between the two great cities of Manchester and Liverpool. Maybe it dates back to early football matches or the docks, but for whatever reason the rivalry has continued for many years. There was often a great dislike on both sides, which never made any sense to me.

For a short time, I worked in a pub close to Liverpool. There, I experienced more than a taste of the banter. I couldn't see myself working as a police officer in Liverpool with my Mancunian accent! It looked as if I would have to wait at least a year before joining the police.

I studied a map of the United Kingdom and counted 45 territorial police forces as well as many other organisations such as British Transport Police and Ministry of Defence Police. I looked down south and saw the county of Hampshire where the force's area includes the Isle of Wight. I thought it would be a really good bet to go somewhere like that. Firstly, because it was down south. In Manchester, everything seems to be grey and it rains a lot. Now I love Manchester and Rochdale and the North West. The people are fantastic, but the weather is miserable. I could see that Hampshire had sunshine, beaches and good weather. What more could I want?

I had no friends or family down there. In fact, I don't think I had even visited Hampshire. I decided that this was where I was going to become a police officer. I called them up and asked if they were recruiting. Luckily for me, they were taking on new constables. They sent me an application form and so started my adventure in the police.

I filled out the form, again all written by hand. I was never the best at writing neatly, and I was the kind of person who had to check the spelling two or three times. However, I figured that a couple of hours of pain would provide me with decades of gain.

I popped the application form into the post and waited. It wasn't long before I received a reply saying I had been successful in the initial application stage. I was invited to attend the Southern Support Training HQ in Netley, near Southampton.

I arranged a coach journey from Manchester all the way down to Hampshire. Then I caught a train connection on an old slam-door train to the very small station at Hamble. It was totally unmanned, without even a waiting room, just a platform. I got off carrying a small bag. Then I walked two miles or so to the bed and breakfast that I had managed to book through a magazine. I unpacked my kit and waited for the following day when my interview process would take place.

I had brought a conservative dark suit for the occasion. My feet were hurting because my shoes were too tight for such a long walk.

The police training centre is in the grounds of an old military hospital. Once inside the imposing building, I stood nervously with about 30 other recruits. We were to be put through various tests and scenarios to see if we would be likely candidates. We were taken to a large lecture theatre, separated between seats so that everyone was kept apart, and given a form to complete.

We were told that we were going to have an observation test, and to watch the screen in front of us. A number of clips were played. We saw simulated crimes taking place. There would be a robbery, including a street scene, then people going in and out of doors, holding objects.

We would be asked various questions about what we had seen. What colour was the woman's hat? What did she say? What accent did the man have? What type of bag was he carrying? How many people were in the car? Registration number? I felt that I had performed well in the test. Then there was a talk about general policing duties and what we could expect to encounter.

Next, we were put into small groups and engaged in conversations. A member of staff introduced questions to the groups. This test was all about uncovering whether you had strong political opinions or views about race and diversity.

I remember one of the questions: which group of people in society did I dislike the most? If they saw hesitation, I knew they would ask why I took so long. I said I disliked students who had been in education for their entire lives, were still young, but believed they knew everything. They thought they were worldly wise, but all they had experienced was the educational bubble.

I said there was no particular group in society that I disliked. I treated everyone as I would expect to be treated myself. Only when people became abusive or disrespectful would my opinion change. I said that, if you treat people well, they would usually return the favour.

I did speak to a WPC later at Ashford, during my training who had made the grade. She said she had been asked what she thought about euthanasia. She said, 'I think we should send them more aid and, if need be, grant them asylum.'

I rolled my eyes and tried not to laugh. She was actually successful with her application, although not with the Hampshire force!

After lunch we then went on to the gym, got changed and prepared for a medical and a fitness test. Now I wasn't too worried about the medical, because as far as I was aware there was nothing wrong with me. I seemed to pass that without any problems. I then went on to do the physical fitness test. At that time, we had to do what most people dreaded, the 'bleep test'. This involves running from one side of the sports hall to the other, with around 100 feet between two lines. You go to the line on the beat. Every minute the bleeps begin to progressively get quicker and quicker.

When I joined, the expectation was for men to do this, flat out, for 10½ minutes. I believe the time for women was 7½ minutes. I had been in training prior to this and was able to accomplish the task without too much difficulty and continued running for about 13 minutes before I stopped.

I saw many men and women stopping well before the allotted times. I thought this seemed quite strange to me, because the exercise was relatively straightforward. I believe the bleep test for new candidates is now about 5½ minutes and I hear there are still many candidates who don't achieve that. What does that say about modern society and lack of fitness?

We then went on to doing sit-ups in pairs. The person you were paired with held onto your ankles while you completed the sit-ups. The task was to get as many done as possible in a minute. I believe I achieved around 50 sit-ups in a minute, so again quite a strong candidate. I'm not sure I'd want to do that nowadays!

The person I was teamed up with put in an impressive number of sit-ups and we were then asked to complete as many press-ups as we could in one minute. My partner smashed out about 40 press-ups.

Press-ups didn't suit my gangly frame. I was really slow to get them done, and managed about 13 in the minute. My partner kindly told the instructor that I had done 26, so that number was recorded. I'm not sure whether the staff cottoned onto the ploy! But I didn't dispute my total. I reckon they realised I was useless at press-ups, but good at the other tasks.

There was also a flexibility test where you sat down on the floor and put your hands towards your feet. There was a wooden panel that you pushed along to show how far you could reach.

I also recall a grip test, involving a device that you pulled with your fingers. No problems there.

I can safely say that the candidate I was paired with, who helped me through, really saved my bacon. I believe he was also successful. Without his help, I might not have made the grade. Sometimes you just need a little bit of luck.

There were two days of these tasks and being asked to discuss various scenarios. At the end of it all, we weren't told whether we had been successful. They just said we would be notified in writing, and that was the end of it for now.

Local candidates would have received a visit from a sergeant to their home address. The sergeant inspected that address and spoke with family members. It was part of a vetting process to see what kind of family you came from, who you associated with, what your house was like and the kind of environment you lived in. Were the surroundings suitable for someone in the local force? They were obviously looking to make sure that there was no chance of you being corrupted. They assessed the values within your home setting.

Many of the candidates who joined at that time had one of those visits. However, with me being nearly 300 miles away, I don't believe they were going to send anybody up north. I just had an extra interview with a sergeant which seemed a little pointless at the time. He asked various questions about my home setting. And, to be fair, he seemed satisfied with what I had told him.

Just before leaving, I was called in before a panel of four senior officers. I sat down in the chair in front of them. It was quite intimidating and scary. I recall them mulling over whether I was a suitable candidate. It felt very much like this was my one and only chance to convince the decision makers that they should take a punt and have a bet on me.

A grey-haired inspector said: 'We've brought you back because we're just not sure about you. We're not sure if you will be the right sort of person and have the right life experience to be a constable.'

I felt some anger rising up inside me. I felt as though he was accusing me of not being good enough and my upbringing wouldn't be suitable. I made an impassioned speech as to why they should select me and the fact that I'd had a number of jobs and met all sorts of people from all walks of life.

I was good at communicating. I could prepare written reports. I was good observationally and my work, in particular in the pub, would put me in good stead when dealing with conflict.

There were a few nods between the senior officers and some glances of eye contact between them and they scribbled down some notes. With that, they said I was free to go free to go and I would be contacted by post.

Off I went home, back on the train and then the coach. A few weeks later I received a typewritten letter saying that my application had been successful.

I would be joining Hampshire and Isle of Wight Constabulary on 14 September, 1992. I was just 21 years old.

Training for my future

I n 1989, a new modular training program had been introduced. This programme required new recruits to attend in-force training venues for up to four weeks during the first module. Although the recommended training period was a minimum of 17 days, this minimum duration was often all that was provided. This discrepancy highlights the conflict between the need for adequate training and the organisational pressure to deploy police officers on the streets as quickly as possible.

I spent two weeks at the Hampshire Police Southern Training Centre in Netley. That was Module One, or Mod One, as we called it.

I stayed in the Victoria House accommodation block, part of the old Netley Hospital. This was never any good, even after being refurbished. Each room had a single bed, table and a sink. There was a thin duvet, with a pillow as thick and luxurious as a cream cracker. The rooms were cold, damp and depressing. I hated having to stay at Netley on courses.

At the rear of the site, D Block (Victoria House) and E Block (Albert House) formed the old psychiatric hospital. D

Block was opened in 1870 as the army's first purpose-built military asylum.

These buildings were also used from the 1950s to 1978 to treat army and navy personnel who suffered from sexually transmitted diseases, drug and alcohol problems, and later housed the Joint Armed Services Psychiatric Unit. The perfect place for new young police recruits.

Hampshire Constabulary wanted us out on the streets and operational as soon as possible, so our 'Mod One' was only two weeks long. That said, we were based at the training centre and not allowed to venture out. It was all very basic stuff, like being issued with our uniform and equipment.

We filed into a classroom one by one and picked up our uniforms, having been previously measured. We then had to try it on, which quite frankly felt like putting on fancy dress, writing our name and 'collar' number inside our hat/helmet. This was advised by our trainers to prevent loss. If found by the public, having fallen off during a scuffle with a villain, the hat would hopefully be reunited with you. However, it turned out in reality that there was more chance of putting your hat and paperwork on top of a police car, getting in and being driven off at speed to the next job, only to see a confetti of paperwork blowing in the breeze behind you. This would be highly amusing for the locals who would see your helmet rolling down the road. The other, more probable reason, was cops in the station picking it up by 'mistake'.

We would learn how to stand up and salute, performed whenever an officer of the rank of inspector or above entered the room.

At this point we were not actually police officers. To be a police officer you need to be sworn in by a 'Justice of the Peace' also known as a JP or magistrate, or known by the criminal fraternity as 'The Beak'.

An Attestation.

Every police officer and special constable is required, on appointment, to be attested by making an 'Oath of Declaration' in a prescribed form before a Justice of the Peace in the force area concerned, implemented by the Police Reform Act of 2002.

Policing Powers.

This Oath transforms the member of the public, becoming a police officer, into an official crown servant – a constable.

A warrant card is presented, and the constable now has the powers of a police officer.

By the end of Mod One, we all attended the ceremony held in the lecture theatre at Netley. Friends and family attended (not mine, as they all lived too far away) but it was a very proud moment to be sworn in and presented with my warrant card. The force photographer took a few pictures to record the event and that was that. I was now a police officer, yet I still had no idea what I was doing or how to do it. Scary!

I looked down at my warrant card that was housed in a leather pouch. This opened up to reveal the warrant card on one side and a large silver shiny Hampshire crest on the other. Cool, I now had a badge I could 'flash', just like the cops on those TV shows and films! I was excited to get started.

During Mod One and Mod Two, I had loads of things happening. I received my posting. This was the police station I would be stationed at during and after my training period. My base would be Portsmouth Central. I was 'well chuffed' as I knew a city centre nick would be busy, providing a lot of work and a good variety of crime and jobs to deal with.

I had moved into a section house to live, having come down from the north. This building was part of Fareham police station. The section house is long gone, and my room is now an office. There was a section house in all the Policing Divisions in the force area. The section house was brilliant, comprising about 10 to 15 rooms, housing mainly all new young constables plus the odd detective who was going through a divorce and been kicked out of the family home!

We were able to mix and socialise. There was a bar at the police station and also a canteen to buy a hot meal. The rooms themselves were very small, with a single bed, a wardrobe, table and chair, with no en-suite facilities, just a shared bathroom. Everyone was in the same boat and it was great to be able to spend time with people in the same situation as yourself.

My first job on moving down south was to head to Fareham Market and buy myself a sad looking tea set for one. A single plate, bowl, cup and cutlery.

I chatted with another recruit called Justin who also was living at the section house, having joined on my intake from a different part of the country. He told me he was being posted to Cosham police station.

Neither of us knew the county and he had looked up the town on a map. Cosham is positioned just north of Portsmouth. He and his family had seen that it was close to the sea, and imagined walking around on foot patrol like *Dixon of Dock Green*, saying 'Hello' to long-bearded fishermen in yellow waterproof clothing, as they sat on the harbour walls, fixing fishing nets while smoking their pipes.

Cosham was, in fact, a small high street of shops and a massive concrete jungle of a council housing estate, mixed in with a few private houses. Not quite the little fishing village he had imagined!

A new language in the police

One thing that worried me when joining the police was not the dangers I might face, but the fact I would have to learn a new language. The phonetic alphabet!

Most people know that the phonetic alphabet is a list of words, each one standing for a letter, like Alpha for A, Bravo for B, and so forth. They are used to spell things out clearly over the phone or radio, making sure there's no confusion, especially when the connection is a bit ropey or it's hard to hear. This is vitally important in the military or the emergency services, when lives can be in danger if the radio message is not clearly sent and received as intended.

Here is the NATO phonetic alphabet, commonly used in the UK and globally:

A - Alpha   L - Lima   W - Whisky
B - Bravo   M - Mike   X - X-ray
C - Charlie   N - November   Y - Yankee
D - Delta   O - Oscar   Z - Zulu
E - Echo   P - Papa
F - Foxtrot   Q - Quebec
G - Golf   R - Romeo
H - Hotel   S - Sierra
I - India   T - Tango
J - Juliet   U - Uniform
K - Kilo   V - Victor

The last time I had to learn a new language was at school. I took French, as I thought it would be easier to learn than German, which was the alternative language studied at Oulder Hill school. I took French as a CSE exam and managed a 'U', meaning 'unclassified'! I am no expert on school exam boards, but I guess I must have spelt my own name wrong with a result like that! I was terrible at languages.

I really wanted to do well in my new policing career, so set about learning the phonetic alphabet even before moving down south. I would practise reading number plates of passing cars in my head, and getting friends to 'test' me down the pub. Somehow, I managed to learn it.

I need not have worried. The phonetic alphabet was not going to be the most difficult language I needed to understand on moving down to Portsmouth. It was going to be the local dialect and slang.

In the UK we have lots of strong regional accents and local dialects that makes each area unique and different. I have a strong 'northern' accent from Rochdale, which can sometimes make it difficult to be understood, especially down south. 'Pompey' is no different, and is a slang term for Portsmouth. As I first stepped out walking on the streets of Pompey, I could hear this whole new language being spoken by the locals. I knew I would need to learn and understand it.

I decided to walk around Pompey city centre before starting my new job, to familiarise myself. I overheard a group of lads chatting as I walked past them in Commercial Road, and the conversation went something like;

'Oi, Oi! You's alright mushty, wot u doin?'

'For farks sake, goin' over Turk town later to do some chorin'. It's noice the gavvers don't nose me for chorin' over there.'

'Don't be a farkin' dinlo. Yoose on bail.'

Translated, that conversation would mean the following,

'Hello, are you okay, friend? What are you doing?'

*Exasperated swearing. 'I'm going over to Gosport to do some stealing (shoplifting normally). It's nice the police don't know me over in Gosport.'

'Don't be fucking stupid. You are on police bail.'

As you can see, like Cockney rhyming slang, Pompey has a whole local dialect I had to get to grips with. Portsmouth is technically an island on the south coast of England connected by bridges to the mainland. Many residents have that island mentality, with some locals rumoured never to have left Portsea Island, even for a holiday! With a vast association with the Royal Navy, it is a diverse city with a unique and fascinating history. This slang was once widely used as a signal of heritage and a sense of pride in the local community.

If you go 'dayntain' (down town) to the Pompey FC stadium, Fratton Park on a match day, or a local market or pub, you will still hear the spoken slang commonly known as 'Pompey Speak'.

The maritime ambiance in Portsmouth has given the Pompey accent its own unique flair, distinct from the more rural-sounding Hampshire accent. It's got a bit of a Cockney flavour, being the closest match, with loads of London slang filtering down to Pompey over time. This makes sense since, after World War II, lots of Londoners were rehoused in Portsmouth, and plenty of East End dockworkers moved there too.

'Pompey Speak' stands out with its diverse structure and phonetics compared to other regional English accents. You'll also hear a mix of borrowed words from Cockney slang and Romany Gypsy origins, especially since some Romany families were relocated to Portsmouth when Gypsy and Traveller sites, particularly in the New Forest, were shut down. There are lots of words and phrases that make up 'Pompey Speak'.

This is a short A-Z selection of the best and most well-known phrases.

Cop the needle – To 'cop the needle' is when someone gets proper narked or wound up about something, often used for someone who's getting a bit shirty or annoyed. It can be shortened to say that someone has 'copped' or 'well copped'

Cream Krackered – To be very exhausted and tired. This is a phrase that has come down from London.

Chore/Chor - Meaning Stolen. 'Chored' is of Romany Gypsy origin. This was a phrase I heard a lot at work. Suspects used it in interviews and even store detectives would use it to describe thefts. Most people who lived in Pompey in the '90s had a pedal bike chored.

Chinny – This is used when a person is not believing in what another person is saying! Or you may say 'Chinny Recon' and rub your chin at the same time. This is the same as saying 'Jimmy Hill' when you don't believe somebody.

Chuffed – When someone is happy or proud of an accomplishment.

Chufty badge – When someone's chuffed to bits about something they've done and won't shut up talking about it, you might ask if they want a 'chufty badge'.

Cushty – Everything is great. Romany Gypsy in origin.

Diamond Geezer – A really great bloke.

Div – Someone who is stupid.

Divvi – A word borrowed from the Romany Gypsy language meaning crazy.

Dinlo – A playful insult meaning idiot or fool. 'Din', and 'dinny' are also used. Like many words on this list, it is Romany Gypsy in origin.

Duff – A term used when something is broken. 'E got duff'ed up real good' would translate as 'He got beaten up badly'.

Eze up – When someone is getting a bit too much in your face and you need them to calm down.

Gavvers – The police. Another Romany Gypsy word.

Gettin' lairy – When someone is being a bit too cocky, or they are being overly sarcastic, or losing their cool.

Got a chuffty on – When you are commenting on a person being proud of something. Sometimes said in a sarcastic tone, i.e. 'I bet you got a chuffty on about it'.

Got a loight? - Asking for a light, usually for a cigarette.

Init – Isn't it.

Knackered – Exhausted, tired, can also mean 'broken' if applied to an object.

Knukledayn – To knuckle down, to get on with a task.

Likes - Adding an 's' to the word 'like' is a very popular occurrence. If you wanted to sound like a local then 'Ts' in words become silent and add an 's'to the end of everything you say. For example, Yous twos.

Well, Mangey – Something looks dirty, ill or uncared for. 'That dog was well, mangey.'

Matelot – Slang for a sailor.

Mush – (Pronounced as moosh). A Romany Gypsy word originally meaning man or good friend, but now used for a mate.

Mush Bird – A rather masculine woman!

Mullered – Another word nicked from the Romany Gypsies, which can mean either proper drunk or someone's been properly battered in a fight.

Noice One Geeze – Good job mate.

Off ya 'ed – Someone who isn't thinking right…likely to be intoxicated!

Oi knows oi dooes – I know I do.

Out of order – Not exclusive to Portsmouth, but a phrase very much used in Pompey. It describes the view that something - or someone - is unfair or has done something wrong, rather than something is not working or is out of sequence. 'You can't nick him! That's out of order.'

Play up Pompey - The famous Portsmouth Football Club chant.

Pompey Pineapple – ladies from Portsmouth on a night out may wear a Pompey Pineapple hairstyle. The hair was pulled up to the top of the head, then a hair band held it in place so it resembled the leaves on top of a pineapple.

Pompey Strut (aka The Pompey Shuffle) – Walking with a swagger that nobody was going to mess with them.

Roight Scank – A disgusting person.

Sort – A person that is good looking.

Scum/Scummer – A Southampton fan, or a resident of Southampton.

Squinny – To complain or cry a lot!

See a man about a dog – Borrowed from Cockney slang, this means to attend a meeting, or an excuse for what someone was doing when committing a criminal offence.

Skive – To take an unwarranted day off work or school, for example, pulling a sickie!

Tain –Town

Taking the piss – Mocking someone.

Tickety-boo – When something is going smoothly without any disasters.

Turk Tain – Is a reference to the neighbouring town of Gosport.

Turned 'round n said – When referencing to how someone had told another person off (i.e. I turned 'round n said to em...).

Well 'ard – Someone who knows how to take care of themselves. Don't mess with them!

You is doin' my swede in mush - You are giving me a headache, mate.

I quickly picked up the local lingo, speaking with the locals while at work. I would often ask colleagues about various phrases if I did not know what they meant.

Particular crimes also have their own sub-culture and language, such as drugs. An example would be cannabis. It has between 50-100 different slang names. If you wanted to get good at nicking people for crimes, it was important to understand and learn everything you could about the subject, including the language.

I tried to learn everything I could about drugs and crime. It was much more interesting than learning French!

Love at first sight

After a few months of living the glamorous life of a rookie copper in a box room at Fareham Police Station, the novelty had well and truly worn off. The section house had been a brilliant introduction to the job, a sort of halfway house between training school and the real world, and I'd made some cracking mates. But sharing a corridor with a dozen other recruits, all on different shift patterns, meant your rest days were punctuated by the sound of someone else's alarm clock or the clatter of boots heading out for an early turn. It was becoming intolerable. A man needs his own space, a sanctuary away from the constant hum of the nick.

Three of us recruits living in the section house: Justin, Scott and I decided to pool our resources and escape the confines of institutional living. We set off on foot and headed for the estate agent's in Fareham, feeling like proper grown-ups. We were presented with a sheaf of glossy printouts, each one a portal to a potential new life. We flicked through them, imagining ourselves in various living rooms, arguing over who would get the biggest bedroom.

Eventually, we found it. A lovely semi-detached, three-bedroom house that seemed to tick all the boxes. The viewing confirmed it, The place was perfect. The house came fully furnished with all the modern conveniences we needed, including a large brown sofa in the living room upholstered in a fabric uncannily reminiscent of Bungle, the large bear from the 1980s children's television show *Rainbow*.

The location was a stone's throw from all our respective stations, and it was nestled in a quiet, respectable neighbourhood. This was crucial, as we knew it wouldn't take long for the locals to clock the constant parade of uniformed officers coming and going at all hours. We didn't want to be living in a neighbourhood full of criminals.

I drew the short straw for the front bedroom. It was a decent size, with a nice view of the street, but it came with a rather peculiar feature: a large, white chest freezer, secured with a heavy-duty padlock. The owners, who had moved abroad for a few years, had left strict instructions with the estate agent. Under no circumstances were we to open the freezer. Oh, and the attic was also padlocked and strictly off-limits.

Now, you can't tell three suspicious coppers not to be suspicious. It's like telling a dog not to bark at the postman. Our minds, trained to look for the unusual, went into overdrive. What on earth was in that freezer? And why was it padlocked? My first thought, naturally, was 'body'. It's always a body. Plus, and this was the real kicker, we were the ones paying the electricity bill to keep this mysterious object frozen. By my reckoning, that gave us a certain right to know what we were chilling.

Unfortunately, no key had been left. The padlock was steadfast. The freezer remained a silent, humming enigma in the corner of my room. The attic, however, was a different story. We were far too curious to leave it be. A bit of gentle persuasion with a screwdriver on the screws holding the bracket, and we managed to create a gap just big enough for a peek. We shone a torch into the darkness, the beam dancing across the rafters. And there, hanging quite proudly from the beams, was a collection of antique firearms.

The look of relief on our faces was almost comical. It wasn't a dismembered gangster or the family's dark secret; it was just a chap's prized gun collection. There was no ammunition, they were clearly just for show, and posed no threat to anyone. We carefully re-secured the attic hatch, the mystery solved, and went back to arguing about whose turn it was to buy the milk.

They say you find love when you're not looking for it, which always sounds like a bit of a cliché until it happens to you. People can spend their whole lives desperately searching for 'the one', trying so hard that they scare off every potential candidate. For me, it just… happened. And it all started with my car.

By now, I was the proud owner of a Toyota Corolla. It was gold, with a 1.3-litre engine, and utterly unremarkable to look at. But it was new-ish, impeccably reliable, and it got me to and from work without any fuss. More importantly, it was my chariot for the long drive back up to Manchester to see my family and mates. It was my pride and joy. Consequently, I spent an inordinate amount of time tending to it. On my days off, you'd find me on the driveway, vacuuming the interior, polishing the dashboard, and waxing the paintwork until it gleamed under the Hampshire sun. I loved that car.

Unbeknown to me, this ritual was being observed. From behind the curtains of the house over the road, a pair of eyes was watching. My future wife, Janet, was having a conversation with her father. As she later told me, he'd spotted my automotive obsession and said, 'Well, if you like him that much, why don't you go and talk to him?' I suspect he was less of a romantic matchmaker and more a father trying his best to get his daughter to finally move out.

Whatever his motive, it worked.

As I was holding my hose pipe in one hand and hosing the suds off the bonnet, she appeared at her front door. I gave a friendly wave, she smiled back and wandered over for a chat. The connection was instant. She was beautiful, with long blonde hair and a laugh that made you want to keep making jokes, however terrible they were. We just clicked.

We arranged a date for a pint at a local pub, followed by a trip to the cinema. Those first few dates went better than I could have hoped. We started seeing each other regularly, juggling my chaotic shift patterns with her university schedule. It turned out we had more in common than just living next door to each other. However, our relationship didn't get off to the best start…

Of all the reasons a woman might reconsider a relationship, I suspect that 'nasal assault' ranks rather highly. I count my lucky stars every day that Janet, my now-wife, has a remarkably forgiving nature and, one must assume, a less-than-sensitive nose. I looked forward to our third date, because things were going swimmingly. She'd invited me back to her house for a coffee – the classic, hopeful end to a promising evening. Her cat, a creature of serene elegance, was padding softly along the back of the sofa, a picture of domestic bliss. I, on the other hand, was a ticking time bomb of gastric distress. Whether it was a dodgy prawn or, more likely, the several pints of bitter I'd cheerfully sunk earlier, a significant build-up of internal pressure was demanding immediate release.

Now, I've always been a firm believer in the 'better out than in' philosophy, but this situation called for a level of stealth which I clearly did not possess. I attempted what I hoped would be a silent, phantom emission. A ghost of a fart, if you will. What emerged, however, was no phantom. It was a poltergeist. A foul, malevolent entity that immediately colonised the entire living room.

There was no blaming the cat. In fact, the poor animal provided a damning indictment of my crime. The cat stopped its graceful padding, its back arched like a suspension bridge, and every hair stood on end as if it had been electrocuted. Then, in a gesture of pure, unadulterated disgust, it began to gag, its little body rippling in waves of revulsion. Mercifully, this confused feline stopped short of being sick, but the message was crystal clear.

Incredibly, Janet stayed. Not just for the rest of the evening, but for the next seven years. After such a trial by fire – or rather, by foul air – it seemed only right and proper that I should make an honest woman of her.

The plan was hatched without Janet's knowledge. A romantic proposal, executed with military precision, was to take place during our holiday in the Scottish Highlands. I visited a local jeweller, selected a ring that felt suitably sparkly, and hid it deep within my luggage, feeling like a spy smuggling state secrets.

We're both keen mountain walkers, you see. We love scrambling, walking, the burn in your legs, the feeling of being miles from anywhere, in the wilderness. Janet also has a real love of maps, and had chosen our first peak to tackle on the holiday. Our remote cottage often resembled a military operations room, with maps spread across the floor, covered in her meticulous pencil markings, plotting our route to victory.

On the chosen day, we set off. The responsibility of guiding us safely was firmly placed in my hands. I always knew that the map reading and compass badge I was awarded in the Boy Scouts was going to be useful! The engagement ring was a heavy, conspicuous lump in my pocket, its weight matched only by the anticipation churning in my gut. Will she say yes? What if she says no? My mind was a whirlwind.

Unfortunately, my stomach was also in turmoil, this time thanks to the previous night's garlic bread. As we neared the summit, I could feel a familiar pressure building, but this time it was heading north. A garlic-infused belch of epic proportions was brewing. I couldn't do it. I couldn't ask the most important question of my life while breathing the fumes of an Italian kitchen over her. I bottled it. There was always tomorrow; I had to do this right.

And so, the next day, another summit was planned. A 14-mile hike around Lochnagar and Loch Muick. The weather was typically Scottish: damp, wet, and windy, but we loved it.

Out in the elements, just the two of us. I kept patting my pocket, checking if the ring was still there. As we reached the top, we stopped for lunch. A rocky tor capped by a trig point that, in good weather, offers amazing views of the Cairngorm mountain range.

This was it. No garlic, no suspicious gurgling. I dropped to one knee, fumbled for the box, and popped the question.

To my eternal relief, she said 'yes'. Shortly followed by, 'We're not rushing into it are we?'

Rushing? We had been together for seven years!

I'd done it. A grand romantic gesture, untainted by any unfortunate bodily functions. Result.

It was only when we were back at the cottage, safely descended and basking in our newly-engaged glow, that we re-examined the walking guide. Janet was tracing our triumphant route when her finger stopped. The mountain cairn, we discovered, had a Gaelic name: Cac Càrn Beag. She looked it up.

It translates, rather poetically, to 'A Small Cairn of Faeces'. Or, to put it more bluntly, 'A Little Pile of Shit'.

It seemed that even when I got it right, I couldn't help but get it spectacularly wrong. We howled with laughter until our sides ached. I had proposed to the love of my life on a pile of dung. It was, I had to admit, perfectly on-brand.

The long drive back down to Portsmouth was filled with Janet's gleeful teasing.

'You still have to ask my dad, you know,' she'd say, a wicked glint in her eye. 'He might say no. He's very protective.'

Janet spent hundreds of miles winding me up, stoking my anxiety.

When we finally arrived, I dutifully presented myself before her father, swallowed hard, and asked for his daughter's hand. He beamed, a look of profound relief washing over his face. He was, I think, utterly delighted to be passing on the responsibility!

Of all the things family and friends tell you before you get married, the one thing that stuck is: it's a team game. Janet and I tied the knot in the early 2000s at a lovely old church in the grounds of Portchester Castle, followed by a proper knees-up at a country house. It was a glorious day, hot and sunny, surrounded by everyone we loved.

But as the vicar sagely advised, married life is long and full of challenges. 'It's about working together.'

Wise words, as it turned out. Life has certainly lobbed more than a few challenges our way, and having Janet by my side has been the one constant that's seen us through. A true rock. I love her dearly.

After the chaos and confetti of our wedding day, Janet and I took a day to lie flat and sober up. Two days after the wedding we had chosen to go on our honeymoon, which was going to be an epic trip to Canada. A road trip around British Columbia, starting in Vancouver.

The plan was to fly in and spend a weekend at a posh, expensive hotel in the city centre. We were then going to hire a car, travel as frugally as we possibly could, staying in small hotels, bed and breakfast and local accommodation, spending nearly a month travelling, returning back to Vancouver and then flying back home. The plan absolutely worked and it was a great honeymoon, which felt wonderfully grand and distant to two people who had mostly holidayed in places where British rain could still find them.

The hotel at the start was something else entirely. It sat inside a skyscraper, all gleaming glass and soft carpets that politely swallowed your footsteps. We didn't even check in at a normal reception desk. We'd gone all out on the VIP experience! We were shepherded into a lift with mirrored walls and gentle lighting, up to a private concierge on the VIP level. Staff whisked us to our room with the solemn air of people delivering minor royalty to their quarters. Not bad for a lad from Rochdale.

The room itself was opulent in a way neither of us had encountered. The resident chef had prepared an individual work of art, made out of biscuit, to show off his talents. Everything was thick. Thick towels, thick curtains, thick silence. There was a view of the city that made you feel clever simply for looking at it. We could see the harbour and watch seaplanes landing and taking off. The room had a flat-screen TV that could have doubled as a respectable window in a Victorian terrace. I thanked the bell boy and the door clicked shut. It was our honeymoon, after all; a time for romance.

'Pass me the remote,' I said to Janet, ever the old northern romantic.

I hit the power button and the screen bloomed into a news broadcast. It took a second to tune my brain from glittering Vancouver to what I was actually seeing. A car on fire, a van turned over and a large, angry crowd with placards. It had the flavour of a witch hunt with raw fury, flashing blue lights and the kind of angry noise you can hear even with the TV volume low. Then a street sign edged into frame: Allaway Avenue. I knew it at once. Paulsgrove, just outside Portsmouth.

'Janet!' I said, beckoning her over in haste. 'You need to see this!'

Paulsgrove was part of the patch my old housemate Justin had been posted to in Cosham. It was no longer a sleepy seaside place with those fishermen fixing nets on a quayside and maybe some gulls, fish and chips, that sort of thing. What filled the TV was anything but sleepy. It had made international news. From our lofty Canadian perch, we were seeing our corner of Portsmouth erupt. The spark? Parents discovered that a child sex offender, several in fact, were living in their community. This was shortly after there had been a high-profile murder case in Sussex; the death of an eight-year-old child, who had been out playing, called Sarah Payne. Her killer had been found and convicted.

Roy Whiting, the child killer, had shocked the world with his terrible crimes. The 'News of the World' newspaper had embarked on its 'naming and shaming 'campaign of suspected paedophiles. Paulsgrove's close-knit community, already suspicious of outsiders and fiercely protective of its own, had had enough. They planned to 'out' as many suspected offenders as they could. It had now spilled into violence. Hundreds had gathered on the grass down by Allaway Avenue, near the shops. One particular suspect had to be escorted from their home under police protection. A police officer was seriously injured during the clashes. There was shouting, smoke and the feverish churn of outrage. The banners were blunt. The message, even more so, to keep children safe – by any means.

Paulsgrove had a reputation; a bad reputation. Low-rise blocks, fearsome edges, a bit run down. Yes, there was crime, as there is in any estate with too many people and not enough chances. But there were also a lot of good people who lived there. Some people who would lend you a jumper if you were cold and share half of their last meal if you had nothing. Watching this from the other side of the world was surreal. Vancouver's skyline outside our window and Portsmouth's anger inside the room.

The strangeness of it all was not lost on me. A hotel that smelt faintly of expensive soap, and a familiar English street lit by burning cars was disorienting. We stood for a minute, quiet, letting the scene tilt into place. Then I did the only sensible thing a newlywed could do in a situation that neither of us could alter from a penthouse suite in Canada.

I switched off the telly.

We got on with our honeymoon. I wasn't going to let police work, past, present, or televised spoil that. There's a time for fury, a time for duty and a time for ourselves. The tiny light on the TV faded to black and the world kept turning, with or without us.

This was never truer than when we were both in the police.

Janet had enjoyed a work experience placement with the police back in her school days and had a quiet ambition to join the force herself. My work experience with the police in Rochdale had been very boring, shadowing a crime prevention officer. However, Janet had been exposed to exciting arrests, traffic patrols and even attending a suicide! Maybe not the most appropriate incidents to respond to, for a 15-year-old girl, but she had been bitten by the policing bug.

In 1994, after finishing university, Janet joined Hampshire Constabulary. She took to it like a duck to water. She absolutely loved it. I would have a partner in life, and a partner in crime-fighting, too. And to think, it all started with a soapy sponge and a nosy neighbour.

The end of my training!

Module Two was delivered at a District Training Centre and lasted for 10 weeks. I attended Ashford DTC in Kent. We were shown to our accommodation where four of us had to share one room. The accommodation was fairly basic with a simple bed and cabinet to store your equipment/uniform. We would often have regular room inspections to ensure we were keeping it relatively tidy.

Meals were prepared in a large canteen and the whole place had the functional feel of a government or military premises. We were split up during the day into classes. We would learn law and case studies, then put what we had learned into practice. These practical exercises tested our knowledge and procedures. Our communication skills were being honed to deal effectively with members of the public.

We also had a swimming pool and a large gymnasium. So there was lots of fitness, learning to swim classes and lifesaving rescuing a brick that would sink to the bottom of the swimming pool. There was a 'dojo' room where we learned Taekwondo. This was an eye-opener for many of the recruits, who had never been involved in any type of conflict or fight. It was a relatively safe way to be involved in physical combat with other people and not get injured. We had to pass our fitness tests during each module. If you failed you got 'back classed' or sent back to your home force to be dismissed. A lot of running was involved but, as the weeks went on, we all became much fitter and stronger.

Some people absolutely hated being at Ashford, because this was often the first time they had been truly away from home. Having grown up to be very independent, and well-travelled, I absolutely loved the place, and enjoyed the freedom it provided.

Some of the training was much more regimented which suited the ex-military who had joined the police after leaving the forces. These people were helpful to the other recruits in learning how to polish and 'bull' your boots so you could see your face in them. Also, the ex-military recruits would show you how to get the creases correct in your uniform. They also assisted greatly with our marching practice on the parade square.

Sergeant Beck was a legend at Ashford DTC and was in charge of teaching Drill, Parades and Marching. Wearing an adapted peaked police cap pointing down, he shouted like some sort of sergeant major in the army. That said, he was funny and had a great sense of humour. Some people couldn't quite understand why we practised marching, especially if they were not from the military.

To me it was fairly obvious that it was all about getting everybody to work as a team, listening to instructions. They were teaching leadership and bonding us as a team. Not only that, but when it came to Public Order situations, you needed to know how to move as a unit of officers, control crowds and be able to take instructions under very high-pressure situations. We were being prepared for lumps of wood and bricks being thrown at us. We were able to practise being in a mock riot with shields, and breaking down barricades as instructors hurled wooden bricks in our direction.

A small group of us recruits were in the same situation. Everyone normally went home on the weekends, except for a small group of student officers who happened to live miles away like myself. We chose to stay and enjoy the delights of the local town of Ashford in Kent. The staff, and even the catering team, did not work on the weekends. So all the usual regimented rules went out of the window.

Saturday evening started with us all in the main hall having wheeled in the large TV on a stand. We would order takeaway pizzas and crack open a few cans of beer, while we watched Cilla Black presenting *Blind Date* and that American '90s classic TV show, *Baywatch*.

Order of the day was then taxis into town to start a pub crawl ending in the local nightclub called 'Flatfoot Sam's'. Then we danced the night away to some cheesy '80s tracks. I wondered whether the name of the nightclub referred to a record by the 1950s R&B singer, T.V. Slim. Maybe 'Flatfoot Sam' was an American slang term for a police officer walking a regular beat?

Module Three was spent with a tutor constable on operational patrol for five weeks. I was delighted with my posting to Portsmouth Central police station, as I knew I would be busy and 'in the thick of it'.

It was a strange sensation, walking out of the back yard of the police station on foot patrol for the first time in uniform with a radio, handcuffs, truncheon and a custodian helmet. In my mind, everyone was looking at me, and I was fearing a member of the public might ask me to deal with a serious crime. Would I know what to do?

I was with my tutor, Nick, and in safe hands as he slowly exposed me to a variety of crimes and incidents. It was expected, at the start of your duty as a new cop, that you walked the beat. That meant not even getting a ride in a police car, never mind driving one. The expectation was you would walk the beat for most of your first two years. To be fair I wasn't really bothered, as I had been posted to a city centre. I would not have to walk far to come across crimes being committed, with the opportunity to arrest a few people who were up to no good. A foot chase would never be far away. I relished the prospect of walking around on nights, sneaking around to catch local thieves and villains in the act of committing crimes. I couldn't wait!

The District Training Centre at Ashford was the base for Module Four, lasting another five weeks. This time we had our own rooms, but we needed those as a quiet space for study. We were being tested with weekly exams. If you failed, like the fitness tests, you would be sent back to the force to be dismissed or 'back classed'!

Knowing this was the last time all the officers from different force areas would be together, we had a final black-tie meal and 'gang show' that was put on by students, with cameo skits by instructors. It was a chance to have a few beers and let our hair down. To be fair, we did not need an excuse for that…

Mod Four ended with a passing-out parade in front of family and friends. These were occasions of celebration and thanksgiving to family and friends, who had supported the new student officers on their journey. My passing-out parade was extra special as one of the student officers had just left the RAF. He had arranged for three low-level fighter planes to fly past during the parade. That was epic!

Module Five is actually a week's leave. I spent mine at home, relaxing. Janet's Module Five saw us both in Gran Canaria for some welcome sunshine. We bumped into a lad she knew from Ashford, who was from another police force. His dad was a big cheese in the police and he wanted to let off some steam and have a good time, which he did. I am sure pulling drunken 'moonies' in public at passing cars and tossing white plastic chairs into the swimming pool is probably an offence on the Spanish island, as it would be at home in the UK!

Module Six, after my holiday, involved five more weeks with a tutor on the city streets of Portsmouth.

Module Seven, or The Foundation Course as it was known, was completed with another week back in the classrooms of Netley.

Finally, came Post Module Training. Three Post Foundation Courses of two weeks each, that were spread through the remaining period of probation for two years.

These were delivered by in-force training, normally at Netley. The courses involved attachments to CID, traffic department and scenes of crime, among many others, to have a full and better understanding of how the constabulary works. It also gave new officers a chance to see departments where you might wish to specialise in the future.

The main idea of this police training programme was the structure. Constables would get a 'taster' of operational work during earlier modules, when they were encouraged merely to observe what the role was about. This would provide a grounding and assist in providing context when learning our powers during Module Two.

In reality, I never went on patrol in 'Mod One', as we stayed at Netley Training Centre in Hampshire, but instead was issued uniform, handcuffs etc. I was taught some basics like how to fill in a pocket book, recording evidence and details of what I had seen and people I met while on patrol. Also, completing my receipt book for when seizing property.

At this time in the early 1990s police officers were not issued with body armour, CS Gas, body cameras, Velcro restraints or electronic tablets. It was a very different police service compared to what it is now, with many current improvements to officer safety.

In 1992 you only had lightweight trousers for the summer time, heavyweight trousers for the winter, plus a blue shirt and a black GORE-TEX jacket to keep you dry. You also received a fluorescent yellow jacket, a flat cap for when you were posted in a vehicle and a custodian helmet to use on foot patrol. We were issued with a set of handcuffs and a wooden truncheon, which fitted into a hidden pocket especially designed to carry the truncheon down the side of your leg.

The concept and idea of this were excellent. However, in reality when you chased after a criminal, the wooden truncheon would constantly bang against your knee! The ladies were issued with the same equipment, except they had to wear a skirt; trousers were only just starting to be issued at that time. The ladies had a bowler-style hat to wear and were issued with a smart, small leather handbag. This was to keep their truncheon in, which was half the size of the male equivalent. Looking back now, quite frankly, it is laughable. How far we have come!

Throughout the training and the two-year probation period, a portfolio was issued that we had to complete. I would record evidence and examples of jobs I had been to, detailing my performance against a set of criteria. This bloody massive ring binder folder was a curse as far I was concerned. Why did I have to reflect and write up my 'learning points' for each incident I had been to? It weighed a ton, and I ended up having to fill it out after my shift. Working at a busy city station, we already had enough paperwork to do.

Some clever professor had identified the skills required of an officer. The service had also offered its view on which tasks a police officer must complete, in order to be judged capable of independent patrol. There were 39 different tasks that a probationer was expected to have experienced during the two years. Many would be completed quite early on in service, such as using the radio and taking details of a crime. Others took a little longer for them to encounter, such is the unpredictable nature of policing.

Officers were also assessed against 'desired character traits'. These became known as 36 skills and abilities, and included traits such as self-monitoring, leadership, collation and analysis of information.

The portfolios were completed both by the probationer and those tasked with assessing their performance such as tutor constables and supervisors. The assessments would be completed at key stages through the probationary period, for example at the point of change from one module of training to another.

I was fortunate, having been posted to a city centre police station, as we had a really wide variety of 'jobs' that needed to be dealt with. I had no problems in getting to grips with the tasks, skills and abilities needed for my future career.

Luckily for me, after those two years, my portfolio was full and positively signed off for independent patrol....without having to carry that enormous binder around!

On the beat at last...

I can clearly remember that first day at my designated station. I arrived at Portsmouth Central, nice and early, to start the day shift. I approached the front counter and was welcomed by the sergeant. He showed me the locker room and gave me a key. The sergeant took me to the parade room where I was introduced to the rest of the shift. Quietly saying 'hello' from the back, everyone welcomed me. An inspector came into the room and everyone stood to attention, saluting. He gave the nod, everyone sat down again and the handover continued. Intelligence was passed on from the previous shift, highlighting crimes of note that had been committed and any prisoners who needed to be handed over and dealt with. Each officer was given duties such as walking through the town centre or another beat.

Every station area was divided into a number of beats. The older officers were given details of which vehicles they would be driving. It could be the area car, van or panda car. A ring binder was opened, marked 'routine orders'. I had no idea what this was at first. It turned out to be a force-wide list of instructions and recommendations about protocol and procedures, updated on a regular basis.

The parade room at Portsmouth Central was a relatively large office with a rectangular table in the middle, a couple of ashtrays available and a haze of blue smoke in the air.

Everything was on paper in those days. A fabric pin board dominated one of the walls. It displayed many of our current targets and photos of wanted criminals. When any visitors appeared, a roller blind was quickly pulled down to hide all of that sensitive information!

The back wall had a white board that was used to display information to the rest of the shift. For example, if a search warrant was due to be executed and the officer in charge wanted to explain about entrances, exits and windows, the details could be drawn on the board very quickly.

Another board on the wall contained small hooks for keys and details about each of the marked vehicles. The driver of each vehicle would write their name against it and select their keys at the start of the shift. Any officer who accidentally took the keys home was fined by having to provide cakes the following day.

The final wall on the parade room was a mass of plastic trays set inside a rack with each officer's name on the front. In the days before email, whenever a message needed to be passed to an officer, a slip of paper was dropped into the tray. It was where officers were meant to keep all their paperwork, investigations and case files so that, if they were off sick, all the information could be found quickly. It was a paper version of a computer database, although not so well organised.

A quick glance of this set-up often gave a visual indication of how busy and productive particular police officers were; on occasion looks could deceive, because an officer might be totally chaotic, trying to get the jobs completed!

During every shift, a sergeant would go through the work to check that it was up to date. For every new investigation, there was a form entitled C1 or Crime 1. This comprised three pieces of carbonated paper, making a copy of whatever was written in pen or occasionally typed on it, forming the basis of all investigations. The top piece was used by an officer to write up notes, while one of the other sheets was sent off to a crime recording index. The third one, I believe, went to CID.

Occasionally these C1 forms would end up on top of an officer's personal locker during the daily rush, falling down the back. This was poor practice. It was surprising, during our japes of hiding lockers, or turning them round for fun, how often we would find a number of old crime reports! Some officers seemed to have quite a few investigation notes, lost behind their lockers. One of the main benefits of computerisation was the fact that it was nearly impossible for these investigations to go missing.

The only other item of note in the parade room was one of the most important pieces of equipment in the building: a gigantic metal teapot that could brew around 20 cups of tea. As the new boy on the shift, it fell upon me to make the teas. After refreshments, everyone would receive their assignments for the day and go out on patrol, also picking up their radios.

It was standard procedure to make sure the control room heard you clearly; your life could depend on that radio. The people in the control room are the unsung heroes, doing a great job behind the scenes. I got to know many personally, and would like to say a heartfelt 'thank you' to them all. It must be so frustrating, behind the scenes, only being able give advice and talk through situations over the telephone. At least, being a police officer on the street, you can help the person in front of you. There was always a test call on the early shift, or early turn as we called it. Instead of testing the radio saying, '1189 (my collar number), can I have a test call', this developed into '1189, can I have a testicle?' Just my juvenile sense of humour. They would often laugh, even though this was the routine almost every day.

On that first day, the sergeant took me on a comprehensive tour of the police station. At the front, through the main entrance, there was a small reception area and a welcoming desk which was manned by the duty station sergeant and the SDO. This was either a civilian and/or a police officer, normally someone of a junior rank.

Nobody really wanted to work in the front office. If people were on restricted duties, say because of an injury for example, they could be posted into the front office. There, they could still be effective without having to deal with confrontation on the streets. However, they did get plenty of hassle in the front office.

People would come in to report crimes, make complaints or show their driving documents if they had been stopped, for example. A form had been issued, a HORT1 but it was mainly known as a 'producer'. This was in the days before insurance databases. People might have to sign on, if they were on bail, to make sure they hadn't left the area. Members of the public who may have found a dog, and brought it in, had to be catered for. It was just non-stop dealing with these enquiries as Portsmouth Central was open 24 hours a day back then.

The station sergeant would stay in the background, conducting duties such as checking the safe contents. If drugs or money had been seized from searches, or handed in, they would all have to be booked into the safe. The sergeant ensured that everything was correctly labelled and marked. Other responsibilities of the sergeant included duty rostering and maintaining the safety and security in the police station. Just off from the front counter was a small interview room. This was a private area where victims of crime could make reports and know that other people weren't listening.

There was also an unusual contraption in the front office called a Telex machine. I was puzzled at first, looking at this thing, spewing out reports from the control room, other police stations and other police forces. It provided a safe and relatively secure method of communicating between police stations. There might be details of wanted people on there or a request to arrest someone. It felt very much like something you might see in a 1950s James Bond film: a large ream of paper with perforated edges being fed into it.

Walking through the building there were a couple of toilets and a tuck shop. This was a small cupboard where you could grab a packet of crisps or a chocolate bar if you missed your meal break during a long shift. An honesty box system was used to pay for the 'nutty' as the ex-Navy lads called it. This honesty box often had a number of handwritten IOUs in it.

Then there was a drying room. This was a large cloakroom where, if the weather was bad with a lot of rain, you could put your boots and uniforms. Strong metal radiators did the rest.

The canteen was a large room with several tables and chairs. There was no dedicated cook. It was a case of bringing sandwiches. There were ovens and hobs, so you could make all types of meals. At night time we would sometimes make substantial curries and invite officers from other police stations in the early hours of the morning.

A small room off from this was the quiet area where officers, if they needed a short rest, could take a break. A lot of people smoked openly in the police station. As smoking became more unpopular, this small room was used for that purpose! Eventually smoking was banned in the police station.

There was a patrol sergeant's office where you would receive praise or a telling off, depending on what had happened that day.

Upstairs, there were a number of offices including the Criminal Justice Unit, that helped process case files ready for court. There were also offices for the superintendent and inspector.

When I first joined the force, the CID office was part of Portsmouth Central upstairs. It was quite dark, with nicotine stains on the walls. As a uniformed officer or what they described as a 'wooden top', you only went in there if invited.

The cork helmet, known as a custodian helmet, was designed in 1863, so they delved a bit into history for our nickname.

If you opened the door and walked in brazenly, many an eye would gaze at you, and the room would go silent. For me, there was an air of mystique about the CID office. I was interested in what they did there. I wanted to be part of that world, investigating more serious crimes and catching real criminals. As such, I took every opportunity to enter the hallowed walls of the CID office. I made my face known in the hope that, one day, I would be accepted into that mysterious world.

The sergeant took me out into the back yard where, as in other police stations, there was little space to move vehicles around. I saw a large police van, like a mini bus, with bench seats in the back. It had metal grilles surrounding all the windows. The bench seats all had plastic-covered foam mattresses.

The vehicle was used to transport prisoners. The sergeant said that, after a difficult arrest, people would go in head first onto one of the mattresses and then be restrained if they were violent.

This particular vehicle was waiting to be collected by the workshop for repairs. The grilles had been kicked out and were hanging from the back window. I thought: what have I got myself into? This job might be far more dangerous than I ever imagined!

My role as a crimefighter

If I could keep my nose clean for two years and not mess up, I would be able to pass my probationary period. In that time I was going to be exposed to most general policing duties and crimes under the watchful eye, initially of my tutor, then closely monitored by my sergeant. There was a real advantage to working at a city centre police station. If an urgent assistant shout went out over the radio, in a city you were never far from a colleague who would rush to your location. As a cop, you would only call for urgent assistance if it was genuinely needed. For a country officer, you might have to wait up to an hour before a unit could get to you.

Your best weapon apart from tasers, gas or truncheons, was your mouth. Your mouth got you out of trouble whether in the city or the country. That said, when I first started, I only had a truncheon and handcuffs.

I recall one occasion on foot patrol in Portsmouth's Commercial Road at the bottom of the M275 motorway. I had been taking a statement from the security guard at a supermarket and was heading back into the city centre. A call crackled over the air, calling for urgent assistance. The officer had managed to give details of his location in Somerstown, about a mile and a half away. I needed to get there quickly, not knowing what that officer was facing. Being on foot, I had to use my initiative.

I stepped out into the traffic and held out my hand with a firm, determined stance. Two lanes of traffic stopped. I spotted a middle-aged man driving a bright red Ford Escort. I walked over to the car and said, 'I am commandeering this vehicle. I need you to drive me urgently to King's Road.' I got straight into the passenger seat and told him to put his foot down. The bloke looked bewildered, then a huge smile appeared across his face. He realised that I had invited him to drive quickly across the city in a police emergency. His mundane start to the day had now totally changed.

For me, this wasn't something we had been trained to do, commandeering vehicles. It was just something I had seen on TV and in films. But an officer's life was at risk. The man asked, eagerly: 'Can I go through red lights?' I said quickly, 'No!' But he did make haste through the city streets. Well, as quickly as you can go through a city without blue lights and a siren as traffic tends to be slow anyway. I directed him to the scene. As his car screeched to a halt, I thanked him and jumped out. I could see the area car had arrived just before us and we dashed over to help the officer. He was involved in arresting a teenager who was struggling, having been seen and wanted on a warrant.

My senses were totally alert now. I had adrenaline running through my veins. A police van arrived shortly afterwards and the youth was placed safely in the back. I realised this was the reason I joined the police in the first place. About 95 per cent of the time the duties were mundane and boring, with plenty of paperwork. Then you had times like this which were so exciting. The upstanding member of the public who had helped us was still sitting in his vehicle; I thanked him again and suggested that he might want to wait a couple of minutes to get rid of his own adrenaline before driving again.

My probationary period of two years exposed me to lots of different crimes and investigations and gave me experience in general. I made my first arrest, a shoplifter, at Allders, a large well-to-do department store in Commercial Road, Portsmouth.

Then another arrest happened under quite extraordinary circumstances...

It was my day off and I was out shopping in West Street, Fareham. As I looked up, our eyes met across the bustling shopping street. His stare was intense, like he was processing information in slow motion. As a young copper, I was still honing my skills and developing my copper's nose. By this, I mean taking in the environment and identifying items, objects or behaviour that are present or not present and whether the scene is suspicious.

The young man must have been 200 metres away, but was running directly at me through the crowds of shoppers who appeared oblivious as to what was happening. In both hands he was clutching a plastic shopping bag, used for keeping frozen food cold. My eyes broke off from his stare as he ran towards me and I noticed, about 50 metres behind him, a woman in her late 20s running in the same direction.

My brain instantly hit the jackpot, processing the scene unfolding in front of me. I recognised the woman as a plain-clothed store detective. She was the head of security at the Allders department store in Portsmouth. I had met her on many occasions, dealing with shoplifters they had detained. It was now obvious the woman was in pursuit of the male, who I also now recognised as a prolific shoplifter called 'Yusuf'. I'd already arrested this male on a number of occasions for bulk shoplifting. He was a professional thief, stealing to order, making a good living from his criminality.

All this had taken place in just a few seconds. It was now obvious she was chasing Yusuf, and I was in the ideal position to stop him. Yusuf darted through the crowds, closing the gap as he approached me. His eyes had stayed locked on me, but it felt like he hadn't recognised who I was out of uniform, and he kept approaching. I formed a very quick plan in my head, that I would grab him in a rugby tackle, as he tried to run past me. It seemed like a strong plan at the time.

The gap between us closed quickly: 10 metres, five metres. I could now hear his laboured breath as he ran.

I made my move….at exactly the same time Yusuf appeared to recognise who I was! I lurched forward with both arms outstretched, ready to tackle him to the ground. Yusuf dropped his right shoulder, moving the weight of his body like a skilled rugby player to change direction. He managed to slip right past me, as I foolishly stumbled forward with both arms outstretched.

I turned around 180 degrees, bursting into a sprint after him.

'STOP, POLICE!'

I bellowed at the top of my voice at him. At this moment, the many shoppers around us stopped and turned around to see what was happening. Only the store detective assisted me, continuing to give chase. I wasn't surprised. Everyone had been going about their normal daily business. They had no reason to react to the incident unfolding in front of them.

Yusuf was fast on his feet. But having recently trained to pass the police fitness tests, I was equally as fast when it came to running. We dashed along the pavement towards the High Street, cutting in and out of shoppers.

I shouted out again towards him, 'STOP, POLICE!'

To my amazement he stopped at the junction. He turned around to face me, raising his arms in front with his wrists together, symbolising he was ready to be handcuffed. I took hold of his upper arm. Before I was able to remove my warrant card, identify myself and give the reason for stopping him, he said words to the effect of,
'The clothes in the bag are nicked. Sorry PC Foster, I knew the game was up when I recognised it was you.'

'No worries. I'm still gonna have to deal with you. You are under arrest on suspicion of theft.'

I went on to formally caution him. The store detective had, at this point, caught up with us and opened the plastic bag. I could see the bag contained a number of items of new clothing, still with labels and tags attached. The inside of the bag had masking tape and copious amounts of tin foil stuck to the sides. This is a method used by shoplifters to try to prevent the alarms going off at the entrance to shops.

'You're also under arrest on suspicion of going equipped to steal,' I said.

The store detective explained which shop she had been working in. The company would recover the property and prepare a written statement, evidencing what had occurred and the items stolen. I agreed to this, but now had another problem. I had no radio to call for a police van to pick up the prisoner. I also had no PPE personal protective equipment, such as latex gloves, handcuffs, and truncation should the prisoner change his mind, cut up rough and try to escape. I didn't even have a mobile phone at the time. Only city bankers and yuppies had mobile phones back then!

I decided I would walk the prisoner back to the police station, about five minutes' walk away. I explained to Yusuf we would be walking to the police station. I searched him to make sure there were no weapons or further evidence on him. I didn't fancy being stabbed on my rest day. I took hold of his hand and arm, placing him in a hand restraint that would cause pain should he try to escape. It was a Home Office-approved restraint technique we'd been taught in basic training. Simple, but very effective.

Yusef said, 'There's no need for that, PC Foster. I'm not going to run off.'

To be fair he seemed more embarrassed that people were looking, than the fact I was restraining him. Some police officers or members of the public may feel my approach may have been a little heavy handed, given the fact he had stopped running for me, and was now being compliant.

However, I had seen many suspects run off after their demeanour changed while in custody, when not being restrained properly. When somebody is arrested, it is important to take control of that person and for them to understand that their freedom is now being restricted. Many a criminal has taken the opportunity when under arrest to either escape, discard evidence, or attack an officer. I was not going to allow that to happen.

We made the short journey to the police station, walking into the rear yard and pressing the buzzer to gain access to the custody suite. Speaking over the intercom I announced who I was, then I was met by two uniformed police officers. I gave the details of the arrest to the custody sergeant and the prisoner was booked in. An officer was allocated to deal with the prisoner, so all I had to do was complete my witness statement.

At the time everything was handwritten, so I grabbed a pen and some MG11 statement forms and detailed the arrest. I handed over my completed statement to the patrol sergeant who was on duty. The sergeant said, 'Don't forget to claim four hours.'

Four hours was the statutory minimum amount of time I could claim for that off-duty arrest. Not a bad result for an afternoon's shopping. The whole incident had only taken about an hour and a half! I can understand that some of you reading this may be feeling that seems like a poor use of public money. Well, if you balance things up, it was not a regular occurrence to deal with a crime on a rest day.

What was a regular occurrence: being late off duty and working overtime to get a job finished or handed over to the next shift. The first time I worked overtime, my tutor constable explained about working the 'first half hour for the Queen'.

'What do you mean?' I asked.

He explained that every time you worked overtime, the first half hour was deducted, and that you never got paid for it! Everything else could be claimed for as time off, or payment, depending on whether it was authorised by a senior officer. Over the years, as more and more government budget cuts came in, officers were only ever allowed to claim overtime as time off. They accrued days and weeks of time off, but were often not authorised to claim the time back. Well, my shopping trip ended well in the end. I had another prisoner to my name, who pleaded guilty at court.

Also, I had some extra hours in overtime. Result!

Back in Pompey I had my own area to patrol, with jobs being deployed over the radio, but there was an expectation to help out other police stations when needed. This was often the case in the city when we were really busy.

One day, while actually driving the police van, a call came in for assistance to deal with a shoplifter in Buckland. The job was on Fratton's patch, but I volunteered as all their units were busy. I arrived at the small corner shop in the middle of Buckland on a typical large concrete council estate. Well, unfortunately the shoplifter had been and gone. So my role was to take a report and gather any evidence to see if we could identify the thief and hopefully make an arrest at a later date.

The whole shop was staffed by women. There was a young girl serving behind the counter and another young girl who was replacing stock on shelves. I was immediately introduced to the manageress, a pretty woman aged in her mid-20s. After initial introductions, she invited me into the back office, so I could take a statement and obtain any CCTV that might be available. We got on very well, laughing and joking while we shared a brew. I took the statement, detailing a local alcoholic who had stolen some bottles of vodka. On the face of it, this looked like a cut and dried job with all the evidence necessary to arrest a local suspect. Unfortunately, I wasn't able to collect the CCTV tape at that moment as they didn't have any spares. In the 1990s most shops operated VHS video cassettes and only had a number of spare cassettes to continue recording if one had been seized. I explained that wouldn't be a problem. I would return the following day to collect the CCTV tape, and hopefully arrest the suspect. Not that there was going to be much chance of getting the booze back! I suspected the vodka would have been consumed quickly after the theft.

The following day, I returned to the store to collect the CCTV. The two young girls were working behind the counter and started to giggle as I walked in. I wasn't 100% sure if they were laughing at me, with me, or if it was something I'd done? One of the girls called for the manageress to join us, which she did. The manageress approached with a welcoming smile and invited me into the back office again. As I completed the paperwork and got her to sign an exhibit label, I mentioned in passing about the shop assistants giggling, and queried what I might have done?

The manageress then giggled herself and blushed slightly. I was now more confused than ever, but she put me out of my misery and told me to watch the CCTV tape, which she placed into the player. The small square monitor flickered and showed a familiar room which was not the shop floor, but instead the room I was standing in. She explained there was a hidden camera in the back office to prevent staff thefts. The manageress pointed to the hidden camera in the roof, which it would appear all the staff members knew about.

I watched on, and could see now clearly what the girls had all been sniggering about. I was mortified, but also giggled and laughed with them as to what had happened. My towering height, as a police officer, would naturally command a presence in a room.

On this occasion, when I went to take the initial report, at six feet and six inches I towered above her as we spoke. But she was wearing a low-cut blouse top. This particular lady was blessed with a large bosom that was naturally on show from my position in the small confined office. Quite frankly, it was difficult to look anywhere else.

Well, the CCTV had caught me 'bang to rights', looking at the manageress's assets. She had obviously shared the footage with the other girls in the shop. I apologised unreservedly to the lady, who smiled and appeared quite flattered at the unexpected attention. You could say I was keeping abreast of local crime…

I arrested the shoplifter a week later and updated the elated staff. At every job I attended after this, I made a conscious note to always consider that there may be a covert camera watching my every move.

Things are not always as they seem. Being a police officer you are often required to work long hours. The clock doesn't turn 5pm and you head home. If you're in the middle of a job or you are dealing with an incident, the expectation is that you stay on duty and see it through. Working at a city police station, you are normally extremely busy and have to grab food whenever you have an opportunity.

On one occasion during a late turn, I was driving the area car. As a shift we had decided to get pizza. Everyone threw a fiver in, then wrote on a piece of paper their favourite pizza toppings. I volunteered to take the money, place the order and collect the pizzas. Everyone agreed we would meet back at the nick at 6pm for our meal.

I drove to the Pizza Hut, in Edinburgh Road at the bottom of the Commercial Road pedestrian precinct in the heart of the city. I parked outside and walked in, placing my order of about eight large deep pan pizzas.

I was in full police uniform, waiting for my order. I glanced at my watch, displaying the time of 5.45pm. Perfect, I thought, I would be right on time. I paid the money and collected the pizzas. As I walked out, I got a radio message. 'Kilo Charlie 52, Can you attend a report of a burglary in progress?'
I opened the back door of the police car and dropped the pizza boxes onto the back seat. I ran around to the driver's side and got into the car. Pressing the microphone button, I confirmed my attendance.

With a rush of adrenaline, I started the car. Checking my mirrors that it was safe to pull out, I switched on the blues and twos and screeched off to the immediate response job. I rolled my eyes as I glanced in the rear-view mirror, seeing the pizza boxes slide across the back seat into the rear footwell. My stomach rumbled. Oh well, I hope they'll be okay to eat later, I thought.

As I raced to that job, I felt mortified as to what the public perception would have been. Seeing a police officer in full uniform, with an arm full of hot pizzas, getting into a police car, to then race away on blues and twos. I'm sure a few people would have suspected I was trying to get back to the nick before the food went cold!

Sadly, that couldn't be further from the truth. It was one of those crazy evenings where I was deployed from job to job, and didn't get back to the police station until about 11 o'clock that evening, absolutely starving…along with the rest of the shift. Everyone ended up eating cold, badly deformed pizza, whilst writing up our reports before going off duty.

When Janet first joined, she was posted to Havant, a sprawling town just outside Portsmouth, home to the mammoth council estate of Leigh Park. Back then, it was one of the largest council housing estates in Northern Europe, a place with more than its fair share of deprivation and the sort of social problems that inevitably land on a copper's doorstep. It was a busy, difficult patch to police, and in the days before encrypted radio channels, you could pretty much tune in to the chaos unfolding across the division.

The job, in its infinite wisdom, had a rule: if you were in a relationship with another officer, you couldn't work together. It made sense, of course. You needed to maintain professional detachment, and the last thing you wanted was to be worrying about your other half while trying to handle a volatile situation. But there was a catch. When a call for urgent assistance went out over the airwaves, you couldn't always tell who was at the sharp end of it. Until you could.

I remember one night vividly. Janet had moved stations to Hayling Island, and I knew she was on nights, same as me. Suddenly, a request for immediate backup crackled through the radio. The location was her patch. My blood ran cold. All I could do was listen, my heart thumping against my ribs, as I heard other units confirming they were 'making' towards the incident. Making towards my wife. It's a unique and terrible kind of helplessness, knowing the person you love is in trouble and being stuck miles away, able to do nothing but monitor the outcome through a tinny speaker.

Thankfully, the cavalry arrived swiftly. The offender was arrested and no one was hurt. It was only later I found out the full story. Janet, on her own, had confronted a man brandishing a sword. A bloody sword! It still makes me shudder to think what could have happened.

The silver lining of our shared profession, however, was the debrief at the end of a shift. We would dissect incidents, celebrate the small victories and analyse the close calls. We'd bounce ideas off each other, moan about the paperwork and generally de-stress over a cup of tea before we collapsed into bed.

It was our therapy. That is, when our shifts aligned. More often than not, we were like ships in the night, passing at the front door with a quick peck on the cheek as I headed out and she stumbled in. We were lucky if we got one weekend a month off together. It was another stressor piled onto an already stressful life.

Till Death Us Do Part

They say humour is a vital coping mechanism for the emergency services, and they're not wrong. It's a strange, dark, and often misunderstood language spoken between colleagues in the face of things you shouldn't really have to see. What passes for a chuckle in the front of a police car might get you sectioned anywhere else! In 'the Job', it's a pressure valve. A way of staying sane. What might be humorous for one person, may not be for another, particularly the dark humour used in that close-knit camaraderie between emergency service workers. I was about to get my first lesson in this unspoken dialect, and it wasn't in the classroom.

I was still a shiny new probationary constable. I was still being 'mentored' by my tutor Nick, and my primary function in life was to impress him enough that he would sign me up for independent patrol. So, when the call came in, a sudden death in a tower block in Somerstown, Portsmouth, I saw it as another opportunity to prove I wasn't a complete liability. The initial report over the radio was brief and sombre. A wife had found her husband deceased in their kitchen. The death was unexpected.

I was reading the graffiti on the walls, as the lift juddered its way up the concrete tower, the air thick with the smell of stale cigarettes and damp, with a sour note of urine. Nick turned to me. 'Right, This one's yours. You take the lead. Talk to the wife, do the paperwork, sort the scene. I'll just be your shadow.'

My stomach performed a nervous little flip. This was it. The real deal. 'No problem,' I said, hoping I sounded more confident than I felt. I had practised this at Ashford, but this would be my first time.

We were met at the door by a woman in her seventies. Her face was solemn, her eyes puffy from crying, but she wasn't hysterical. There was a quiet dignity about her as she invited us into the small, tidy flat. She explained that her husband had offered to make breakfast that morning, a simple cup of tea and a bit of toast. He'd gone into the kitchen while she sat in the living room. There, he must have felt unwell. He'd pulled a chair out from under the small kitchen table, sat down, and simply… passed away.

I stepped into the kitchen, my heart thumping a nervous rhythm against my ribs. There he was. The first proper dead body I had ever seen. An elderly gentleman sitting upright on a wooden chair, partly leaning against the kitchen wall, his eyes closed. He looked surprisingly peaceful, as if he'd just nodded off mid-thought. There was nothing to suggest anything untoward, but because the death was unexpected and sudden, a post-mortem would be needed. We later learned it was a massive heart attack. Quick, quiet, and painless. As a peaceful way to go, you could do a lot worse.

After calling the undertakers, who were about twenty minutes away, I returned to the living room. The widow was sitting on the sofa, a fragile but composed figure. I settled into an armchair opposite her, pulling out the requisite form – Form G28, the official document for the coroner.

'I'm very sorry for your loss,' I began, my voice sounding unnaturally formal. 'I just need to ask a few questions about your husband and what happened. It's standard procedure for the coroner's report.'

She nodded, ready to perform this final, bureaucratic act of love. As I started filling in the boxes with my neatest handwriting, I was acutely aware of the scene behind her. Through the open kitchen doorway, I could see the back of her husband's chair. I could also see Nick, who had gallantly offered to make us all a cup of tea.

He called out from the kitchen, his voice full of practised gentleness. 'Would you like sugar in your cuppa?'

The widow agreed with a soft, 'Oh, one please. That would be lovely, thank you.'

And then I saw it. As Nick put the kettle on, out of view of the widow, he glanced over at the still figure in the chair. He gave a slight, almost imperceptible nod towards the corpse, his eyebrows raised in a silent, visual offer. '*You want one, mate?*'

It was a tiny, absurd, and utterly inappropriate gesture. A flicker of gallows humour in the quiet sadness of the room. My professional mask remained perfectly, solemnly in place, but inside, a bubble of laughter was fighting its way up my throat. I kept my head down, focusing intently on the form, my pen scratching against the paper, a smile playing on my soul. It was my first real glimpse into the strange, necessary comedy that keeps the darkness at bay.

The trouble with bubbles

As a copper, I've always found I can get my head around most crimes. Theft? Well, that's often down to desperation, greed, or simply seeing an opportunity. Assault? Usually a flare-up of anger, revenge, or a pint too many. There's a logic to it, twisted though it may be. But the one thing that always, without fail, got right under my skin was criminal damage. Specifically, the mindless, pointless vandalism perpetrated by someone drunk on their way home from the pub.

In a city like Portsmouth, with its tightly packed terraced houses, cars are parked nose-to-tail down every street. Seeing a row of wing mirrors snapped off for a cheap laugh used to properly incense me. It was the sheer futility of it that fired me up.

During my first two years in the service, while still on probation, my tutor and I were often tasked with walking the beat. The patch was usually Commercial Road, the town centre precinct. You always knew a foot patrol there would end with a prisoner. It was a conveyor belt of minor criminality: shoplifters, dodgy credit cards and other petty offences that I needed to tick off my probationary checklist to prove I was a proper bobby. I even had to report someone for the serious crime of cycling on the pavement.

It was on one of these patrols that my tutor introduced me to a peculiar form of criminal damage I hadn't yet encountered. In the heart of Commercial Road stands a large, circular fountain. It's a tiered structure with a wide, two-foot-high rim at the base, and a taller, six-foot-high central pillar rising from the water. At the top, a ring of eight stone-carved lions stands guard, with water cascading from a pool just below them, into the main basin below. On a hot summer's day, it was a genuinely pleasant spot for shoppers to sit and eat their sandwiches.

The local oiks, however, had other ideas. They found it endlessly amusing to buy a bottle of washing-up liquid or bubble bath – and tip the entire contents into the fountain. The result was a spectacular, Ibiza-style foam party. If there was a bit of a breeze, colossal clouds of bubbles would drift down the pedestrianised road, engulfing unsuspecting shoppers. I'll be honest, a part of me found it hilarious. My tutor, however, was quick to point out that our foam-loving youths were, in fact, committing criminal damage. Each time they did it, the council had to switch off the fountain, drain it, and clean the pumps, all at considerable expense. The damage, as the law states, need not be permanent.

But it wasn't the bubble bath bandits that led to my most memorable encounter with this particular landmark. It was a warm summer's evening, around 8 or 9pm. A call came over the radio reporting a male causing damage to shops in Commercial Road. A drunken lad, no older than twenty, had decided it would be a laugh to lob a paving slab at a shopfront window. Mercifully, it hadn't gone through, but his antics had been captured beautifully by the council's all-seeing CCTV system.

The CCTV operator radioed us his location, and we deployed from the station in a flash. There were about five of us, fanning out in a classic starburst pattern to cut off his escape routes. What followed was a scene straight out of a Benny Hill sketch. The lad, who was surprisingly athletic for someone so clearly well-oiled, led us on a merry chase, running in circles and taunting us as we lumbered after him. We weren't overly concerned; our pincer movement was slowly closing in.

Just as we were about to grab him, he made a dash for the fountain. With a surprising show of agility, he stepped onto the low outer rim and launched himself up to the central tier, landing among the lions. The fountain was off for the night but still full of water. He stood there, dancing about, swearing and goading us as we surrounded him. Escape was futile, but he seemed to be enjoying his moment in the spotlight, kicking water at us and shouting obscenities.

After five minutes of this pantomime, I'd had enough. A whole shift was being tied up by this one idiot. I was young, fit, and frankly, I was beginning to lose my rag. I decided it was down to me to take this master criminal down.

Taking a short run-up, I prepared to recreate his grand leap. I propelled myself towards the fountain, my foot hitting the lower rim perfectly. I catapulted into the air, soaring towards the upper level. It was only as my other foot was about to land that I noticed something: the upper surface was coated in a thick, green, and treacherously slippery layer of algae. My Doc Martens boots were no match for it; I could see now that he was wearing a pair of grippy trainers.

In that split second, I flung my arms out, aiming to grab the stone lions on either side of me for balance. Looking like I was doing my best aeroplane impression, I missed both of their heads completely. My foot was already sliding. As I began to topple backwards, one leg shot forward, kicking the offender squarely in the shins and knocking him off balance. But it was too late for me. In what felt like cinematic slow motion, I plunged backwards, head first, into the icy water below.

The splash was monumental, swamping the surrounding paving stones. A moment of stunned silence was broken by an eruption of laughter. From everyone. Including the drunken male.

I clambered to my feet, utterly soaked, as if I'd just gone for a dip in the Solent. My police radio was silent; I suspect they aren't fully waterproof. While I stood there dripping, one of my colleagues calmly asked the lad to get down. Still chortling, he duly complied and was promptly arrested.

By the time I squelched back to the nick, a welcoming party had formed. Colleagues from my station and the surrounding ones were there to greet me with the kind of uproarious laughter reserved for the misfortune of a fellow officer. It wasn't long, of course, before the arresting officer had obtained the CCTV footage and shared my Tom Daley impression with every shift in Portsmouth. My pride was the only casualty that night, but you live to tell the tale, don't you?

And yes, the drunken offender was charged. Not for burglary, but for attempted criminal damage. It seemed fitting.

There are certain unwritten rules in the police. Don't volunteer for anything. Never say the 'Q' word (quiet). And most sacrosanct of all: never, ever mess with an officer's meal. In the old days, this was less of an issue. The station canteen was the heart of the nick on a night turn, a brightly lit sanctuary where the smell of frying bacon and strong tea momentarily banished the ghosts of the shift. Meal breaks were staggered, of course, so the city was never left entirely to its own devices, but those overlapping moments were golden. Around a Formica table, you'd decompress, swap war stories, maybe play a dodgy hand of cards, and generally remind yourself that you were part of a team.

By the time I joined, however, most of these hallowed institutions had been shuttered, victims of budget cuts and changing times. We were left to fend for ourselves. The culinary landscape of a night shift officer devolved into a grim choice between home-packed sandwiches and the questionable embrace of a late-night kebab van.

To combat this gastronomic despair and keep the flame of shift camaraderie alive, we instigated a tradition. On one of the quieter nights, usually a Monday or Tuesday, as it was quieter than the weekend, we'd organise a shift meal. We'd even invite a neighbouring station over, say, the Southsea lot would pop over to us at Portsmouth Central. One brave soul would take on the role of chef, rustling up a vat of curry or a cauldron of chilli. The deal was that the third station on the island would cover all our patches, but if a truly serious call came in, we'd drop our forks, leap into the cars, and race to the scene, leaving a table of half-eaten dinners behind. It was a brilliant system, a chance to properly connect and share stories.

It was after one such magnificent feast that I found myself, as the junior officer on parade, relegated to the kitchen sink. It was like I had gone back in time to washing up pots and pans in the chippy again! I was faced with a stack of stainless-steel pans the size of satellite dishes, each caked with the burnt-on, congealed remains of a particularly enthusiastic chilli. Elbow-deep in a bowl of lukewarm, greasy water, where rogue grains of rice bobbed like tiny buoys in a murky sea, I scrubbed with the vigour of a man possessed.

Lost in a frantic rhythm of sponge and scourer, under the deceptive cover of a mountain of washing-up bubbles, I felt a sudden, sharp pain in my hand. A rogue knife, lurking like a shark in the soapy depths, had sliced into the fleshy bit just under my thumb. It was a clean cut, only about a centimetre long, but it bled with a surprising determination. I tried to soldier on, dabbing it with bits of paper towel, but the blood just wouldn't quit. I applied a plaster, but the wet work of the washing-up rendered it useless. It seemed there was no other option. This was clearly a job for the professionals. It might even need a stitch.

I announced into my radio, trying to sound nonchalant. 'My Panda will be off the patch for a short while. Attending hospital for… a knife injury to my hand.'

They duly noted it down, and then a colleague drove me up to Queen Alexandra Hospital. Now, the A&E department is a place we knew very well. We had a great rapport with the staff, who worked tirelessly in the face of Pompey's nightly parade of the drunk, the disorderly, and the downright daft. We were their cavalry, frequently called to help security remove violent individuals or drug addicts demanding their fix. They were always grateful, and in return, they were our lifeline during the soul-crushingly dull hours of 'constant obs' – babysitting an arrested suspect who'd decided to get themselves injured or had a medical episode. For this grim duty, the nurses would furnish us with a comfy chair and, most importantly, endless cups of tea and biscuits. It was a fine working relationship.

We parked the Panda in the emergency vehicle bay and strolled into reception. The waiting area was a familiar scene of overcrowded human misery. I instinctively started playing 'spot the injury': the man with a makeshift bandage around his head, the woman with her leg stuck out at an odd angle, and the obligatory chap slumped in a corner, smelling like a brewery and snoring for England.

I announced myself at the desk, and the receptionist's eyes widened slightly. 'Right this way, officer,' she said, ushering me straight through the double doors into the main department. Before I could even get my bearings, I was whisked into a treatment room. Suddenly, the curtain flew back and the room was filled with a flurry of activity – doctors and nurses rushing in, a consultant striding purposefully towards me. I was utterly flummoxed. This seemed a rather dramatic response for a minor cut.

'Right,' the consultant said, his expression grave. 'So, where have you been stabbed?'

The penny dropped with a clang that echoed around the suddenly silent room. My message to the control room, intended to be a simple log entry, had been helpfully passed on to the hospital. In the telling, 'a knife injury' had morphed into 'an officer has been stabbed,' and they had, in effect, scrambled the crash team.

All eyes were on me. I meekly held up my hand, revealing the tiny, centimetre-long gash. 'I, erm… I cut myself,' I mumbled, the words catching in my throat. 'Washing up.'

Stunned silence, and then the room erupted. The doctors, the nurses, my own colleague – they were all roaring with laughter. The tension evaporated in a wave of collective mirth. One by one, the emergency team filed out, chuckling and shaking their heads, leaving me with a single, smiling nurse.

'Don't you worry,' she said, patting my arm kindly. 'We'll get you sorted.'

She cleaned the cut, applied a couple of butterfly stitches, and wrapped it in a proper bandage. To say I was embarrassed is an understatement of colossal proportions, but as I walked back to the car, my hand neatly dressed and my face bright red, I had to admit it was funny. It taught me a valuable lesson about the perils of police communication. And, perhaps more importantly, that if you're going to get injured on duty, it's best to have a story with a bit more grit than a battle with a burnt chilli pan.

Who framed Roger Rabbit?

Sometimes, no matter how hard you try, you can't help but take your work home with you. It seeps into the quiet moments, turning a peaceful evening into a tactical operation. I was living with Janet over in Fareham, near Portsmouth at the time, in a lovely, respectable close where the most dramatic event was usually a missed bin collection.

One evening, just as we were winding down, Janet called me into the bedroom. There was a real urgency in her voice. 'Listen,' she whispered, 'can you hear that?'

I strained my ears. At first, nothing. Then, a faint but distinct noise. A sort of rhythmic thudding, like someone trying to force a gate or jemmy a door. It was just muffled enough to be unsettling. I unlocked and opened the bedroom window, and the sound became much clearer. *Thunk. Thunk. Thunk.* Definitely not the wind. My copper's intuition, that little alarm bell that had saved my skin more times than I could count, started ringing. A burglary in progress, I thought. Next door!

'Right,' I said, a plan already forming in my mind. 'I'll go and check it out and contain the back of the house. You call the police.'

That sounded strange, as we were the police! Janet, already in her pyjamas and a pair of frankly ridiculous novelty dinosaur slippers, nodded and grabbed her phone. The plan was simple: a classic pincer movement, waiting for the burglar to appear. I would slip out and cover the rear of our neighbour's house, where the noise seemed to be coming from. Janet, our slippers-and-pyjamas-clad sentry, would guard the front. Our house was a semi at the end of the close, and there was no other way out. We had them cornered. All we had to do was hold the line until the cavalry arrived. I pulled on my trainers and crept out into the cool night air, heading for the back service road. As I got into position, I heard it. Not a siren, but a sound just as familiar to anyone in my line of work. The low, purposeful growl of an area car's engine, the specific hum of its tyres on the tarmac as it swept into the street. You become attuned to it, a sixth sense for the sound of approaching backup.

The car parked at the bottom of the close and two officers emerged. I recognised them immediately and they, seeing me lurking in the shadows, recognised me too. A quick, hushed explanation followed.

'Think we've got a burglar on the premises next door,' I murmured, feeling a strange mix of professional calm and neighbourly panic.

One of them produced a Dragon light, a torch so powerful it could probably illuminate the dark side of the moon. We unlatched the back gate and slipped into the garden, the beam cutting a brilliant white swathe across the lawn. It swept over the back of the house, lighting up the windows and the patio door. Everything was intact. Not a scratch, not a mark. We crept along the side of the house, the beam dancing ahead of us, but found nothing untoward. As we rounded the corner to the front, I saw the tips of Janet's dinosaur slippers poking out from behind our own front door. She peered around, a picture of domestic vigilance, and gave a slight shrug. Nobody had passed her, she confirmed, not that I imagine she'd have given much of a chase in that footwear. I walked back with the officers, apologising for what was looking increasingly like a false alarm.

'I was so sure,' I insisted, feeling a bit of a prat. 'It was a really clear banging noise.'

And then, as if on cue, it started again. *Bang. Bang. Bang.*

I shot a look at one of the officers. He glanced back at me, his expression a perfect mirror of my own renewed suspicion. His eyes then darted towards the source. A small wooden shed tucked away down the side of the house. Of course. They weren't after the telly; they were after the bikes or the power tools. The officer moved towards the shed, hand ready. He swung the door open, aimed the Dragon light inside, and we all peered in, ready to apprehend the culprit.

Inside, sitting in a large cage, was a giant, fluffy white rabbit. It stared back at us, its nose twitching, before lifting a powerful back leg and thumping it furiously against the side of its hutch. *Bang. Bang. Bang.* It turned out he was on heat and, feeling particularly fruity, was simply venting his romantic frustrations.

The silence was broken by a snort from one of the officers, which quickly escalated into full-blown laughter. Soon, all three of us were doubled over, the tension of the last ten minutes dissolving into helpless giggles. I apologised profusely, my cheeks burning, but they were good sports about it. We all agreed it was far better to call and be wrong than to ignore a suspicious noise and wake up to a crime scene.

Needless to say, word of my dramatic encounter with Thumper the amorous rabbit spread like wildfire within local policing circles. For the next few weeks, I had the piss taken out of me relentlessly at the station. But even now, I can't hear a sudden thumping noise in the quiet of the night without a small smile and a brief, vivid image of a very frustrated bunny.

I almost lost my wife and daughter

As the 'noughties' drew to a close, we decided it was time to throw an even bigger challenge into the mix: children. To our delight, Janet fell pregnant quickly. Like all first-time parents, we were a delightful cocktail of excitement and sheer terror. We dutifully attended every antenatal appointment and sat in a circle with other bewildered-looking couples, trying to get our heads around how a tiny person was about to turn our world upside down. You soon learn the big secret of parenthood. Everyone is just making it up as they go along, doing their best to provide a home filled with love, safety, and vaguely acceptable moral values.

Janet's pregnancy went well, from my perspective at least. She would vehemently disagree. For nine months, she was in a near-constant state of nausea. The slightest thing would set her off. A lifelong Portsmouth fan, she'd insist on going to the matches at Fratton Park, only to spend 90 minutes with a sick bag clutched in her hand (is that normal for a Pompey fan?), the aroma of pies and pre-match pints sending waves of nausea over her. Now that's dedication.

As the due date approached, the nesting instinct kicked in. The house was cleaned, with a bag packed and waiting by the front door. I'd marvel at the feeling of a tiny foot kicking against my hand through her belly, giddy with the prospect of becoming a father.

Then, the day came. The contractions started slowly, late in the evening. We tried to get some sleep, but by two in the morning Janet was in considerable pain. It was time. We grabbed the bag and set off on the slow, quiet drive to the hospital in Winchester. The roads were deserted, the world was asleep, but I was buzzing with adrenaline and excitement.

At the maternity ward, the midwives welcomed us in. It was confirmed she was in labour and I would soon be a father. I sat by Janet's bed as the hours crawled by. This was not going to be a quick birth. The air was thick with the rhythmic beeping of monitors, the hum of a tea urn, and the distant sound of other people's babies crying down the corridor. With every passing hour, the contractions grew stronger and Janet grew weaker.

We tried music. She was offered various forms of pain relief, but nothing touched the sides. At one point, a fresh-faced midwife breezed in and chirped, 'Have you considered aromatherapy?' The volley of sweary abuse she received from Janet in response confirmed that, no, some nice-smelling oils were not going to cut the mustard.

After nearly 24 hours, something felt wrong. We both said as much to the staff, with a growing sense of unease settling over us. Janet was exhausted, pushing with all her might but making no progress. Finally, a consultant arrived, took one look, and identified the problem. The baby was in the wrong position, twisted in such a way that a natural birth was impossible. The next bit was a blur of focused activity. A suction cup – a ventouse, they called it, was produced to help turn the baby and guide her out. I was parked on a chair in the corner, given a front-row seat but told to stay out of the way. The suction cup worked a treat, and with a final, monumental effort, our first child was born.

She was whisked to a side table, and I saw she had what I can only describe as a perfect conehead, a temporary side effect of the suction.

'It'll go back to normal,' a nurse reassured me, so I wasn't too worried.

The skull of a newborn baby is not totally solid, as the bone slowly hardens and fuses together to allow the head and brain to grow rapidly during those early years. The medical team cleaned her, swaddled her, and announced, 'It's a girl!'

I heard a tiny cry, a reassuring sign. But the atmosphere in the room was tense.

I looked over at Janet. Her skin was waxy and pale, almost translucent. Similar to the many dead people I had seen through work. Fear flickered in her eyes. Our birth plan, which had optimistically included a water bath, had long since gone out of the window. I was, however, permitted to perform my one requested duty: cutting the umbilical cord. The sensation was bizarrely like slicing through bacon rind, but I enjoyed the experience. As I sat back down, I saw it. A terrifying amount of blood was pouring off the end of the bed. Unbeknown to us, Janet was suffering a postpartum haemorrhage. A life-threatening bleed. Janet now had a matter of minutes to live, unless the doctors and nurses could stem the flow.

Suddenly, the room filled with medical staff working frantically. An emergency alarm had been pressed. They wrapped Janet in a foil blanket attached to a machine that billowed hot air, a desperate attempt to keep her body from shutting down. Her speech became slow and confused. The consultant, calm and swift, began an emergency procedure to stem the bleeding while nurses threw absorbent pads onto the floor to soak up the blood.

Janet looked like a waxwork model of herself. She told me later, in that moment that she looked across at me huddled in the corner and thought, 'I can't die. I can't possibly leave that bloody idiot in charge of my child.'

Charming. But if that's the motivation she needed to hang on, I'll take it.

Then the consultant said something that made the hairs on my arms stand up. 'Can you start bagging up all the pads and weigh them, please.'

A little bit of knowledge can be a dangerous thing. I knew this was for two reasons: to calculate how much blood she'd lost, and to provide evidence for a coroner's court, should the worst happen. As they started gathering the blood-soaked pads, a grim accounting of what we stood to lose, I just prayed it wouldn't come to that. The consultant, a chap who clearly knew his stuff, did an amazing job and finally managed to stem the blood flow. But it had been a near-run thing. Janet was critically ill, having been just moments from death after losing a staggering eight pints of blood. To put that in perspective, the average bloke has about eight pints in total. She was, to use the medical vernacular, running on empty.

The staff, having performed their minor miracle, got her comfortable then hooked up to a constellation of transfusions and saline drips. She was alive, which was the main thing, but she wasn't going anywhere. She'd be under their constant, watchful eye for at least the next day or two.

And so, with Janet out for the count, it was time for me to step up to the plate. My parenting duties, previously a rather abstract concept involving flat-pack cots and arguments over paint colours, were suddenly, terrifyingly, put into play. A nurse handed me this beautiful, crying bundle of joy, a baby we would later name Anna. She was perfect in every way. Apart, that is, from having a head shaped like a particularly pointy traffic cone. She was crying her little lungs out, desperately trying to communicate that her grand entrance into the world had left her famished.

A midwife, sensing my novice-level panic, warmed a bottle of formula and passed it to me. And there it was. I was the first to feed our daughter. She sat on my lap, snuggled into my chest, and the world just…stopped. The frantic beeping of the ward and the gnawing worry for Janet all faded into a low hum. It was just me and this tiny, cone-headed person, a truly magical moment amidst the chaos.

We never even told anyone for about 24 hours that Janet had given birth. It was so traumatic at the time and we did not want to tempt fate by telling family too soon. But eventually I did make some calls to our parents who were overjoyed at the news they had become grandparents.

As the hours turned into days, Janet began to recover very slowly. My life became a relentless triangle of driving from home, hospital, and work, with work quickly becoming the disposable point. I'd arrive on the ward to find Janet hollow-eyed and exhausted. The maternity ward is not a place of rest. It's a cacophony of crying babies, clattering trolleys, and the general, well-meaning hubbub of a system at full tilt.

It was only when I was there, a sentry at her bedside, that Janet felt safe enough to finally drift off, having spent most of the night wide awake and terrified. The police were brilliant, allowing me some time off and to take paternity leave, which really helped.

The haemorrhage had another cruel trick up its sleeve. The sheer fluid loss meant Janet's body, quite understandably, had put milk production at the very bottom of its to-do list. So, for the first few months, Anna was bottle-fed. It was another blow, but thankfully, as Janet's strength returned, nature eventually found its way, and she was able to feed our daughter as she'd always wanted.

It was a traumatic time, no two ways about it. The long hours driving back and forth, fuelled by hospital coffee and pure adrenaline, gave me far too much time to think. The thought that I could have lost both of them, a possibility so horrific I'd never even allowed it to form, played on a loop in my head. But we got through it. Together, somehow, we muddled through. You'd think, after the drama of our first daughter Anna's arrival, that fate might have cut us a bit of slack. That we'd served our time in the maternity ward filled with high anxiety. For a while, it seemed that way. Janet and

Anna both made a spectacular recovery, and I settled into the simple, profound joy of being a father. Life was good.

So good, in fact, that we started to think about doing it all over again. The conversation about a second child was surprisingly straightforward. We both wanted one, but this time we were determined to do things differently. There would be no repeat performance of the last-minute panic. We returned to the hospital, a united front, to have a frank discussion with the maternity consultants. Our one non-negotiable demand was a planned Caesarean section. It took a bit of persuading; consultants can be a stubborn bunch, but eventually they agreed. A wave of relief washed over us. Janet fell pregnant quickly, and we embarked on another nine-month-long vigil. This time, however, the anxiety was tempered by the reassuring presence of a date circled in red on our calendar. When the day came, I found myself kitted out in surgical scrubs, standing in a brightly lit operating theatre. It was the most bizarre, surreal, and utterly incredible experience. One minute, Janet was lying on the table, awake and chatting; the next, a doctor was lifting a small, squawking person from an incision in her abdomen. It was clinical, yet profoundly emotional. We named her Eleanor.

With only two years between them, Anna and Ellie, as she quickly became known, were destined to be thick as thieves. But if we thought our second child would quietly follow in her sister's footsteps, we were sorely mistaken. Ellie, it turned out, had her own unique talent for plunging us into worry and grief.

I'd been at work all day, probably wrestling with paperwork or some minor crisis of law and order, blissfully unaware of the domestic drama unfolding at home. When I walked through the door that evening, Janet met me with a look I knew all too well. There had been, she explained, 'an incident'. Ellie, not much more than a year old, had been sitting in her high chair in the kitchen. Having finished her meal, and clearly bored of the view, she'd decided to engage in a spot of light acrobatics. Using the kitchen cabinets as a launchpad, she'd braced her little legs and feet then pushed, hard. Janet had only turned her back for a second, but it was long enough. The high chair tilted, hung in the air for a heart-stopping moment and then crashed backwards onto the tiled floor. Janet scooped up a startled and wailing Ellie, gave her a thorough check-over, and found her seemingly none the worse for wear.

Later that evening, with Janet taking some well-deserved downtime, I took over bath duties. I was perched on the edge of the toilet next to the bath, happily washing shampoo out of Ellie's hair as she splashed about, when my fingers brushed against something on the back of her head. It was a large, soft, squishy lump. My stomach lurched. I gently felt it again. It was huge, easily the size of half a grapefruit, and it had a terrifying, boggy texture.

'Janet!' I yelled, my voice tight with a sudden, cold fear. 'Get in here, now!'

She appeared in the doorway, and I saw her face drain of colour as I pointed to Ellie's head. My hands were dripping with soap and water.

'Call an ambulance,' I said, trying to keep my voice steady. 'Right now.'

I knew, with the grim certainty of a police officer, that this was serious.

Janet, ever the calm one in a crisis, made the call, relaying the details with a calm composure. The ambulance arrived in a shriek of sirens and a flash of blue lights. After a swift assessment, the paramedics confirmed our fears. 'We need to get her to hospital. Urgently.'

Janet climbed into the back with Ellie, and I watched them disappear into the night, promising to follow on.

What followed was a blur of hospital corridors, hushed conversations and the relentless hum of medical machinery. Ellie was whisked away for a battery of scans while Janet and I were plunged into a new kind of hell, the waiting game. We were questioned repeatedly about what had happened. Sometimes together, sometimes separately.

The staff, quite rightly, had to rule out a non-accidental injury. It was a strange and deeply uncomfortable position to be in. As police officers, we were used to being the ones asking the questions, the ones harbouring suspicion. Now, the spotlight was turned squarely on us. We understood the process, of course. We accepted it. But it didn't make it any less galling. Our main difficulty was that neither of us had actually seen the fall. We could only piece together what we thought had happened – that the force of the high chair hitting the tiled floor had caused the injury.

The diagnosis, when it came, was brutal. A massive fracture down the back of her skull had caused a haemorrhage. The grotesque, squishy lump was her body's own desperate attempt to protect the brain, a build-up of blood and fluid outside the skull. Ellie was admitted, and Janet began a bedside vigil, sleeping in a blue padded plastic-covered chair, exhausted but unable to rest, her world shrunk to the four walls of that hospital room. I split my time between looking after Anna, trying to maintain a sliver of normality for her, and making the daily pilgrimage to the hospital. My heart was in my mouth every time I walked through the doors. We didn't know if she would survive, or if she did survive, whether she would have brain damage.

Then, just when we thought things couldn't possibly get any worse, they did. We were called into the family room. That dreaded, softly furnished room where bad news is delivered. The consultant sat us down. He explained that Ellie's blood tests had shown a remarkably low white blood cell count. They suspected, on top of everything else, that she might have leukaemia. The room went quiet for me. Everything else the consultant spoke of felt like 'white noise', as my thoughts focused on that term, leukaemia.

We were stunned into silence. It felt like a physical blow, knocking the last of the air from our lungs. A fractured skull was one thing, but cancer of the blood was another entirely. It was too much to comprehend.

And then, as the hours and days passed, a small miracle. Just as we were bracing for the worst, Ellie started to improve. The colour returned to her cheeks. She began to seem more like her old self. Further tests were run, and the news, when it came, was delivered not in the dreaded family room, but by a smiling doctor on the ward. It wasn't leukaemia. Her body, in fighting the immense trauma to her head, had simply thrown all its resources, including its white blood cells at the site of the injury.

We were told her skull would heal naturally, and it did. After a few weeks that had felt like a lifetime, we were allowed to bring her home. We were also, officially, cleared of any wrongdoing, a fact we'd never doubted but which was a relief to have confirmed in black and white. It's a strange sensation, being the one who normally points the finger of accusation, only to find it pointing at you. I suspect, in the long run, that unnerving experience made us both better police officers. It certainly taught us a thing or two about how it feels to be on the other side of the desk.

We were both just overjoyed that Ellie would be safe and well.

The smell of death

Anyone who works in the emergency services will be exposed to death. No one joins because they fancy a weekend dealing with death, but it's part of the job. Police officers, ambulance staff, fire officers and first responders of all types will all get called when life tips over at its most vulnerable and critical moments. Sometimes it's not a rescue, it is picking up the pieces that may have ended with fatality.

I've had my fair share of witnessing serious injury and death. People sometimes ask how I deal with it, as if there's a secret technique tucked into a pocket of my uniform. For me, it's quite simple. I detach myself. Especially when someone has died. As far as I'm concerned, the person has gone. What remains is a body, a shell. My job then becomes professional and practical, to secure the scene, gather evidence, be respectful. Treat the deceased, their family, their friends, and those who first found them with dignity – the sort of dignity I would want if it were my own loved one. It's not coldness, it is a form of professionalism and care. It is also a way to cope with the kind of trauma most people are never exposed to.

That said, some incidents etch themselves in your memory for all sorts of strange reasons. The smell, for one. As a cop, you never forget the smell of death. It clings to your clothes and your thoughts and turns up, uninvited, at the oddest moments. Even barbecue smoke, under a certain breeze, can carry a hint of it. For me, rotten chicken has a similar smell. You learn to breathe through your mouth and get on with it. Then, later, you talk. Some officers on shift used to carry a small tub of menthol vapour rub to mask the smell. Having Janet around made things easier for me, as I could chat about some of the grim realities of attending such incidents. She had witnessed many of the same experiences and had a knack for telling a grim story without turning it into a horror show. We'd often sit after a shift and offload: what we'd seen, what we hadn't expected, the little details that lodged. Janet had a few particularly memorable tales, and one of them still makes my skin crawl.

It was the middle of summer at a caravan park. Families sprawled in deck chairs, sausages sizzling, kids shrieking around inflatable crocodiles. The sort of place that smells of cheap sunscreen and burnt burgers. The site owner had been worried about one of the long-term residents, a man who'd stopped paying his bills and hadn't been seen for a while. Janet arrived and, before she even crossed the threshold of the caravan, she knew. There was a sweet-sour note that announces itself. Death had been there for some time. Everyone else in the caravan park was blissfully unaware that death was less than 100 feet away.

With the help of a colleague, she forced the door of the caravan to gain entry. As it swung open, the floor moved. Not because the caravan was on a slope or poorly built, but because it was alive. A slow, rippling mass of maggots and dead flies shifting as if the lino itself breathed. The man had been dead for six months.

The really sad element to this was that he wasn't missed. The absence of anyone to notice. No friends, no family, no regular knock at the door. There was no foul play at hand and the man had just died from natural causes. The team dealt with it quietly, discreetly, trying not to attract attention from holidaymakers who were cheerfully ignorant, licking ketchup from their fingers while, a few metres away, life's end was being carefully tended to.

It was bizarre and tragic, like a play with an audience on the next stage, laughing at the wrong time. Janet would often threaten to throw away her uniform or her boots (which we had to buy ourselves) after attending a smelly incident like that. She described to me once, having to attend an incident where a male was having a mental health episode. On entering the flat, she was overcome with a foul smell of human excrement.

Many people have hobbies such as collecting stamps or coins, but this particular individual enjoyed collecting his own faeces. It was like something out of a horror film. There were faeces smeared on doors, on the internal walls of the house. As she spoke to the male, she inspected the house further to see how he was coping with life. On opening the fridge there was plate after plate stacked with human excrement. Both Janet and her colleague were holding back a nauseating wretch.

To complete the bizarre scene in the centre of the living room was a model. Yes, you guessed it. There was a model of a mountain created from human shit, that resembled a scene from the film, *Close Encounters of the Third Kind*, where one of the characters becomes obsessed with UFOs and a subliminal image of a mountainous shape, repeatedly making models of it. The man was taken to hospital for a psychological assessment. Janet took her clothes and boots to the nearest rubbish bin after that job.

On another occasion, Janet was sent to deliver a death message. We're trained for that. At training school, you practise with role-plays. It is important as a police officer to be clear and unambiguous as to what has happened, providing clarity and compassion. But you can only prepare so much. Telling someone their husband, wife, child, parent has died: there's no simple or tidy way to do it. You go, you say what's true, you stay long enough to anchor them, and you gather what you need to help with the paperwork and the practicalities. You resist the urge to fill silences you can't mend.

On this occasion the circumstances were complicated. The husband had died away from the area he lived with his wife, and the circumstances were…unhelpfully specific. At the moment he had died, he'd been with a prostitute. He'd had a heart attack mid-act and passed away. Traumatic for the woman he was with, I imagine. Potentially devastating for the wife who knew nothing about any of it and was about to learn the worst thing anyone can learn.

What do you say? You're carrying a bomb of information into someone's lounge. Do you set it off all at once? There's the ethicist's answer, then there's the human one. On that day, I was relieved it wasn't my call. Janet told the wife her husband had died. She said which city, that it was known he'd suffered a heart attack, and where he'd been taken. The rest would come out inevitably, and soon, but not in that first, shattering moment. There's a duty to truth, yes, but also a duty not to injure without necessity. The wife would find out. But she didn't have to find out everything at once, like a trapdoor giving way beneath both feet.

These are the sorts of decisions that don't appear on the forms. No manners of training or briefings can prepare you for those types of decisions. They happen in the pause between sentences, in the way you hold your hands, in the pitch of your voice. They happen because you walk into people's lives at the very moment those lives are tipping, and you can steady the fall a little, or you can make it worse.

There's no glory in it. Just a hope that you handle the worst moments of someone's day with care and compassion.

It's a rotten job at times

My first sudden death was, for want of a better word, a textbook case. Straightforward, simple, and a gentle introduction to a side of policing that many never see. It was a neat, if sombre, beginning to a long career of dealing with the decidedly less straightforward sudden deaths. As I would soon discover, death, much like life, rarely sticks to the script.

One such incident took me to a block of maisonette flats down in Portsea, off Cumberland Street. The call from the control room was a 'concern for welfare'. A chap hadn't been seen by a friend for a while, and his phone was ringing into the void. I climbed the internal communal stairs to the first floor, the air already still and heavy, with each footstep creating an echo. A few sharp knocks on the door yielded nothing but silence.

I was used to this. Many people, especially criminals, got used to the way the police knock on a door. Often with a sense of authority, using a rhythmic hard rap of the knuckles. Those who were wanted would often remain silent and not open the door. I chose to knock, often with a cheery tune in the hope somebody would come to the door, as I held my finger across the spy hole. As I waited, I scanned the windowsill for the tell-tale signs; a congregation of flies is usually a dead giveaway, pardon the pun – but there was nothing.

Crouching down, I flipped open the letterbox and peered into the gloom. 'Hello? Police!' I called out the man's name, my voice swallowed by the sparsely furnished flat. No reply. Just an eerie, listening silence. But then it hit me, the smell. An unmistakable, cloying stench that cuts through everything else. At that moment, I was fairly certain my 'concern for welfare' had become a 'confirming the inevitable'.

I radioed the control room. 'I'm forcing entry,' I announced, then took a few steps back.

With the full force of my size 14 boots, I gave the door a proper introduction. It flew open, slammed against the hallway wall, and then bounced right back into its frame. The lock surround was utterly mangled. I squeezed inside, my boots echoing on the tiled floor. The flat was freezing, I guessed the heating had long stopped working, once the electric meter had used up its credit.

'Hello? Police!' I called again, the words feeling foolishly loud in the quiet. There's nothing quite so unnerving as searching a property on your own, not knowing what's around the next corner. Every shadow plays tricks on you: every creak of a door makes you jump. It's like being the star of your own low-budget horror film, minus the dramatic music.

I moved methodically down the corridor, checking each room as I went. The kitchen, a bedroom, and finally the main living room. Nothing. The man was nowhere to be seen, yet that smell lingered, thicker now. I was still deeply concerned. In missing person enquiries, you learn that people, especially children, often hide in the most unlikely of places, seeking comfort in small, enclosed spaces. So, I started again, more thoroughly this time: opening cupboards, peering behind the sofa, checking inside cardboard boxes, anywhere a person might conceal themselves.

As I made my way back towards the entrance, I noticed a small service cupboard tucked away beside the front door. I shoved the broken entrance door out of the way and pulled the cupboard open. There he was.

It appeared he had chosen to end his own life, using a length of electrical flex from within the utility cupboard. He was a man in his thirties. In a strange way, he looked at peace, though his eyes were open and staring directly at me. The cold of the flat had partly preserved him, holding off the worst of decomposition, but he'd been there for a few days. There was no note, no explanation. Just a profound, silent sadness.

I updated the control room, requesting a CID officer and a photographer to ensure everything was properly documented for the coroner. It didn't look like foul play, just a tragedy. As I sat there alone with the deceased, I began filling out the requisite G28 form. One of the questions was 'Ethnicity of the deceased'. I looked at the man. His skin was a deep, dark black. I recorded 'IC3' – the police code for someone of Black Afro-Caribbean ethnicity.

As I continued with my paperwork, I kept glancing over at him. Something wasn't quite right. A detail nagged at me. Then I saw it: an unusual mark on the very top of one of his ears. It was a different colour from the rest of him. Curious, I went over for a closer look.

The tip of his ear was, in fact, white. It turned out the man was white European. 'Lividity' is the term for the settling of blood after death. In this case lividity had turned his skin such a dark, uniform black that he appeared to be of a different ethnicity entirely. That tiny patch of skin on his ear was the only clue to who he had been before. It was an unusual quirk I had never seen before, and have never seen since.

When CID arrived, they agreed there was no foul play, and the undertakers were cleared to attend. The next of kin would be notified, and I would move on.

My very next job, as it happened, was dealing with some kids swearing and kicking a football against a wall. From the profound to the profane in the space of an hour, such was the rhythm of my beat work.

Of course, not all endings are so quiet. I recall another man, who had died in his bath. It's a surprisingly common occurrence. The heat, the change in blood pressure all can lead to a sudden fall or heart attack. This poor soul however, had been there for some time. In his final throes, he had kicked the plug out, draining the water away and leaving him exposed for several weeks. Decomposition was, to put it mildly, well advanced.

After my initial enquiries, the undertakers arrived and asked for a hand moving the deceased. The guy was quite large and they needed all the help they could get to lift this dead weight. The plan was simple, we'd lift him from the bath and place him in the body bag waiting on the floor. Donning surgical gloves, we each took a limb. On the count of three, we lifted.

Unfortunately, the man's body was so putrefied that it simply… split. He broke in half with a sickening gush. His liquefied remains poured out of his torso and straight into the plughole he'd accidentally opened weeks before. Even the undertakers, men who did this for a living, looked a bit green in the face. A change of plan was required. We used two body bags and were able to move the deceased, rolling him onto a bag while still in the bath and then lifting him out and into a second bag lying on the floor. It took a great deal of grim determination to move him, with what little dignity for the deceased we could muster.

Needless to say, I took a leaf out of Janet's book of advice in these situations. My first stop after that job was the police station, to put in a request for a new uniform, as mine was going straight in the bin. Some days, you just can't wash the job off.

Staying in control under stress

In the police, I was always known for being very calm and in control. Nothing would phase me and I felt comfortable in dealing with any 999 police emergency. Similar to the pilot Tom 'Iceman' Kazansky, portrayed by Val Kilmer in the '80s film *Top Gun*, I always remained calm under pressure.

My voice would be calm on the radio during the craziest of police pursuits and I always gave the impression of being in total control, even if inside I was flapping like mad! Over the years, I have attended a large number of incidents, building up resilience to deal with what I would be exposed to in the future. But what effect does this have on the human brain?

Imagine an alarm system designed to protect your home. When it detects a threat, it blares loudly, alerting you to danger and preparing you to act. Once the danger has passed, you disarm the system, and silence is restored. But what if the alarm became stuck? What if it continued to sound, long after the threat was gone, triggered by the slightest noise or the faintest shadow?

This is the essence of Post-Traumatic Stress Disorder (PTSD), a profound mental health condition that can develop in the aftermath of a terrifying, stressful, or distressing event. While a period of shock and distress is a natural human response to trauma, PTSD occurs when the mind's alarm system fails to reset. It is a persistent physical and emotional response that keeps a person locked in the trauma, long after the moment of impact has passed. I am no expert on the subject and have not knowingly suffered from PTSD.

In the '90s, officers were mainly told to 'just get on with it'. Of course, having a dark sense of humour really helped, and sharing details of incidents with colleagues, as they would be able to better understand incidents you had attended. Help with mental health in the police has improved, but it could still be much, much better.

The University of Cambridge has published research suggesting that, for the UK Police workforce, almost one in five employees suffer with a form of PTSD. Police officers are exposed to significantly higher levels of trauma compared to the general public. To give you an idea of scale, research by the FBI and Boston University suggests that the average volume of traumatic events encountered by police officers is 10 to 900 events throughout their career. This is obviously role-dependent.

The average volume of traumatic events encountered by the general public is two to three traumatic events in a lifetime. As you can see, it's not surprising police officers are more likely to suffer from PTSD at some stage in their lives.

To understand why this happens, we must look at the intricate machinery of the human brain. Two key structures are central to our experience of trauma: the Amygdala and the Hippocampus.

First is the **Amygdala**, which can be thought of as the brain's immediate and instinctive *alarm system*. When faced with a perceived threat, it is the Amygdala that sounds the siren. It triggers the primal fight-flight-or-freeze response, flooding the body with adrenaline, raising blood pressure, and sharpening the senses into a state of hyper-vigilance. It is our raw, unfiltered reaction centre for fear and stress.

Working alongside it is the **Hippocampus**, the brain's diligent *memory filter*. The Hippocampus is responsible for taking our experiences, making sense of them, and filing them away in the correct place. Critically, it gives our memories context, stamping them with a sense of time and place. It is the part of the brain that turns the present into the past.

In a healthy response to a stressful event, the Amygdala fires its alarm, we respond to the danger, and then the Hippocampus steps in to process the experience and store it as a past memory. This is what helps to create resilience, being exposed to events and then learning from them. For professionals in high-stress fields, such as policing or emergency services, the risk is compounded. Their daily duties can keep the Amygdala in a near-constant state of arousal, making it exceptionally difficult for the brain to contextualise and process the relentless stream of stressful events.

As a tutor constable, teaching new police officers how to operate in a real environment on the street and not in the classroom, I would often talk about the need to be in a state of readiness to stay safe.

Green would mean everything is relaxed with no threats. Maybe, sitting in the police station, the only threat is being on the lookout for colleagues playing a practical joke on you!

Amber would mean to be prepared. No immediate threats, but keeping all your senses alert to possible threats. Every time an officer goes on patrol, they should be at this level of readiness.

Red would mean a threat is present or imminent and you need to 'Fight or Run', taking immediate action. The 'Freeze' option is not really a good situation for an emergency responder.

Being alert would often prevent yourself, a colleague or member of the public from being hurt, because you were ready for that sudden headbutt or hidden weapon a prisoner may be concealing. The simple truth of this job is that no one ever calls us because they're having a good day. You're dialling 999 because you're a victim, you're terrified, or you're in the middle of a crisis. We are steeped in that, day in, day out. That constant exposure to trauma and distress inevitably shapes how you see the world. It has to. It builds a library of worst-case scenarios in your head, and it can breed a cynicism that's hard to shake.

Then, you find yourself on a street in the middle of the night, in a dynamic situation where a life-changing decision has to be made in a split second. Your training and knowledge of the law are the foundation, of course; they're the bedrock. But when the pressure is truly on, what really comes to the fore is the sum of every similar job you've ever been to. It's that gut instinct, honed by years of seeing how things can go catastrophically wrong, that ultimately guides your hand. And that doesn't just dictate how you do the job. It shapes who you are when you take the uniform off.

Only a few years before I was due to retire, I fully understood and experienced my own brain's Amygdala flooding the body with adrenaline, raising my own blood pressure. That created a 'life or death' experience, as you will discover later, turning out to be the fight of my life…

When football fans go to war...

My first ever football match was a rather underwhelming affair. My brother Geoff took me to see Rochdale AFC at the Spotland Ground when I was about 10 years old. I remember it being bitterly cold and I certainly wasn't dressed for the weather. The quality of play, I must say, was equally uninspiring. It's fair to say that, after that chilly Saturday afternoon, I wasn't exactly rushing to join the ranks of football fanatics.

Years later, however, football found me again, this time in Portsmouth.

When I first started in the police, my tutor Nick was a Pompey fan of the highest order. For Nick, any opportunity to see the Blues play at Fratton Park was not to be missed. As my tutor, he was an experienced officer and, at the time, an area car driver, which meant we spent our shifts cruising around in one of the force's high-powered Volvos.

One evening, on a late turn, Nick turned to me in the car. 'Ever been to Fratton Park?' he asked.

I hadn't the foggiest what he was on about. I gave him a blank look, which I imagine confirmed his suspicions that I was a complete heathen. A slow grin spread across his face.

'Right,' he said, 'I'll show you. There's a game on tonight.'

So, at about quarter to eight, we drove the area car round to Frogmore Road and parked up. In full uniform, we walked over to a gate at the corner of the ground. A steward spotted our uniforms, gave a knowing nod, and ushered us in. The game had just kicked off and the stands were already packed. This was back in 1993, when most of the ground was still standing terraces, but there was some seating. Nick led me to a metal staircase that snaked its way up the side of one of the enormous floodlight towers. Near the bottom was a small platform, and from there we had a perfect, elevated view of the entire pitch and ground.

The first thing that hit me was the noise. It was a physical presence, a colossal, unified roar that seemed to shake the very air. Thousands of fans were singing in unison, the chorus of 'Play Up Pompey' driven by the deep, rhythmic thud of a large drum somewhere in the crowd. The pitch was bathed in the brilliant glare of the floodlights, and the air was filled with a blizzard of homemade ticker tape. These were just little strips of ripped up newspaper, which had been hurled into the sky as the players ran out from the tunnel. Now, these drifted gently around the ground like paper snow. I remember thinking, this is more like it. This was the spectacle; the raw, captivating excitement I had expected to find at Rochdale all those years ago.

We were only visiting, not on official football duty, so after a brief chat with some other uniformed officers, we had to leave, ready to respond to the next call. But in that moment, I was hooked. I had a feeling I was going to become a Pompey fan, whether I liked it or not.

Policing the football soon became a regular part of the job, and I have to say I really enjoyed it. Most of the English football season unfolds from the end of summer through the bleakest parts of winter, so we quickly became experts in layering. Long johns, extra jumpers, anything to fend off the bone-chilling cold was fair game. The duties were often paid overtime, so it could be a nice little earner on a rest day.

The main part of the job, of course, was managing the fans. Before the game, during the game, and after the game, our role was to keep a lid on things and ensure everyone got home safely. Fratton Park has four stands. The North Stand has two tiers; the South Stand houses the players, staff, and a family section; the Milton End is for the away supporters; and then there's the famous Fratton End, home to the most hardcore, and usually noisiest, Pompey fans.

Our shift would typically start with a briefing. Our unit, or 'serial', would file into the seats of the upper South Stand, a sea of high vis jackets and custodian helmets. Sometimes, if serious trouble was expected, we'd be told to bring our NATO helmets. A senior officer, the silver commander, would outline the plan for the day, cover any intelligence about potential troublemakers, and assign us our positions.

Before kick-off, we'd patrol the streets and pubs around the ground. Fans would be having a pint or two, and the atmosphere was generally good natured. There were strict rules about taking drink into the stadium, and anyone who was too drunk would find themselves arrested and missing the match entirely. We'd occasionally have to walk through the pubs, often to a loud cheer and the odd shout of 'Here come the strippers', but it was all part of the banter.

I remember one Saturday afternoon, my serial was positioned near Priory Crescent, monitoring a couple of pubs. It was all fairly quiet, but something caught my eye in the bookmakers on the corner. The shop was full of punters, some studying form cards, others staring transfixed at the TV screens, waiting for the latest results. At the back, a counter was protected by bulletproof glass, with little metal trays for passing money and betting slips. The wastepaper bins were overflowing with discarded slips, the ghosts of failed bets. But from one of these bins, I saw a wisp of smoke. Someone had carelessly tossed a cigarette in. The smoke thickened, turning black, and then, with a sudden whoosh, the contents of the bin burst into flames.

I confidently strode into the shop and shouted, 'Fire! Everybody leave!'

To my utter astonishment, a few people glanced over, but nobody moved. It was as if I was invisible. They were completely mesmerised by the races on the screens.

'There is a FIRE!' I boomed, in my best police voice. 'Everybody OUT!'

Still nothing. It seemed the prospect of their horse finishing the race was more compelling than the prospect of being burnt alive. There was nothing else for it. I walked over to the flaming bin, grabbed it by the base and carried the whole blazing thing outside onto the pavement. I then nipped back in, grabbed the fire extinguisher from by the door and put it out myself. I stood there, perplexed, at the sheer power gambling held over these people.

On another occasion, I had to arrest a fan after a scuffle broke out in the stands. This was fairly routine. I cuffed him and led him down to a small, makeshift custody area near the Frogmore Road entrance. I say 'custody area' in the loosest possible terms; it was really just a sergeant behind a temporary desk with some paperwork forms next to the toilets. The custody sergeant gave my offender a 'gypsy's warning'. He was de-arrested and sent on his way, minus the rest of the match. For a more serious matter, he would have been transported to the main police station.

The most violent match I ever policed was, surprisingly, Portsmouth versus Leicester City. I say surprisingly because we always expected trouble from the Southampton games, our fierce south coast rivals. But this Leicester match descended into what I can only describe as a full-blown riot. Unfortunately for me and my colleagues, nobody had a NATO riot helmet with them! The men had just custodian helmets to wear and the ladies had bowler-style police hats.

On that day, there was a cry for 'chin straps down'. There were straps inside the helmet to stop them easily being knocked off. These were normally kept inside your helmet, so you didn't look like a bit of a plum walking the streets, but in a scrap like this, you needed your chin straps.

I vividly recall being part of a public order unit, a line of officers holding onto each other's belts, using the crowd control techniques we'd been taught back in Ashford. After the game, the Leicester fans made their way onto Goldsmith Avenue, heading for the train station, and running battles broke out in the street.

We formed a line across the road. I was standing next to our chief inspector when a half brick came flying out of the darkness and hit him square in the face, cutting him open just below his eye. To his immense credit, he just shook his head and carried on, a true example of leading from the front. We had no shields that day, just our batons drawn. As people ran at us, we'd strike and push them back. I've never been so relieved as when a couple of land sharks (police dogs) arrived, their snarling teeth quickly persuading some of the more idiotic supporters to reconsider assaulting us.

Troublemakers started ripping planks of wood from garden fences, using them as weapons. It was pure bedlam. The noise was intense, a cacophony of shouting, sirens, and flashing blue lights. It was one of the most frightening incidents I ever had to police. Eventually, we managed to contain the violence, escort the genuine fans to the train station, and restore some semblance of calm to the streets of Portsmouth.

Of course, the goal was always to avoid such chaos. A quiet word in the ear of a potential troublemaker early on could often de-escalate a situation before it began. I remember one fan, a middle-aged man, which surprised me, as you often expect it to be youngsters. But at football, passion can get the better of anyone. He was wearing a blue Pompey top and giving some very expressive hand signals, mostly aimed at the referee or the number 2 player, as he was holding up two fingers!

I made my way through the seats, having radioed the control room to get a CCTV camera on me just in case. I tapped him on the shoulder. He looked around, a little shocked to find a police officer at his elbow. I warned him about his language, explaining firmly but fairly that he'd be arrested if he continued. He managed a smile and agreed to tone it down.

About fifteen minutes later, after a controversial decision on the pitch, I heard a familiar voice from a few rows behind me. I knew it was him. I turned, putting on my most severe expression, ready to march over and arrest him if he uttered another swear word.

He caught my eye, shouting directly at me, 'It's your hat! He can't see, it's your hat!' and then broke into a huge grin, as did his mates. The phrase he'd been using before was a rather derogatory term that rhymed perfectly with what he'd just said. 'He's a tw**!' I had to laugh.

It was genuinely comical and I let him off, one more time. Sometimes, a little bit of humour is all you need.

The tragedy of the Tricorn Centre

Ah, the Tricorn. Now *there's* a building that could start an argument in any Portsmouth pub in the '90s. Built in the mid 1960s, the Tricorn was a brutalist beast of concrete and ambition. Designed by architects Owen Luder and Rodney Gordon, it was meant to be a shining example of modernist architecture, all bold lines, exposed concrete, and the sort of uncompromising geometry that seemed to come straight out of a sci-fi novel.

Some locals saw it as daring and futuristic – a proper statement piece for a city that had seen too much war damage and was itching to move forward. Others…well, they thought it looked like a collapsed car park. And, to be fair, they weren't entirely wrong. But I loved it!

The Tricorn Centre got its name because, when viewed from above, its layout resembled a three-cornered hat, a classic tri-corner shape such as the hats Admiral Lord Nelson would have worn. Made almost entirely from rough, grey concrete, the Tricorn was as much a feeling as it was a building. Its 10-storey structure loomed over the northern end of the city centre; a tangle of multi-storey car parks, ramps, stairwells and dead ends. There were shops too, at least at first: a barber's, some greasy spoons and off-licences, and even a nightclub hidden away on the upper floors. I recall a vinyl record store just off Charlotte Street, where a woman would read tarot cards and tell you your fortune.

At its peak, it housed the largest Laser Quest site in Europe and even a market. The upper floors had storage units for the market traders. I'm told that in the 1980s there was even a Virgin Megastore record shop in the Tricorn. There was a snooker hall, and the Tricorn provided a base for a surprising amount of life, especially the more alternative or 'fringe' types. Some kids hung out there because it was edgy, urban, and a bit grimy; the perfect place to skulk with a skateboard and a bottle of cheap, strong cider. Especially those who loved to skate or cycle down the car park's spiral ramps at high speed. Others wouldn't go near the place after dark, as it was poorly lit and had a threatening feel about it.

Some saw it as a bold attempt to bring modern urban life to Portsmouth, and a kind of working class cathedral to modernity. But, to many, it was an eyesore, a failed experiment in urban planning that never quite delivered on its promise. Rain would collect in the walkways and bits of concrete would flake off; it always seemed just a bit too dark and a bit too damp. Over the years, it became a symbol of neglect as much as of innovation. By the late 1990s, public opinion had turned solidly against the Tricorn. The shops had mostly shut, vandals had moved in, the smell of urine was strong and it started showing up on 'ugliest buildings in Britain' lists. There were still those who defended the place passionately, calling it a misunderstood masterpiece.

For me, I loved its edgy side and the chance to deal with any criminality that occurred. On one such occasion, the shift was called in by the duty inspector to close down an illegal rave taking place in part of the abandoned structure. It was the late '90s and the ecstasy rave scene was well and truly at its peak, with illegal raves popping up at locations most weekends.

On entering the building via a first-floor doorway, there was a heavy repetitive thump of dance music. A few flashing lights cast shadows as ravers ran and scattered, like rats. There was no resistance from the youths who had attended, making it a simple operation. But the writing was on the wall for the Tricorn.

Every unit in the Tricorn was now filled with flying rats. The pigeons had moved in and left huge amounts of toxic bird poo on any available space below where they would perch. This was disgusting and made it dangerous to enter any of the internal units.

Being such a well-known building in the city that was tall and easy to access, the Tricorn Centre unfortunately became a location for people to take their own lives. During my policing career, I attended many suicides at the Tricorn. Particular stairwells, standing tall throughout the building, became regular locations for police officers to attend. There would be regular reports of bodies found at the bottom, or searches for missing persons who may have been threatening to take their own lives. These events were traumatic for everyone involved. The victim must have felt so helpless, that they felt death was the only option. I cannot even imagine how desperate they must have felt.

The person finding the deceased body would suffer a traumatic experience; it didn't matter if you were a passing member of the public or a police officer. The effect on the person who witnesses that scene is still the same. Police attend the scenes of suicide on a more regular basis, so become more resilient, but not immune to the effects. Then there is the effect on families and friends, who may or may not have been aware of how the victim was feeling prior to taking their own life. Suicide is heartbreaking on so many levels.

On one such occasion, I received a call from the control room to attend a particular stairwell of the Tricorn near Landport View. The body of a young man had been found on the ground floor. It was dark, in the early hours of the morning. As with any sudden death, the police were called on behalf of the coroner to ensure no foul play had occurred.

I attended on 'blues and twos', racing to the scene in the area car. Occasionally, people would find a body and think they are dead, but in fact they may be alive. It's important to arrive quickly and establish if the person is alive or needs medical treatment. On arrival, it was fairly obvious that this young male had received catastrophic injuries after falling from a great height. His arms and legs were grotesquely contorted as they pointed in unnatural positions, having been broken. There was, surprisingly, only a small pool of blood where the body lay motionless. Even though the person obviously looked dead, I checked for his vital signs, such as his pulse, by pressing my fingers against his carotid artery or evidence of any breathing, watching for a rise and fall of his chest. Unfortunately, he was dead.

As other officers attended, I asked them to place a 'scene on'. This just meant stopping anyone walking into what could be a crime scene, normally by unrolling long lengths of plastic 'Police - Do Not Cross' tape and tying them to door handles, police traffic cones or cars to create a secure scene. At this point, we did not know: had he jumped or been pushed?

What made this tragic event stick in my mind was the young man's face. He had a full face of theatrical make-up on. His features were haunting to look at; his complexion was very pale with white and black 'Goth' style make-up. His look was compounded, as it was dark and gloomy, with only the weak street lights casting a dim yellowish glow over the tragic scene. We examined the staircase above for any evidence of foul play, but there was none.

On returning to the ground floor, facing up towards us next to the man, lay a solid mobile phone like a Nokia 3310. Famous for being indestructible, this early mobile phone had just survived a 100-feet fall onto concrete. Made of a strong plastic body and firm, clicking keypad, its small, luminous green screen offered a world of simple joy, providing a perpetually full battery bar and a signal that never failed.

We all glanced at the screen as it started flashing while it sang its four-note jingle. The joyful ringtone broke the sombre mood. The screen flashed a simple word, 'MUM'. I felt a wave of emotion and a pain in my gut, as I realised the young man's mother had probably woken up, worried that her son had not returned home from a night out.

We just let the phone ring out. Now was not the time to answer that call. The police will always try to deliver a death message face to face, ensuring they have all the facts in place before breaking such devastating news. The man was quickly identified and his parents were told, in person, what no parent wants to be told: that their child has died.

It transpires that the young man had been to watch a Marilyn Manson concert. Manson was infamous for his striking and eerie appearance: pale foundation, heavily-applied eyeliner, mismatched contact lenses and jet-black lipstick. His costumes ranged from fetish-inspired leather to Victorian gothic attire. There was no direct link between the man's death and the concert he attended, but it did explain the unusual appearance.

On another occasion, I was called by the control room to attend Pye Street, next to the Tricorn centre, to a report of a body at the back of the shops. It was about 8.30 am and shop workers had been turning up to work, when someone spotted a body near some industrial bins.

To be more precise, it was a report of a pair of ladies' legs sticking out from the rubbish bags and discarded cardboard boxes. I raced to the scene in the area car, arriving by the large spiral 'up' ramp to the Tricorn car park. The member of the public, who had called the police, pointed out where the body was and I went to investigate.

I quickly spotted the motionless legs protruding stiffly from the flattened cardboard boxes and rubbish bags. Red high heel shoes covered her feet, with stockings or tights covering the pale skin of her legs, which I could see glimpses of through the occasional small hole and ladder in the nylon. The woman's legs were not what I would call slender, but a bit more 'chunky'. This woman obviously had a bit more 'timber' on her than most local girls. I braced myself for the worst as I reached down to pull back the cardboard to reveal the body. Using my right hand, I peeled back the cardboard sheet.

Immediately, I stepped back in shock. The body moved suddenly and her head turned to look directly at me. It took a split second to realise that this lady, who might have been attacked and dumped, was in fact a bloke with a five o'clock shadow. He was wearing eyeshadow and bright red lipstick. It wasn't pretty, but at least this person was not dead! I assumed he'd been wearing a wig, but this was now missing and his hair looked dirty and unkempt in a short crew cut style. Aged in his early twenties he was wearing a short black mini skirt and a light-coloured blouse to finish the look. As he tried to speak to me, I was hit by a stench of foul-smelling stale alcohol mixed with vomit on his breath. He was definitely going to be suffering with a hangover.

'Where am I?' the man asked, total confused.
'Pompey by the Tricorn,' I confirmed. 'Are you okay?'

I noticed he was now shivering and appeared to be very cold. He glanced at a large chronograph watch on his wrist. This would have ruined the appearance of being a woman, in my humble opinion. I assume that he wanted to look 100% like a female the night before.

'FUCK! FUCK! FUCK', he said in a panicked voice. 'I'm late back to ship!'

It quickly became obvious he was a matelot in the Royal Navy, had been on a very, very heavy night out, and was now late back to ship. He confirmed the ship would still be in the dockyard and had not yet sailed, but he should have returned hours ago. Maybe not classified as a deserter, but he was definitely going to be in trouble. Other than hungover and feeling extremely cold, the man was not harmed or injured.

Now normally, the usual way of dealing with such matters would be one of two ways. The first would be to call up the 'Provost', the Royal Navy's own police force and let them deal with the sailor. We, as the civilian police, worked closely with the local Provost. The Provost had a number of powers and punishments we could only dream of, to help deal with members of the Royal Navy who had broken the law or brought the service into disrepute. This was great, because most members of the Royal Navy understood. When ashore, they blew off some steam, but would always be respectful if they had interactions with the civilian police, and so avoiding the wrath of the Royal Naval Provost.

If a sailor failed the 'attitude test' with the civilian police for a minor fight or drunkenness, the Provost would be called in. If the matter was of a more serious criminal nature, they would be arrested by the civilian police and dealt with accordingly. When finally released, they would be passed to the Provost to collect. If the sailor passed the attitude test, we would either give them a warning and send them on their way, or escort them back to the ship. This would ensure they got home safely and did not cause any further problems.

Now this lad (or lass) had caused no real problem, so I would normally have returned him to ship. However, I had a dilemma. I had found the man at the back of a pub/club called Martha's, a well-known LGBTQ+ venue.

Legally speaking, openly queer men and women were banned from serving in the Royal Navy until the year 2000.

This ban from Her Majesty's Armed Forces was only lifted following a European Court of Human Rights ruling.

On speaking with this young lad, he explained he had spent the previous night in Martha's, drinking. He may or may not have been questioning his own sexuality, rather than being on a drunken stag 'do', dressed in fancy dress as a woman. I wasn't concerned about his motives. I was more worried that, by taking him into the Royal Navy base in this state, it could well affect or end his career. There was a real threat of him being dismissed or placed in custody.

I knew a few cops who would have just taken him and let him face the consequences. I didn't want to be the executioner, so I had to think a little 'outside the box'.

Next to Martha's pub at the time, was a McDonald's and a charity shop. I told the lad to stay where he was. I went to the charity shop on Commercial Road and asked if they had any old clothes that might be suitable for this lad to wear, having explained his predicament. The staff agreed without hesitation, finding some trousers, a T-shirt and an old pair of shoes for him to wear. They also showed kindness in opening the rear doors of the shop to let the man in, so he could get changed in private and use the staff toilet to wash his face. He discarded the women's clothing in the bin. Ten minutes later, he was ship-shape and ready to be returned to his vessel. I drove him back onto the base and to the quayside. I left him to walk the final part up to the ship and give an explanation as to why he was late back. That, I felt on this occasion, was not for me to do!

In the spring of 1997, I attended an early turn parade on shift. Little did I know what the sergeant had in store for me.

He had already read out the intelligence reports and previous jobs of note from the last shift and proceeded to issue each officer with their postings for that day.

There were instructions for the area car, van, panda car, walking beats, dealing with a prisoner in the bins (or should I say in the Bridewell), but my name was not read out. What was I doing today? The sergeant had some bizarre news for me.

'Fozzie. I want you to let the control room know you are committed at the Tricorn for the day with a TV film crew. You won't be available for general deployment.'

The morning parade was over and everyone put their empty mugs on the wooden tray, sitting next to the big battered metal tea pot. The sergeant went on to explain to me what my role was. As the TV film crew were using pyrotechnics, they required a police officer present to update the control room, should members of the public start calling the police or fire service on seeing smoke or hearing explosions.

He also said, 'Oh, don't worry about lunch. A meal will be provided.'

RESULT! This was going to be an unusual shift. Maybe I would find fame and fortune on the film set?

I put on my uniform waterproof black jacket and conducted a radio test call. Donning my custodian helmet, I set off on foot patrol to the Tricorn centre. On arrival I set about finding the Assistant Director (AD) on the set, who would be my contact for the day. I was genuinely surprised at the amount of crew and vehicles on the site. It was really busy with people wearing radio headsets and clutching clipboards. The whole operation was being managed professionally, with private security preventing access to the film set. Lorries were parked on the surrounding roads, with a spaghetti of cables snaking from them into the Tricon centre. I located the Assistant Director on the first floor where the market traders lock-up units were situated. He briefly introduced me to the Director, who kindly thanked me for my attendance. The AD then explained what would be happening that day. We looked over one of the concrete balconies to an inner square below on the ground floor, including an underpass of derelict shops.

The shops would normally have been boarded up. But the TV film crew had removed the large panels of chipboard from the windows and doors. Instead, the industrious set designers had been busy creating signs for each shop front. They had painted each one, with bistro cafe tables and chairs in the underpass.

The AD explained they were recreating the inside of a modern-looking shopping centre. Briefly looking down that street, they had done an amazing job. The Tricorn appeared to have been reborn. But this was just the magic of TV. In reality, the Tricorn had been left abandoned, and the local talk was all about when the place would be demolished.

The AD continued, 'We are filming an episode of *Casualty* where a bomb goes off in a shopping centre. Look carefully through the upper windows of each shop. Internally you will see large cannons facing each shop window.'

I could see what looked like metal wheely bins positioned at a 45% angle facing each main shop window. The AD explained each one was full of rubble with a pyrotechnic charge. This would simultaneously blow rubble through the windows into the inside of the shopping centre, to create the effect of a bomb exploding.

It all made sense now. In 1997, the UK was still very much in the centre of 'The Troubles', with attacks from Irish Republican paramilitaries including the IRA and splinter groups carrying out bombing campaigns on the UK mainland. Portsmouth was home of the Royal Navy and would have been a high-profile target for these groups. I had been deployed to many suspect packages during my career, but most turned out to be discarded old suitcases, misplaced shopping bags or a homeless person's holdall hidden away. All had to be treated with respect, as if they were real devices. We would place large cordons on streets to protect the public and call in the bomb disposal teams, who would confirm the area was safe. Occasionally they would carry out a controlled explosion, taking no chances.

The police in Portsmouth had also got used to dealing with finds of real unexploded ordnance, because the whole region was a favourite target of the Luftwaffe in World War Two. It was a regular occurrence for unexploded bombs to be found, even after such a long time. Bigger explosives, once removed, would often be towed out to sea and detonated by the Royal Navy.

The current threat was brought into sharp focus on 9 February 1996 when the IRA ended its 18-month ceasefire by detonating a massive truck bomb in the Docklands area of Canary Wharf in London. The explosion killed two people, injured several others, and caused extensive destruction with damage estimated at around £150 million.

Then, on 15 June 1996, the IRA detonated a huge truck bomb on Corporation Street, near the Arndale Centre in Manchester. I knew this area well, having shopped there on Saturdays as a teenager. The lorry contained over 3,300 pounds of explosives, being the largest bomb the IRA ever set off on English soil. The blast caused widespread destruction across the heart of the city. Over 200 people were injured. There were a number of smaller bomb attacks claimed by the IRA during 1996, with many more hoax bomb calls in 1997 aimed at causing disruption and terror.

The AD explained he would give me a 'heads up' when they planned to detonate the charges, so I could update the control room. Apart from that, I didn't have a great deal to do. I was able to chat with the stars of the medical drama TV show, who were all really nice. To be honest, I was probably a bit star struck! I enjoyed the best hot lunch ever on the job from a catering truck that also provided all the meals for the actors and crew.

Then, late that afternoon, as the sun started to hang low, I got the nod that the pyrotechnics were due to be fired. I took up a position on an upper floor to get a great view of the action. There was a loud explosion as the cannons fired, throwing rubble into the shop windows and causing them to smash. The bistro tables and chairs were sent flying and it looked like a scene of total destruction. Then all was quiet. A large cloud of grey smoke drifted softly and eerily from the Tricorn towards the Royal Navy base. Set against the backdrop of the troubles, the scene sent a shiver down my spine.

The crew broke the silence. as they all started clapping, happy with the results captured on film. I updated the control room, giving the all-clear. It had definitely been a totally different shift for me.

'Give My Love to Esme' was the title of the BBC episode of *Casualty* that aired on 11 September 1997.

In 2004, after decades of controversy, they finally knocked the Tricorn down. The council had no choice. It was too far gone, too hard to redevelop, and hated by the public. There were plans for all sorts of fancy replacements but, like a lot of Portsmouth projects, it spent years as just another empty space with promise. Finally demolished and flattened, the area is now just a wide expanse of car parks for shoppers. But for anyone who grew up or lived in Pompey between the 1960s and the 1990s, the Tricorn is etched in their memory.

Whether you thought it was a monument or a monstrosity, you couldn't ignore it!

The use of discretion…up to a point!

Back in my day, police officers had a great deal of discretion. We could make sensible operational decisions. Part of a constable's probationary period was to fine-tune that ability. Perhaps the offender was a child who had stolen 10 pence worth of sweets. Maybe it would be better to take them back to the parents and establish the lay of the land. How was the child being looked after? Were there issues in the home environment? On the other hand, was this someone with a foil-lined carrier bag to prevent the shop alarm going off? They could be using tools to take off tags from clothing, stealing in bulk, then selling to fund a drugs habit.

At the same time, people didn't get off scot-free. As a probationer, you needed to get your numbers in the book, with offenders in custody. You had to demonstrate your competence in arresting people, saying the caution, so that the arrest was procedurally correct. You had to learn how to search suspects, also completing the necessary paperwork.

Arresting officers had to take people into custody, building up a rapport with the detainee. We had to interview our own prisoners, and learned how to use the 'peace' model of interviewing where you gather as much information as possible. PEACE is a mnemonic, which is a well-known framework used in investigative interviewing.

P.E.A.C.E. stands for:

P – Planning and Preparation
    Decide interview goals
    Review evidence
    Plan questions and strategy

E – Engage and Explain
    Build rapport
    Explain the interview process
    Ensure the interviewee understands their rights and role

A – Account, Clarification, and Challenge
    Let the interviewee give their free account
    Clarify details
    Challenge inconsistencies without being confrontational

C – Closure
    Summarise the interviewee's account
    Check for additional information
    Explain next steps

E – Evaluation
    Evaluate the information gained

Assess interview effectiveness
Plan any follow-up actions

We had to deal with the challenges of the custody suite, observing time limits, speaking with the custody sergeant and jailers, then preparing all the evidence. We spoke with solicitors, deciding if there was enough evidence to charge a suspect.

CPS were only called in for really serious matters. The police prepared most of the prosecutions. I would deal with shoplifting, criminal damage, fights, stabbings, domestic incidents and the occasional robbery.

Being the '90s, we had a lot of car crime to deal with. There were plenty of thefts from motor vehicles. We had people taking vehicles without consent, often by joyriders. Car security back then was poor. Most of the thieves would use a screwdriver to break the door lock. Once inside they would break the cowling underneath the steering wheel and pull out the ignition barrel. They would stick the screwdriver into that. They turned the starter and away they would go. The only real way to prevent this was to use one of those massive yellow steering wheel locks. They were simple and effective. The way I've just described breaking into a car, and stealing it, was known as 'black boxing' in the criminal fraternity. That name was certainly familiar to me, having worked in the Black Box in Rochdale.

Having dealt with a few of these incidents and interviewing the suspects, I enjoyed learning about the modus operandi. For me, knowledge was power. Understanding how criminals thought and behaved, and the tools of the trade, made it easier for me to catch offenders.

There were officers on the shift who I would describe as 'thief takers'. This was what I aspired to becoming; someone who could identify crimes and suspects, even before most people realised something was awry.

Another trick I learned: how to break into cars in the '90s, involved packing tape that came from large parcels. Don't worry, readers, these methods will not work on modern cars! The tape could be used for sliding in between windows of a car and the seal. You pushed the tape down to the bottom of the car door, creating a loop with the tape, which would then make contact with the catch on the door lock. With a small tug on the tape, you could gain access to the car. On learning this, I had my helmet filled with packing tape. Sounds bizarre, I know. I was often called out to cars with pets or children stuck inside during hot weather. No need to smash the car windows and cause lots of inconvenience. My method of using the thieves' trick avoided a lot of mess and achieved the same result. Sometimes babies and children were left locked in the back of vehicles, and my trick to rescue them worked without any trauma. It was bad enough that they saw my face at the window!

A lot of the miscreants that you deal with tend to be career criminals, but they're not always the sharpest tools in the box. I always found it interesting, coming across villains with good imagination when committing their offences.

Car crime, as I said, was a massive problem in the 1990s. To back up what I said earlier, if you were driving a Ford Fiesta, Ford Sierra, Austin Metro or a Vauxhall Astra GTE after 9pm at night and you looked under 30 years of age, it was most probably a nicked motor! I would be on the lookout for those cars to ensure they hadn't just been stolen.

Looking for stolen cars often resulted in offenders trying to make off and attempt to outrun the police. I was involved in many police pursuits, chasing stolen cars or going after wanted criminals. But unlike playing computer games like *Grand Theft Auto*, police pursuits can be really dangerous and occasionally deadly if there is an accident. Don't get me wrong, they can be very exciting too. I think nearly all cops enjoy being involved in those chases. But, unlike computer games, you don't get a second chance if you make a mistake.

On one occasion, during the daytime I was involved in the pursuit of a stolen Astra GTE. I'd followed the car north in Commercial Road, past St.Paul's Church. I had my 'blues and twos' on, but the vehicle failed to stop. The rogue motor drifted around the roundabout and entered the Buckland estate. There were three teenage lads inside and they knew where they were going. The car turned left into Wingfield Street and left again into Nelson Road. Then the 'pursuit' became interesting.

As Portsmouth is a densely packed city on an island, most roads can become quite congested at times. Buckland had become a rat-run for vehicles. So the council fitted a number of traffic calming measures, including speed bumps – also known as sleeping policemen – all across the Buckland estate. As the stolen Astra and my police car entered the estate, I can only describe the scene as being from the '80s TV show, *The Dukes of Hazzard!* On hitting each speed bump, both cars became partially airborne, bouncing over each bump and crashing down on the other side in showers of sparks.

I'm not sure if it was the dust being kicked up from the underside of the cars, or my tears of laughter, but it became difficult to see anything. The Astra screeched to a halt in a dead end, and the three youths decamped from the vehicle. They did a 'starburst', running in different directions. Nick, my tutor, always said in these situations, just keep your eye on the driver, which is exactly what I did. I chased him down on foot and arrested him shortly afterwards.

On another occasion I attended a street in the Landport Estate following a report, from a member of the public, of a male youth trying car door handles. I spotted a young lad of about 17 years of age who fitted the description. I stopped the police car and went to speak to him.

He came across as very nervous and, as he fitted the description of the youth, I told him I was going to search him. I explained the search procedure and the reasons for it. I said he would have a copy of the search record on completion. The lad was compliant and, as I went through his pockets, I came across an unusual item. I saw a number of flat, thin strips of stainless-steel metal, bound together on a key ring.

'What are these, then?' I asked.

He replied: 'I dunno, just found them.'

I knew exactly what they were and what they were used for. It was a set of feeler gauges. A tool used to measure the thickness of gaps. But these had been adapted and filed down slightly, creating a set of skeleton keys to bypass car locks.

I took hold of the lad by his right arm firmly, saying, 'You're under arrest on suspicion of going equipped to steal' and cautioned him. It was quite rare to catch a criminal with a set of skeleton keys. Most would just pick up a stone off the street and smash a window or use a life hammer nicked from a bus. Occasionally offenders would carry a spark plug from a car engine, using the fine tip to break the glass easily. A car thief would have a plausible reason for carrying spark plugs. Back at the police station during a tape-recorded interview, the lad made a full and frank confession.

My favourite modus operandi involved a burglar. I don't know anybody who likes burglars. They are horrible people who invade your personal space, a space that should be a safe sanctuary for you and your family.

One winter's night, I was assisting in an area search for a burglar, just off Somers Road in Somerstown. A resident in one of the terraced houses had been woken to the sound of an intruder in the house. The intruder fled, and the occupant called the police immediately. All available units had quickly attended the scene, to start searching for a suspect. I got out of the police car and was walking on foot. My senses were alive, and I was listening for any sound that might give away the location of the suspect. It was so cold that my breath released as a steamy mist in the night air. Luckily I was wearing my thick woollen NATO police jumper, thermal vest and long johns to keep warm.

I opened up nearby bins and cycle sheds, looking for the suspect in vain. I could not understand it. We were in the area at the time of the call, but had seen nobody. The area was swamped with cops in minutes. I thought he must be hiding nearby. I shone my torch into some bushes at the corner of the street. Nothing.

My colleague further up the road shouted, 'I got him.'

I ran up the street to assist. The burglar was lying down on the back seat of a car that was parked in a row of vehicles. The suspect had the stolen property from the burglary on his person, so was arrested and taken into custody. The car was only 20 yards from the victim's house. On checking PNC, the car was registered to the suspect. This career burglar confessed all during his interview. He said he had learned that, when it was going to be cold and frosty, he would park his car earlier in the day near the house he planned to steal from. He would then wait for a frost to cover the cars before going to commit the burglary. If disturbed, he could quickly hide in the frosted-up car and not be seen. He would normally wait until the police had left the area, before defrosting the windscreen and driving home. A truly well-planned crime.

Unfortunately for this burglar, my colleague had spotted the frost had been moved off the door handle, making it look suspicious. The officer tried the car door, which was unlocked and the rest is history!

A full and frank confession from this criminal still led to a prison sentence for his crimes

.

And then I was upwardly mobile...

When I was walking on the beat during my probationary period, I would often dream of driving police cars. I had learned how to chat with people. In particular, shop workers and store detectives were really helpful. They gave me cups of tea to keep me warm and, most importantly, provided vital intelligence about criminal activity.

As I walked around Portsmouth, if I was fortunate on a quiet day, another officer would pick me up to ride in their police car and help with their duties. This was much appreciated, allowing me to get dry and warm.

I kept thinking: it would be grand if I could get behind the wheel!

After about three years in the police, I passed my basic car course. This allowed me to drive low-powered panda cars such as Ford Fiestas and Escorts. I had a blue light on the top, allowing me to pull vehicles over. This was of great assistance, especially while working nights, although there was no siren. The sirens were only allowed on the area cars, traffic cars and the police van.

I dealt with road traffic accidents, driving offences, speeding and out-of-date tax discs. Traffic offences seemed really boring to me. However, I used these as a tool to catch real criminals. If I pulled someone over, and I could see this was a law-abiding citizen, I would often give them advice and a word of warning. That seemed the right tactic for minor issues such as a defective brake light. Soon they would be on their way to get the problem sorted. I always believed in having a good relationship with the public because they needed us, and on occasion we depended on them to help solve crimes.

Of course, I encountered motorists who would be totally anti-police. They would often have a long criminal record once you did a PNC check against them. These were career criminals who flouted the law. If they committed any minor traffic offence, I would happily follow it up because I could prevent them from being able to cause more serious trouble. That vehicle was often the way they would get from A to B to commit criminal offences. If I could stop them, it was a job well done.

On patrol in my panda car, I pulled over a sporty yellow SAAB convertible because of the way it was being driven. I asked the motorist why he had been going along slightly erratically, but not to the extent where he could be prosecuted. This man was well known to me. He had previously been convicted many times of supplying Class A drugs.

His appearance was particularly menacing and intimidating. He was a bodybuilder, about six feet tall with a shaven head and tattoos. He wasn't the type of person who would come with police quietly if arrested. I suspected that he was still involved in drugs, but I didn't have reasonable grounds to search him or his car. That wasn't going to stop me having a look around to see if other offences were being committed, such as how much tread he had on his tyres. I noticed that his tax disc was out of date by a couple of months. I pointed this out to him and he was very blasé, swearing in my face.

I warned him about his language, saying if he continued, he would be arrested, but he always knew how far to push things without being detained. I wrote him out a document which was called a CLE 2/6. This was a small notice that informed the driver they were being reported for having no tax disc.

I handed the notice to him, which he just screwed up and flicked into the middle of the road. I wasn't perturbed by this, as was the expected reaction. But I did say, 'Come on, you need to pick up the litter.' The screwed-up form was now classified as litter. He said, in a few abusive words, that he wasn't going to pick it up.

Therefore, I was left with no option but to explain I was going to report him and he would receive a summons to appear in court…unless he picked the item up. This was becoming a bit like a Mexican stand-off. The suspect was now out of the car and puffing out his chest like a pigeon. We could have been two gunslingers in a Western film, waiting for the first person to go for their pistol. Was he going to pick up the litter, or was I going to report him?

He was much stronger than me and muscular. But, at six feet six inches, I towered over the suspect. He made no move to pick up the discarded form, so the drama in the road continued. I explained that I was reporting him for the litter. As part of that process, I needed to have the correct details so that the summons could be served on him. I wanted his name, address and date of birth. At this moment the suspect refused to give me his address. I knew his name, but did not know where he was currently residing.

I repeated, under the Police and Criminal Evidence Act that, unless he was willing to give me his current address, he would be arrested until we could obtain that information. This caused him to become quite agitated, mouthing off, shouting and continuing his acts of intimidation.

Quite frankly, my patience had failed. I was having none of it. Out came the cuffs, and I slammed one of them straight onto his wrist. I started to say, 'You are under arrest…'

At that point he started to react violently, thrashing out with his arms, trying to knock me off balance. I decided to use a jiu-jitsu move that I had learned during training at Ashford. It was called a knee strike, and it came in very useful. Using the full force of my leg I kneed his upper thigh, and the effect was instant. A radiating wave of pressure against such a large muscle mass caused him to collapse to the ground and cry out in pain. After that it was easy for me to straddle on top of him, put his arms behind his back and continue cuffing the suspect as I called for a police van to take him into custody. On this occasion, I managed to place handcuffs on the offender. With some huge bodybuilders, their arms were too thick and we had to improvise, using two sets of handcuffs!

The suspect was taken back to the police station. He was released after about half an hour, once he had given his correct details and they had been checked out. It was a totally lawful arrest and prevented him from conducting his suspected criminal business. It was also a reminder to that particular male, a well-known villain, that he was not in charge of the city. His bullying and intimidation tactics were not going to work against this police officer.

He did end up paying the fine for not having a tax disc, which was a result. Yes, and he had to pay the litter fine as well!

I became an advanced driver and also took the van test about five years into my career. Driving vans was particularly difficult as they were large vehicles. I started off with Ford Transits, going onto Mercedes Sprinters. They were set up with cages over the windows for use in public order situations. They also had a metal cage built into the back with a section in the centre to carry officers. There were a few seats in the front to carry police, equipment, cones, or whatever else was needed. The police vans were tricky to manoeuvre because of their size. There was a lot of skill involved in negotiating the back yards with all the other vehicles at the nick, getting prisoners closely and safely to the back doors and custody suites as soon as possible.

My stint at Portsmouth had elements of a rollercoaster ride. One really embarrassing incident happened while I was driving a patrol car in the city in the early hours of the morning. At about 3.00am, the Fratton area car reported a stolen vehicle failing to stop. The rogue car was heading out of Portsmouth at about 70 miles an hour in the 30 limit. I headed off at speed, as I was close by on London Road, which is one of three main roads that lead north out of the city. The plan was, I would try to cut him off, by getting ahead and box him in, as the other police vehicles involved were directly behind the suspect. As an advanced driver in this BMW 330 Estate, I felt confident in my ability. I knew that I had to act quickly; these joyriders in a stolen car could cause havoc and kill someone in the built-up city streets, or drive at excessive speeds, dangerously trying to evade the police on the motorway.

However, at speed, I drove across a manhole cover. It was wet and greasy, on a sweeping bend in the road. The car was on the edge of its limits and the sudden change in surface from tarmac to iron was enough for me to feel the back end of the car start to drift out. It was all over in a split second but it felt like slow motion as the BMW slipped and span round 180 degrees. I managed to control it a bit, but ended up hurtling backwards at about 70 miles an hour into a bus stop. For me, the pursuit was over.

Everyone on the radio could hear everyone else, so I could hardly keep my nightmare a secret. Fortunately, at that time of day there were no other people or vehicles around. The bus stop was demolished, while the car ended up with a V-shaped back end and had to be written off. Calm as anything, I walked away uninjured and provided a brief update on the radio that I had suffered a PVI (Police Vehicle Incident).

A sergeant came out to take the accident report, but my actions were totally exonerated and I was back driving the next night. It had been a close call all round! For some time afterwards I had to endure comments about a police chase in reverse, greasy manhole covers and demolished bus stops. You can just imagine!

Often police cars, particularly on nights, would drive in Portsmouth's pedestrian precincts. Certain routes were accessible to us. We could slip between large metal barriers and slowly patrol the pedestrianised areas, catching people trying to commit burglaries, fighting or dealing in drugs. You would drive slowly, knowing you were in an area designated for pedestrians. The van was a totally different kettle of fish. Very often, you wouldn't be able to drive such a large vehicle into pedestrianised areas. There was one route available to test the driving skill of a van driver. That was around the Henry V111 castle on the seafront at Southsea, by the promenade. A pedestrian walkway, round back of the castle, was just wide enough to allow the police van in, and I mean *just* wide enough!

One evening, during a late turn on a Saturday night, we were deployed to deal with any fights within the city. I was in the back of the police van, being driven by one of my colleagues, and we were ready to jump out at a moment's notice. We were prepared for the exodus from certain pubs descending into a Wild West-style brawl.

The driver decided to take the tricky route at the rear of Southsea Castle. Travelling slowly at about one mile per hour, the van inched forward in the darkness. It was a dry night, but the sea was crashing against the railings and rocks on our right-hand side. All of a sudden, the van stopped. From the back, we asked what was going on. We were told that the driver did not feel confident in moving forward. He had lost his bottle and become stuck.

Because the vehicle had cages fitted against all the windows, the driver could not adjust the mirrors to show how close he was to the railings and rocks. Not wanting to cause damage to the van, railings, or his own reputation as a police driver, the constable felt he could go no further forward. Reversing was impossible. He called for us to get out and walk. However, the front doors of the van were almost touching large rocks and railings. The mid compartment had a sliding door, but was so close to the rocks that we couldn't open it. So, in effect we were trapped inside the police van.

Panic started to set in as we tried to work out what to do. We better not get a bloody shout on the radio now! Then someone in the van remembered that the keys to the ignition also included a key to open an internal door to the custody cage. An emergency escape route!

Having called up a second unit, we managed to open the rear doors and we escaped one by one via the prisoner's cage, breathing in the sea air with relief.

We walked the last 500 metres to outside the Time and Envy nightclub and the Royal Navy's 'school of dance', Joannas, where the trouble was expected to break out, rather than risk getting trapped in the van again.

I believe that the driver still gets the occasional ribbing to this day!

A dab of damage control

For anybody behind the wheel of a police car, Sunday mornings were governed by an unwritten but ironclad rule: the pilgrimage to Kingston Crescent Police Station in Fratton, for vehicle maintenance and cleaning.

Tucked away in the backyard, like a mechanical baptismal font, stood a formidable jet-washing machine surrounded by an arsenal of vacuum cleaners, chamois leathers, and buckets. It was here that we observed the sacred duty of delivering a good impression. The philosophy was simple: a police car ought to look the part. It should gleam with authority. It should smell of lemon disinfectant and wax, not stale kebabs and pasties.

Every time you got into a police car, there was a check sheet of things you had to note, like the depth of tyre tread, tyre pressures, water and oil levels. Many of these would be legal requirements. It would be wrong for police officers to be driving vehicles that were not legally roadworthy.

But once a week, we went deeper. We scrubbed. We polished. This ten-minute frenzy of cleaning served a dual purpose, beyond mere vanity. Prisoners, you see, are a crafty bunch. The back of a police vehicle is often treated by arrested persons as a sort of mobile amnesty bin.

If you've just been nicked, the natural instinct is to ditch yourself of incriminating items: knives, wraps of drugs, needles, or other vital bits of evidence, by stuffing them down the back of the seat. By ensuring the car was spotless before your shift started, one could confidently assert in court that whatever illicit treasures were discovered post-arrest belonged solely to the passenger.

However, amidst the sea of sweet wrappers and crumpled crisp packets tipped into the bins near the washing bay, a peculiar item kept appearing with suspicious regularity: small, empty bottles of Tipp-Ex.

For a long time, the presence of correction fluid in the car park was a mystery. We were policemen, not typists. Our paperwork was usually done with a pen and a heavy sigh back in the report writing room. It wasn't until a more seasoned veteran took pity on my naivety that the penny dropped.

In the eyes of the force, there was no such thing as an accident. It was a 'Police Vehicle Incident' (PVI), the underlying logic being that accidents are unavoidable, whereas smashing a wing mirror off on a gatepost is generally the result of someone being a clot. The procedure for reporting such a mishap was draconian. You had to confess to the sergeant, fill out a mountain of forms, and face immediate suspension from driving duties while an investigation determined your level of blameworthiness.

For a major collision, this was fair enough. But for a microscopic scrape against a bollard? A tiny graze on a kerb? The punishment hardly fitted the crime.

The accessory to these dodgy practices? Those tiny bottles of Tipp-ex!

Urgent assistance

One Sunday in September 2004, I was crewed with a WPC from the shift in a Panda car, and the initial plan, as always, was to chip away at the mountain of paperwork that never seemed to shrink. You've got statements to take, witnesses to see, suspects to hunt down. You try to get these inquiries ticked off with ruthless efficiency, because you know that at any moment, the radio will crackle to life and your carefully laid plans will be cheerfully lobbed out of the window. The day progresses, the immediate response calls pile up, and suddenly you're drowning in a sea of other people's emergencies. So, it was always prudent to get a head start.

On this particular Sunday, our investigative trail led us over to Gosport. We were collecting statements about a brawl at the Tiger Tiger nightclub down at Gunwharf Quays – a fairly standard entry in the Portsmouth weekend diary. Nothing too remarkable. With that sorted, we drove back into the city, and I dropped my crewmate off at a newsagent who had been plagued by shoplifters.

And so, at about 7pm in the evening, I found myself pottering around on my own. It was then that the radio broadcast two words guaranteed to make the hairs on your arms stand up to attention: *"Urgent assistance."*

The location was Commercial Road, the main pedestrianised shopping artery of Portsmouth. I knew that at the very bottom, it led into Edinburgh Road, allowing for vehicle access. I had no idea what I was driving into, but with an 'urgent assistance' call, you don't hang about to ask questions.

As I swung the Panda into Edinburgh Road, I clocked a British Transport Police van parked up near the junction with Surrey Street. It was empty, abandoned-looking. I glanced down Surrey Street, a pedestrian-only zone from my side, and saw it: two figures wrestling on the pavement.

I ditched the car and sprinted over. The scene crystallised as I got closer. Right outside a pub called The Surrey Arms, a BTP officer was on the floor, locked in a desperate struggle with a man I recognised instantly. Let's just say he was a regular and enthusiastic patron of Portsmouth Central's five-star cell block. He was in his mid-thirties, sporting a scruffy tracksuit and a fresh cut above his eye that was bleeding sluggishly. He was no athlete, this one; his tracksuit was less for hitting the gym and more for legging it from the law.

But I digress. The offender was on his back, and the BTP officer was lying across his chest, facing me. The officer had an arm wrapped around the man's torso, but the man's own arm was curled up in a strange, tight position near the officer's head, his fist clenched. He was shouting, agitated, a ball of pure fury.

What struck me first, though, was the BTP officer's face. It was a ghastly, unnatural shade of pale, and his eyes were bulging from their sockets in a way that was utterly bizarre and terrifying. Then, in a quiet, rasping voice that was barely a whisper, he croaked something to the effect of, 'Get him off me. He's got my throat.'

The look in his eyes was one of sheer, unadulterated terror. My gaze dropped, and I saw it. Just under the collar of his uniform, the thin wire cord from his radio microphone, the one that usually clips to a lapel, had been wrapped around his neck. Our tracksuit-clad villain was using it as a ligature, pulling it taut and methodically strangling the life out of him. The officer's face was scratched, his shirt smeared with blood. It all registered in a fraction of a second.

There was no time for a committee meeting. I drew my CS gas canister from my belt, aimed it at the suspect's face, and channelled my inner drill sergeant. I've got quite a deep voice, and when deployed with sufficient authority, it can have a wonderful 'shock and awe' effect, breaking their deadly fixation.

'LET GO OF THE CORD! GIVE ME YOUR ARM NOW OR YOU'LL BE SPRAYED!'

It worked. He released his grip. I lunged forward, grabbed the wire, and yanked it away. The officer gasped for air, and the suspect, his primary objective thwarted, immediately began thrashing about again, now more focused on escaping than finishing the job. Using my quick-cuffs, I managed to get his arms secured behind his back, double-locking them so they wouldn't tighten.

The threats began, as they always do. 'I'll fucking have you! I'll rip you apart.' It was nothing I hadn't heard a thousand times before, but he was still a live-wire, kicking and spitting, looking for any opportunity to bite or kick. The BTP officer and I pinned him down, waiting for the cavalry.

Just as we thought the situation was vaguely under control, a woman appeared at our side. She was also in a tracksuit, not a matching set, you understand, but they were clearly a pair. She began shouting and swearing at us.

'Let him go!' she shrieked, inching closer. Every time she did, our man on the ground became more violent, feeding off her energy. The BTP officer, still trying to catch his breath, managed to inform the suspect he was under arrest for criminal damage to his van.

At that exact moment, the area car screeched to a halt and other officers piled out. Seeing them, the woman decided it was time for direct action. She charged at us as we lay on the floor, pulled back her right arm, and swung a clenched fist with all her might, connecting squarely with the BTP officer's face.

The newly arrived officers were on her in a flash, bringing her to the ground , cuffing her and arresting her for assaulting a police officer. This, predictably, sent our subject into a fresh rage. Apparently, seeing his companion getting arrested made him hungry. He twisted his head, opened his mouth, and bit down, hard, into my upper arm.

I felt a sudden, explosive burst of pain. He clamped his jaw down for what felt like an eternity but was probably only two or three seconds. When he released his grip, I looked down at him, still struggling beneath me.

'You're also under arrest for assaulting a police officer,' I said. I didn't bother with the caution. It seemed, at that point, rather impractical.

We eventually hauled them both to their feet and bundled them into separate police vans. I glanced at my arm. The skin was broken, blood welling up around an angry, bruised indentation of a full set of teeth. Marvellous.

On my journey in policing, it seemed the cell blocks got progressively busier and the booking-in process progressively slower. On this particular evening, there was no room at the inn at Portsmouth Central. My prisoner and I were destined for the Waterlooville Bridewell.

En route, I was dropped off at the Queen Alexandra Hospital to have my new bite mark examined. A human bite, as any nurse will tell you, can be far nastier than a dog's. My wound was cleaned, dressed, and I was given injections for tetanus and a course of antibiotics. Suitably patched up, I carried on to Waterlooville.

Later, I went to his cell. I slid open the small hatch in the door, used for passing through meals and checking on the occupants. He was sitting on the wooden bench inside.

'You're also under arrest on suspicion of attempted murder,' I told him.

His only reply was a monotone, 'I want my solicitor.'

The severity of the offences meant we had to seize all his clothing for forensic evidence, carefully bagging each item. I finally got back to Portsmouth Central around midnight, booked in all the property, and wrote up my notes. It was a late one.

I spoke to the BTP officer a few days later. He thanked me, his voice still shaky with the memory. He told me, quite matter-of-factly, that he genuinely thought he was going to die that day. As a police officer, you just never know what's waiting around the next corner.

And what became of our tracksuit-clad couple? The attempted murder charge was, inevitably, dropped. I believe it was downgraded to a simple assault on the BTP officer. He was also charged for the assault on me. Both he and his partner received relatively mediocre sentences which, if I recall correctly, involved no prison time. The court did order him to pay a small amount of compensation—less than £100—to myself and the other officer. We both knew we'd never see a penny of it. Offenders would often make a token payment of maybe £1 to show willing, then the payments would just stop, and the orders would drift into administrative oblivion.

It often felt frustrating at the time. But, then again, it was just another Sunday evening in Pompey.

Murder on the seafront

Back in May 2001, I was on patrol with my crewmate, Simon, in a BMW 330 Automatic Estate. It was a lovely warm evening. We were just cruising around when a call came over the radio. Staff at a hotel were reporting that a man had killed his wife. The location was the Post House Forte, now the Holiday Inn on Southsea seafront.

On the way there, we formulated a plan. We didn't want to just turn up and see what happened. We put on the blues and twos (blue lights and two-tone sirens) and discussed a plan of action.

At any crime scene, you have to consider forensics. One of the first things I learned from my tutor was to keep my hands in my pockets at any crime scene. It might not look very professional, but you didn't want to go around accidentally touching things and disturbing any evidence.

So, we discussed who was going to deal with the body and who was going to talk to the suspect. Simon said he would go to the body, leaving me to find out what had happened from the potential killer. The idea was that we wanted to keep the two scenes apart, preventing cross-contamination.

This meant that we would have the area of the hotel with the body and, separately, the scene with the suspect. We arrived at the hotel and a member of staff greeted us in the reception area. We were given scant details, just that a man had killed his wife. The staff had already taken the suspect to an empty room on the same floor as the body. I went to the room where the suspect was waiting, while Simon headed for the room containing the body.

I was surprised when I opened the door. A fairly elderly man, about 70 years old, was standing inside. I told him that I was there to find out what had gone on. I was acutely aware that anything he told me had to be recorded as evidence, being such a serious matter.

There are various rules about how to conduct an interview away from the police station. I wanted to make sure we didn't overlook any evidence. So the two of us sat down and he was like a rabbit in the headlights. I cautioned him, using the standard statement that everyone will be familiar with.

I recorded in my pocket book what was called a contemporaneous interview with the pensioner. At this stage he wasn't under arrest. I just wanted to find out what had happened. I asked various questions and he answered. I allowed him to elaborate, repeating back his answer and allowing him to respond with more details.

He said that he and his wife had gone to the hotel to resolve some differences in their marriage. They had only recently become man and wife, but things weren't working out.

'Yep, I killed my wife,' he told me. 'I used a draught excluder.'

A draught excluder? I wondered what he was on about. It transpired that he had brought this heavy draught excluder from the bottom of a door at their home address. It was like a heavy sack; an unusual murder weapon, to say the least. There was an element of premeditation in my mind. A most peculiar case.

At this stage I didn't know for certain that his wife was dead. I contacted my colleague on the radio. Yes, the lady had passed away and Simon was waiting for scenes of crimes officers to secure the room and carry out forensics.

The suspect signed what was, in effect, a confession given under caution. Then I arrested him on suspicion of murder. I called for a police van for transport which arrived quickly. I escorted the man downstairs.

I still kept him apart from my colleague because we needed to keep the two scenes separate with no cross-contamination. I went to Portsmouth Central police station where the suspect was booked into custody. The usual procedure was followed, where his outer clothing was removed and everything bagged up and sealed.

I produced a statement and took a photocopy of my pocket book for the handover, which was due to go to CID in the morning.

My handover didn't go down too well. It was rare for CID to be given a prisoner arrested for murder, with a signed confession from the start. They were quite peeved because they had little investigating to do; we had nearly sorted everything out for them.

There was still one intriguing detail to emerge from the case. In court, it was revealed that the pensioner had become involved in a row with his new wife over the cooking of scrambled eggs.

He said that his previous ex-wife had made a better job of scrambling the eggs, leading to an almighty argument…and a tragic death.

A madman with rage in his eyes

To be a good thief-taker, you have to be always observing. Looking for what is abnormal in the normal or vice versa. What do I mean by that? For example, driving down the street you might see a young male dressed in the latest designer gear. He's riding a bicycle, but the unusual thing is, the bicycle is a 'lady's shopper' with a wicker basket on the front. That's what I'll describe as abnormal in a normal street scene.

The chances are that any self-respecting Pompey youth, dressed in designer gear, would not have gone to the local bike shop and bought a lady's bike to get around the city. The chances are that the lad was probably on a nicked bike. But he might have 'borrowed' it from his mum or his sister, I hear you say. I agree, but the chances are pretty slim.

It would certainly be enough for me to spin the police car around and stop to find out more. You might have heard of coppers having a 'sixth sense' or a 'copper's nose'. Very often, you make your own luck in catching criminals in the act of committing offences.

One evening in 2002, I was with my crewmate Simon again. He was also an area car driver, and we made a formidable team in catching villains. We would often patrol the streets of Portsmouth in the evening or during the night, looking for suspicious characters who were up to no good.

To stay awake during the early hours when your natural body clock is telling you to go to bed, we would play games such as 'The human sat-nav'. This was before the days of smartphones in everybody's pocket. Sat-navs had recently been invented, but they were the type that stuck onto the windscreen, easily nicked, and sold down the pub for 40 quid.

To play the human sat-nav game, you would start in a known area of the city with your crewmate driving, and the 'player' would be the passenger. The player would have to close their eyes. As the police car slowly manoeuvred around the quiet streets turning left, turning right, navigating around roundabouts and car parks, the driver would suddenly announce, 'What street are we in?'

Hopefully the passenger, using their levels of concentration, would be able to work out the exact street with their eyes still closed. It was so important, as a police officer, to know exactly which street you were in at all times, in case you had to call for assistance. This was just one of the many ways that we maintained a level of alertness during the night when the city had gone quiet.

On other occasions when it was stormy, the waves would often crash against the sea defences along the esplanade. Driving slowly along this stretch of road, the area car driver would use the electric switch on the driver's side to open the passenger window. This allowed the spray from large waves crashing over the car to also engulf and soak any unsuspecting passenger. This was always guaranteed to get a laugh and many probationers, including myself, were exposed to the harsh spray of the Solent.

I digress. On this particular evening it was getting dark and we were driving west along Goldsmith Avenue, just past Fratton Station railway bridge. There used to be a 'TK' at that location. TK is an abbreviation for telephone kiosk, which I would always look into whilst on patrol. This was where Class 'A' drug users would loiter, huddled inside phoning dealers or waiting to be served up 10-pound or 20-pound bags of crack and heroin. This was common practice as many heroin addicts only had access to phone boxes to contact their dealers. Mobile phones were not commonplace at that time.

On this occasion I could see a single female in the phone box, but something just didn't seem right. I said to Simon that we would pull over and check it out. I couldn't quite put my finger on it, but she had a look of distress in the way she held her shoulders and head. I got out of the police car and walked over towards the phone box. The woman looked towards me, and I could see a real look of fear and terror in her eyes.

There was certainly something abnormal about her appearance. The top of her head, her face and most of her hair and shoulders were covered in curry. Curry sauce and meat was dripping off her upper body. The woman, who was white and aged about 40, was understandably distraught and crying.

'Are you okay? What happened?' I enquired.

The woman went on to explain that she had an almighty domestic argument with her ex-husband, who threw curry all over her in a fit of rage. We took a large roll of blue paper towels from the back of the police car and passed her some, to help clean the curry off. We quickly obtained details from the lady who was called Julie Sheppard. She gave the name of her ex-husband as Howard Woodin. They lived in a terraced house together, in Francis Avenue. We could see the house, as it was close to the junction where we stopped. Julie appeared absolutely terrified and, as far as we were concerned, Woodin had committed a nasty assault on his ex-wife. He was about to get nicked.

I called up on the police radio, asking for a police van to attend our location. I had the impression that he wasn't going to be coming quietly following the heated domestic incident. On arrival of another police unit, Simon and I went to the address and knocked on the front door. There was no reply although it was obvious a male was inside, as we could hear him moving around. I rapped on the door with my knuckles and shouted, 'IT'S THE POLICE. OPEN UP THE DOOR.'

A male shouted some unpleasant words towards us, which I took to mean he wanted us to go away and that we had both been born out of wedlock.

I explained quite forcefully that we were coming in, with or without an invite, but there would be less damage if he opened the door.

'F*** off,' was the response.

I obtained a key from Julie to unlock the front door so that we could gain access. I placed the key into the lock and opened the door, which led into a hall with a flight of stairs going up to the first floor. I was hit by the smell of curry, and could see food splattered on the floor and walls. The place was in a bit of a state following the violent argument and assault that had occurred. I caught a glimpse of Woodin at the top of the stairs and then I could hear a bedroom door being slammed shut. 'You ain't f***in' takin' me.'

I shouted up, 'It's the police. We need to speak with you.'

Woodin continued to shout and swear towards us. It was obvious he was never going to come quietly. I then heard the screech of wood against wood. A heavy object was being moved in the bedroom. He was barricading himself inside, pulling the bed and wardrobe against the bedroom door.

Simon and I rushed to the top of the stairs. I tried to open the bedroom door but it was jammed shut. I gave the door a subtle shoulder barge to see if I could move it, but no success.

'I'll F***IN' SHOOT YOU IF YOU COME IN,' Howard shouted, and I could hear him pulling out drawers and discarding them as if searching for something.

I am no hero when it comes to firearms, and we both quickly ran down the stairs, adrenaline pumping.

'HE'S GOT A GUN!' we shouted to the other units, warning them as we ran out of the house.

They scarpered for cover, and immediately started to shout towards members of the public to stay back. Simon was on his radio, updating the control room.

I quickly spoke with the victim, Julie, asking if she knew whether Howard had any guns.

'Only an air pistol. It's on top of the wardrobe.'

The 'red mist' had come over me, and I was pissed off and angry at Woodin for being a bully and assaulting a woman like he had, messing us about, not letting us in and threatening us. How dare he! Looking back now, we should have contained the scene, waited for armed back-up and a negotiator. We should have followed procedure, but you make decisions at the time to the best of your knowledge and ability. It was only an airgun, hopefully.

We got the 'big red key' from the back of the area car, and put on the only two body armour jackets we had. Later on, all police officers were provided with personal issue body armour, but at this time we just had two in the area car. Luckily, they were both size 'large' or we would have struggled, both being well over six feet tall.

We returned to the address and climbed the stairs at speed, two steps at a time. Simon swung the metal battering ram at the internal bedroom door. It was no match. The wood splintered on the edge of the door as the ram penetrated the internal cavity, creating a large hole.

Woodin was shouting, 'STAY BACK, I'LL SHOOT!'

We hoped that this was all bluster ,and the intelligence on the firearm was correct. A deafening bang rang out in the enclosed hallway as the ram hit the door, again cracking it down the middle. Simon hit the door a third time, and the top half bounced open like a Wild West saloon door. A bed was pushed up against the lower half of the door. The wardrobe was partially blocking the entrance, with clothing strewn across the room.

Our eyes met for a split second. Woodin looked like a madman with rage in his eyes, his face red with a sheen of sweat. He glanced at a white cardboard box on the bed. The lid was ajar. Inside the box, the handle and trigger of a handgun was visible.

Immediately, he pounced for the gun, I leapt forward through the ruined door, and grabbed Woodin around his upper torso with both arms. He was unable to grab the gun and Simon climbed in after me, kicking the firearm out of his reach. Rolling him onto his front, he was shouting and struggling wildly. I 'cuffed' him behind his back, then brought my face so close to his I could smell his breath. 'You're nicked, mate!'

Once we had double locked the handcuffs and he had calmed down, I formally arrested Woodin on suspicion of causing actual bodily harm and cautioned him.

The gun was an air pistol, and seized as evidence. We marched him out to the van and placed him in the rear cage. He immediately started kicking the internal cage and continued to swear and make threats towards us.

Julie had a look of relief on her face; now he was locked up, she was safe.

The difficulty with policing domestic incidents is that both parties normally live with each other. So when the incident is over, be it an argument or assault, one or both parties are arrested and the incident is normally dealt with by the courts the following day. Often when the dust has settled, couples decide to get back together.

This may be part of a longer-term controlling behaviour by one person in the relationship. It might be that one party is too scared to leave, or feel they cannot leave due to financial problems. Whatever the reason, once dealt with by the justice system, many couples find themselves back together, for better or worse. In Julie's case, it was for worse.

About six months later, in 2003, Howard and Julie had another domestic argument. He brutally murdered his ex-wife.

Howard Woodin, then aged 45, stabbed Julie Sheppard 26 times. Although the couple had divorced, they continued living under the same roof for the sake of their children.

Woodin claimed he acted in self-defence, but a text message found on Ms Sheppard's phone painted a chillingly different picture.

Sent on the day of her death, the message read:

'20 March 2003, twice 2 day howard threatened to knife or stab me put hand round my throat tried to push me b-wards into kitchen. Said he would say self def.'

Judge Michael Brodrick, delivering the sentence at Winchester Crown Court, described the attack as 'savage,' stating:

'You persisted until she was dead, severing three separate blood vessels. You are a devious, domineering, manipulative, self-centred man determined to get your own way.'

The pair had originally met at a singles club in 1998 and married in early 1999, but divorced three years later. Despite their separation, they remained in the same home – an arrangement leading to escalating tensions that I had seen with my own eyes.

On the day of the killing, an argument turned deadly. Woodin first stabbed Ms Sheppard in the stomach with a five-inch vegetable knife. When the blade broke, he continued the assault with a 10-inch bread knife, targeting her face, neck, and shoulder.

Just 20 minutes before the attack, Ms Sheppard had called police expressing fear for her safety, but hung up when Woodin returned home.

After the murder, Woodin contacted his solicitor and daughter before finally calling emergency services. He claimed Ms Sheppard had attacked him and then stabbed herself – a version of events dismissed outright by medical experts.

Pathologist Dr Hugh White confirmed the wounds, some as deep as 12cm, could not have been self-inflicted. Forensic scientist Clair Galbraith testified that Ms Sheppard had likely been on the floor and defenceless during the attack, with cuts on her hands indicating that she tried to shield herself. Dr David Chilvers, a police surgeon, concluded that Woodin's injuries were superficial and likely self-inflicted.

The investigating officer for the murder, Detective Sergeant Dave Sackman, said after the trial, that it was the worst domestic violence he had seen in his 22-year career.

'If you were to punch the palm of your hand 26 times and imagine it was a stab wound, it must have been a terrifying last few moments for Ms Sheppard.'

The story does not end there. Woodin was sentenced to life in prison for this brutal and savage murder. While serving time at HMP Wayland in Norfolk, as an inmate he became known for frequently voicing his dissatisfaction with prison conditions.

According to *The Telegraph*, by 2010 he had been restricted to submitting just one complaint per day, after repeatedly raising the same concerns through the official prison grievance system.

Among his complaints were objections to the 'tasteless' food served in the prison canteen and the practice of officers opening his mail.

He also protested about being transferred between facilities. In February 2013, *The Daily Star* reported his latest grievance: the lack of butter in his sandwiches. He also criticised HMP Erlestoke in Wiltshire for spending money on Christmas decorations, arguing it should have gone towards improving the food.

Woodin, aged 56, died on 14 September 2015 at Abbas Combe Nursing Home in Chichester, while under the custody of HMP Coldingley in Bisley. He had been moved there to be closer to family in his final days.

During a hearing at Woking Coroner's Court on 25 May 2016, Assistant Coroner Dr Karen Henderson referred to a report by police and probation ombudsman Nigel Newcomen, stating Woodin had been experiencing troubling symptoms prior to his diagnosis.

Initially suspected to have suffered a mini stroke, a CT scan at Frimley Park Hospital on 18 June later revealed a possible brain tumour. Follow-up tests confirmed it was terminal. He was given a prognosis of six months to live.

Woodin's condition deteriorated rapidly. On 13 July, he was admitted to St Helier Hospital in Carshalton, where doctors revised his prognosis to just two weeks. He was transferred to Rowans Hospice in Waterlooville, before returning briefly to the healthcare unit at HMP High Down. On 8 September, he was moved to the nursing home in Chichester, where he died six days later.

A statement from his daughter, Gemma, expressed her satisfaction with the care he received at the end of his life.

The coroner returned a narrative verdict, ruling that Howard Woodin died of natural causes.

The Wheel of Fortune

There was a time when the seafront at Clarence Pier felt like that great British seaside holiday destination. A place you remember as a kid, during hot summer holidays. Back in the 1990s, before trendy coffee shops and artisan doughnuts arrived to civilise the promenade, you could smell the candy floss, sea salt and chip fat the moment you opened the car door. The Isle of Wight hovercraft would belch and sway like a dragon with the wind. There was a Wimpy restaurant that made a burger which tasted exactly like those I had enjoyed in America.

Next to it, the amusement arcades sang their familiar chorus of coins and cheap prizes dropping in metal trays accompanied by blinking lights promising riches. The chance to win big on the grabbing claw machine that always seemed to drop the prize, just before it swung over the exit chute! The futuristic sound of Oxygene, by Jean-Michel Jarre, played loudly from within the arcade, creating a sense of mystique from the outside.

The main building, known as the 'Golden Horseshoe' also had a small bowling alley. The 'Wheel of Fortune' stood proudly to one side of Clarence Pier, with its small collection of rides and rollercoasters overlooking the sea. The Wheel of Fortune was another children's arcade, all cheerful bulbs and stickily varnished plastic, the sort of place where a ten pence coin felt like a ticket to glory. A mecca for those gamblers clutching a small plastic tub full of two pence pieces. Even the 1993 Mr. Bean episode 'Mind the Baby, Mr. Bean' was filmed on location at Clarence Pier and the Wheel of Fortune.

Above the Wheel of Fortune on the first floor was Jurassic 3001, a grandly named ghost-style train with a dinosaur theme that I never got a chance to ride, despite my persistent curiosity. What did prehistoric terror look like, when rendered in plywood? A giant plastic Triceratops dinosaur head poked out of the corner of the building, scaring children inside.

One evening, down by the D-Day Museum, one of the area car drivers, Tommy, had parked up out of sight to be proactive, in an attempt to catch some drink drivers or joyriders that evening. His plan was simple. Let the pubs and nightclubs empty, then wait until Clarence Esplanade became a runway for the fast and the foolish. After that, pick off the ones who treated speed limits as a challenge to beat. Hopefully bagging a drink driver or two. As a strategy parked next to the sea, it had a sort of fisherman's patience to it. Throw your line. See what bites.

I was out on patrol in the van, Kilo Charlie Double Nine, the call sign, making it sound more glamorous than the reality of a Ford transit van, with a rattling steel cage in the back and a smell of policemen's boots and damp coats. The radio crackled with Tommy's voice. 'Fail to stop, Clarence Esplanade'.

The words sharpened my senses as it sounded like he had a bite! A car had blast past him at an astonishing clip and, when he lit up the blues lights on the police car, it simply kept going. There was a pause, then his tone changed from businesslike to urgent.

He had 'eyes on', but the suspect car crashed. Not just crashed, it had driven straight into the Wheel of Fortune at nearly 100mph!

The next moments unspooled with a kind of dreadful choreography. I switched on the blue lights to the van and swung around towards the pier, tyres squealing as I took the corner. I saw a small fire licking from the remains of a car at the front of the building, housing the Wheel of Fortune. Tommy was first on the scene. He would later describe the impact as if the car had tried to swallow the arcade whole.

When I arrived, the scene was all noise and rubble. Broken glass scattered underfoot. The air was hot with burning plastic and that bitter smell of deployed airbags. An intruder alarm rang out. I looked over twisted metal and gaudy arcade colours and, bizarrely, a pile of pink tickets scattered like confetti.

The vehicle had crossed the pavement and buried itself so deeply into the frontage that, for a moment, it was hard to take in where the car ended and the arcade began. I expected tragedy. Instead, the driver, astonishingly, was on his feet. He emerged as if he had simply popped in for a packet of crisps and taken a wrong turn. He was shaken, grey faced, but upright. Driving at that speed, straight into a building, it was nothing short of miraculous.

On the roadside, away from the smoke, he told us quietly that he had not intended to survive. It came out that, following a bad run of days, he had been in a dark mental place with the kind of despair that narrows the world to a single, terrible idea. He had chosen to end his life in a blaze of glory. The Wheel of Fortune, of all places.

We did what we could. The ambulance and fire service were called out. Some gentle words over the top of the paperwork and he was taken to hospital for treatment. He was given another chance whether he liked it or not. In the aftermath, the council installed bollards along the pavement, a neat row of sentries to keep the next misjudged driver from becoming headline news. The Wheel of Fortune was patched up and returned to its cheerful clatter. If you did not know, you would never guess what it had swallowed and survived.

On another occasion, one summer's evening I was back on the same stretch, this time driving the area car. The police radio chirped with an urgent call for me to attend.

'RTA. Vehicle on its roof outside the Wheel of Fortune'.

I felt my stomach do a small and unhelpful acrobatic turn. My mind flashed back to the previous accident. Was it going to be the same driver attempting to take his life again? Would I be looking at a fatal accident? The thoughts flashed through my mind as I accelerated hard, making the BMW 330 roar in protest at the low gear I had selected, over the car's own automatic gearbox choice.

I hit the blues and twos and headed for the pier. Sure enough there it was. A car on its back like a stranded beetle, wheels still spinning a little in the evening sun.

Not quite a full car by modern standards. It was a three-wheeled Reliant Robin in a shade of yellow you could have spotted from space. A relic from a more optimistic era, made of fibreglass and faith.

I got out and went to assess the scene. Through the open passenger window I found the driver suspended by his seatbelt, upside down and entirely unbothered. A middle-aged male, but not Del Boy from the TV show *'Only fools and horses'*. He looked at me with the bright expression of a man who has lost a fight with physics and found it mildly amusing. 'Alright mush.' he said in a Pompey accent that belonged behind a market stall. 'Any chance you could push me over?'

The male appeared totally uninjured. There is something undeniably charming about a vehicle that can be righted like a garden ornament. Reliant Robins are light, and with only three wheels they have all the stability of a drunk on a tightrope. I put a hand on the top of one wheel, gave it a firm shove, and over it went, a tidy half turn, back onto its tyres. The driver checked his hair in the rearview mirror, brushed himself down, grinning as if we had just completed a small magic trick.

He explained he had taken the roundabout a bit too enthusiastically and the Robin had just rolled over. No harm to anyone, no damage to anything except his pride and a little scratched paintwork. I breathalysed the driver because it was routine after an accident, but the SL-400 (The Lion Alcolmeter) showed a green light confirming he was sober.

A few details were taken, a few final checks, and I sent him on his way holding the plastic disposable tube from the breathalyser and some advice about corners and centre of gravity. He patted the roof of the Robin with affection. I watched him pull away with the tentative care of a man escorting a tipsy aunt home from a wedding.

On a subsequent occasion, I was directed to a report of a car fire in the Hovertravel car park at that same location. It was a dry but extremely windy night. The wind was howling off the sea whipping in a northerly direction across the common. I arrived within minutes on blue lights to see a parked and unattended car on fire. It was well ablaze but 'Trumpton', better known as the fire service, was already on the way.

The flames licked and danced in the night air, being fed by the strong winds and all the combustible parts of the car. I watched on in amazement, as the flames leapt from the original car, to the one parked next to it, and so on. The first fire engine arrived only a few minutes after me, but now approximately 10 cars were all fully ablaze! Nobody was hurt, but luck was not on the side of the owners who had parked their cars there that night. I was later informed that the fire was caused by a simple electrical fault.

It struck me then how that patch of road had become a tiny theatre of chance. One night it tried to swallow a life and gave it back. On another, it turned a car on its head and made us both laugh. On this occasion many cars had been written off in minutes. The Wheel of Fortune kept spinning above it all, lights winking, coins chattering, oblivious to the stories it hosted.

If there is a lesson to be learned, perhaps it is this. Some nights the house takes everything. Other times, you walk away with your pockets fuller than you dared hope.

Occasionally, with a gentle push, the world simply lands the right way up. We all need a little bit of luck at times!

Knives and swords in the streets

I was always reminded, quite rightly, that Portsmouth was the home of the Royal Navy. Alan Ball, while managing Portsmouth Football Club, famously stated, 'This is Portsmouth, people went to war from this city.'

Many brave people did go to war from Portsmouth. Historically famous leaders like Admiral Lord Nelson, armed with a sword, set off from these shores. Then in more recent times, troops have departed from Portsmouth for D-Day, the Falklands and the Gulf war.

Like all military cities, the people are tough, but I don't expect them to carry swords like Admiral Lord Nelson.

One Sunday afternoon, I was back at the nick, finishing off a bit of paperwork and just about to grab a sandwich for lunch, when a call came in on the radio. 'Charlie One, any units free to attend a report of a fight at the Home Club, Portsea?'

I confirmed my attendance and jumped into the area car.

I switched on the 'blues and twos' and made my way at speed towards the Home Club on Queen Street. This club was formerly known as the 'Sailors' Home', and is now called the Royal Maritime Hotel.

This historic hotel and conference centre was originally founded in 1850 to serve sailors who were between ships, offering respectable home comforts and a safe place to leave their money.

I drove down Queen Street towards the building and saw outside a group of men fighting and brandishing weapons. There was a group of approximately 10 males, aged in their late teens to early 20s. All were dressed smartly in traditional Sikh clothing. Now. being just a simple lad from Rochdale, at the time, I had no idea about traditional Sikh clothing and what it consisted of, but I do now.

It centres around the Five K's: Kesh (uncut hair), Kangha (comb), Kara (iron bracelet), Kachera (underwear), and Kirpan (sword).

It turns out I was driving towards a Sikh wedding reception. It had ended up becoming a massive tear-up between the younger males there. I have no idea what started the fight, but I was more concerned with the Kirpan element, especially as I was on my own.

Everyone at the scene seemed to be armed with either a short sword or a curved dagger that was sheathed to their lower leg. As I approached, most people in the fight were chasing each other, while making threats with swords and daggers that glinted in the afternoon sun. Everybody seemed to be armed with a bladed weapon of one type or another, apart from myself. How the hell was I going to stop this lot, without getting myself injured?

Thank goodness for the siren on the police car. As I approached with the siren wailing, most of the offenders ran off in various directions, many scurrying swiftly back into the building. An elderly man, also in traditional dress, was shouting at the younger males to get back inside and stop disgracing themselves.

By the time I got out of the police car, the street scene was once again calm. The elderly gentleman greeted me, shaking my hand. He apologised profusely for the disturbance. It was apparent he was embarrassed by the behaviour of others at the event.

I wanted to know if anybody had been hurt during the fracas. 'I need to have a look inside to make sure nobody is injured.'

The elderly man agreed and led me into the building through a fire exit that many of the fighters had just used.

The scene inside the building was most bizarre. It was as if there had never been a fight. Everybody had put their weapons away. All daggers had been placed back in their sheaths. Music played softly, while groups of guests sat around large round tables covered with white linen tablecloths.

They were sipping drinks and I could see plates of half-eaten curry on the tables, balloons on the walls and paper streamers on the floor. Two small children ran hurriedly past us, playing a game of tag.

The old man, who was obviously a respected elder of one of the families, was doing a great job in restoring normality. 'You can see, officer, that all is calm now and nobody wants to make a complaint. Certainly, all was quiet, there were no obvious injuries and nobody wanted to complain to me. What a bizarre scene.

Then the elder, like a psychic, said, 'You must be hungry, officer. We have all finished eating, but we have lots that will go to waste. Please take some back to the police station and eat with everyone on duty.'

'I can't, really,' I answered, caught in this difficult situation, knowing that police officers could not accept gifts to prevent allegations of corruption. He passed into my hands a large cardboard box with various foil trays containing curry and rice dishes.

'It is up to you. It will go to waste now. Throw the food in the bin or eat it while it is still good.'

Reluctantly, I thanked him. After all I did not want to offend the families celebrating a wedding. I reported on my radio that the job was finished and returned to the police station. As soon as my shift and the other officers working at the police station saw or smelt the box of curry, I was treated to a hero's welcome. They attacked it like a swarm of locusts!

On another occasion, a call had been made to the control room reporting a suspicious male with a knife at the back of Tesco in Crasswell Street. I was driving the area car, with another experienced area car driver called Stevie. A fellow northerner, we would always have a good laugh, sharing the same sense of humour.

From Arundel Street, I turned into Buckingham Street. I immediately spotted the male, standing by an alley which ran the whole length of the supermarket to the front of the store in Crasswell Street. To the left side of the man was a tall brick wall. To his right was a ramp for vehicle access into a multi-storey car park, but it was closed with large metal gates. The alley was behind him and we were in front of him.

This was definitely our suspect. On occasions, 999 calls from the public get lost in translation, like a serious game of Chinese whispers. This was one such occasion. The man did not have a knife. He had a metre-long Samurai sword in his hand. There was no sheath and he held it in one hand by the handle, slowly dragging the tip against the pavement.

I immediately stopped the area car at the junction, preventing traffic entering the street, but more importantly providing us with distance between the suspect and ourselves. Luckily there were no other members of the public nearby. The man looked up at both of us, taking hold of the sword with both hands and brandishing it like an oriental warrior from the 1980s film, *Shogun*.

The BMW 330 estate had a boot full of equipment for dealing with a variety of incidents. It had a first aid kit and two body armour jackets. Our short-sleeved shirts and clip-on ties would not offer us much protection in these circumstances.

Unfortunately, we could not access the body armour, due to a metal grill sectioning the boot off. This grill would be helpful in the event of an accident with items being thrown around, but not so helpful now. We would have to leave the relative safety of the car to open the boot. Not ideal.

Stevie looked towards the equipment in the boot, obviously thinking the same but placing his hands on his door handle.

'Stay in the car,' I said quickly.

I figured that a man wielding a Samurai sword in the street, mentally speaking, was probably not in a good place. We would be safer in the car.

Our options, should he attack us or a member of the public, were very limited. I pressed the transmit button on the car radio, updating the control room that the male was in sight. I gave his description, in case he ran off, and the details of the threat he posed.

The control room confirmed they had the details, stating they would deploy an ARV (Armed Response Vehicle) towards us. I could hear the control room deploying other police units to 'place a cordon on', closing nearby streets to prevent the public entering. In the '90s, not many police units patrolled the county carrying guns. It would probably take at least half an hour before they arrived. We were on our own.

The male suspect was white and slim build. He swung the sword in a circle over his head like some sort of Ninja, watching us all the time, but unfortunately he must have missed the memo about what to wear. Instead of a black cotton traditional Ninja costume with a black balaclava, he wore a pair of white Reebok Classics, a pair of navy-blue Adidas trackie bottoms and an oversized baggy Nike T-shirt.

I had an idea. I picked up the in-car microphone to the loudhailer and pressed the talk button just as the man started to step forward towards us.

'STOP, POLICE! PUT YOUR WEAPON DOWN!'

The sound of my voice boomed out across the street, over the loudhailer. The suspect hesitated but held on strongly to the sword above his head, pointing it in our direction.

I tried more verbal commands, as he started to walk towards us, closing the distance.

'DON'T DO IT, BOY! GIVE IT UP NOW. IT'S NOT WORTH IT!'

For some unknown reason, my last instructions came out with an American accent, like I was the cop, Sheriff Buford T. Justice, who famously uses a Southern accent in the *Smokey and the Bandit* films.

The man paused. The engine of the police car was still running and I said to Stevie, 'If he comes at us or attacks a member of the public, he's going over the bonnet and I'm running him over!'

One hit from that sword could have easily killed a person.

I'm fairly sure my suggestion was not a Home Office approved self-defence move, but I would rather be alive and explain my decision-making process to a coroner's court.

He continued towards us and I revved the engine as a warning and made one last plea over the Tannoy system.

'DROP THE WEAPON NOW!'

Amazingly, he complied with my command…

'KICK THE SWORD AWAY AND GET ON YOUR KNEES, WITH YOUR HANDS ON YOUR HEAD.'

Again, he did as I had asked.

'CROSS YOUR FINGERS AND FACE AWAY FROM US.'

On doing this, we both exited the car and approached him. I had my ASP baton ready, while Stevie had 'quick cuffs' ready in his hand. As I covered Stevie, he placed the suspect in handcuffs to the rear, arresting and cautioning him at the same time.

We called for the police van and the male was taken to custody. I'm not sure what the final result was for him. I think he might have been sectioned under the Mental Health Act for a medical assessment. A good result for him, as he was due to be another road traffic collision statistic.

We never did see an ARV that day. The strangest thing about that job was: nobody at the nick mentioned it. Not the sergeant, inspector or anybody above. We just got on with the rest of the shift. No 'well done' or tea and biscuits for us.

Also, TRiM assessments had not been introduced back then. TRiM stands for Trauma Risk Management. It is a process designed to support individuals and teams affected by potentially traumatic events at work, ensuring early identification and intervention to prevent long-term mental health issues.

I'm pleased this is an option offered to officers in the modern-day police service. We could have done with some of that during my days in the force!

The day we saved a life

In the police, summer evenings are packed with surprises. I loved working them, out on patrol just wearing trousers and a blue short-sleeved shirt. If the temperature was hot, you didn't even have to wear a tie.

In those days we didn't have body armour. The heat of the sun can do strange things to some people in Portsmouth, or so it seemed. That could be drinking or just doing something a little bit crazy.

One night, at about 9pm, a call crackled in on the police radio, 'Somebody trying to kill themselves at the back of the police station.'

I'd just been taking a comfort break and enjoying a well-earned cuppa. I dashed to the rear entrance of the police station at Pompey Central and the back yard. I could see nothing obvious. Had the caller got the location wrong?

Behind the police station was a large multi-storey car park. Roughly rectangular in shape, it reached five storeys high, made of concrete, with several staircases. I walked around the side and could see a male sitting on the very top near the central staircase. His legs were dangling precariously over the edge, facing towards the police station.

I've never been sure what causes people to want to take their own life. They must be at such a crisis point, feeling that the only way out of their problems and situation is to end it all. The emergency services know that there will be a time when they're called to try to help these people.

You never want to make the situation worse when dealing with any emergency. The last thing I planned to do was to run towards the male who could clearly see me approaching. And I certainly didn't want to get hit by him if he jumped!

I let the control room know I could see the male, and walked slowly towards him. I watched him all the time as I approached. Carefully, I negotiated the staircase at the front of the car park. The staircase was open to the elements with just a short wall surrounding it. With me being so tall, the slightest push could quite easily have tipped me over the edge if there happened to be a disagreement with the male.

I calmly tried to engage the man in conversation. He was only about my age, in his early 20s, a thin chap, wearing just jeans, a T-shirt and a pair of trainers. I was standing about half a level down on the staircase. The male had warned me not to come any closer. I was close enough to chat to him comfortably without having to shout. I could also see he was alone and, fortunately, there was nobody else in the car park behind him.

I reached for my radio microphone and explained to him that I was going to let the control room know I was there, and everything was okay at the moment. I could hear on my earpiece that the control room had been organising a trained negotiator to attend. An ambulance had been called and asked to park just out of sight, in case they were needed quickly. I could also hear other officers closing roads and footpaths nearby.

Until the police negotiator arrived, which could take anything up to an hour, I would have to negotiate with this man to stop him taking his own life. Quite frankly, it felt like a rather large weight of responsibility on my shoulders. If he jumped, it would be down to me, and I didn't want that.

I asked him about why things had got to this stage and to talk to me about his problems. I was honest and said I might not have all the answers and I certainly might not be able to solve the problems; the one thing I could do was listen and hear what he had to say.

This worked a treat and the man started chatting with me. We started to build some form of rapport and he told me all about his problems, his work, his relationship and how he felt everything was going wrong. The male spotted a police officer on the ground below and started to shout that he didn't want any others near him. This had spooked the male, causing him to shuffle closer to the edge of the concrete wall.

Often these suicidal incidents, when people are threatening to take their own lives, tend to end with a better outcome the longer the incident goes on. I did not want to make things any worse than they were. I also wanted to make sure everything was done by the book because I was acutely aware that, if the man fell, my actions would be under the microscope.

I had been negotiating with him for approximately an hour. At this time, we still didn't know when the negotiator was due to arrive.

It was now becoming dusk as the light fell with the sun setting. I noticed movement in the distance behind the male who was looking towards me. I could see it was an experienced police officer. I recognised him from one of the other shifts at the police station.

I did not want to draw attention to the officer, who was slowly walking up the vehicle ramp towards the top level of the car park behind the person in crisis. I continued to talk to the young man, while all the time I could see this police officer who by now was about 50 yards away.

I was in a tricky situation. If I had asked the officer to stop, it would alert the man to his presence and might cause him to jump. My colleague did stop and crouched down. I relaxed for a moment.

The officer then took off both of his shoes, leaving him standing there in just a pair of socks. At first, I was confused. Why the hell had he taken off his shoes? It then dawned on me, as then he slowly padded towards us both, like a big cat on a game reserve hunting its prey. He was going to wrestle this man to the ground.

I had no option but to keep the man talking and occupied, praying he would not turn around. I could see what was about to happen. It certainly wasn't going to be a conventional

'Home Office-approved' manoeuvre to bring a crisis negotiation to an end.

The officer quickly approached, silently, making no noise in his socks.

Closer and closer...20 feet, 10 feet, five feet. Then without warning the officer grabbed the man by his shoulders, pulling him backwards and onto the car park floor. The man was detained safely, winded a little by the sudden fall of five feet behind him.

I ran up to assist my colleague. We placed the man in handcuffs, more for his protection (and ours) so we could safely walk him out of the car park to the waiting ambulance.

The incident was brought to a successful conclusion, but it could have gone horribly wrong. The male was taken by the ambulance for a psychiatric assessment and I never did see him again. We updated the control room and that was it. I just went on to deal with the next job. There was no debriefing; it was just another incident.

At the end of the day, a life had been saved. I felt we had achieved a successful outcome.

A sergeant in trouble

In the early to mid 1990s, when I started work, we would begin a shift with a 'parade'. This involved a short handover from the previous shift, a check on the intelligence in the last 24 hours, being assigned your roles for the day and highlighting any particular tasks that you might have to get completed.

This was done on every single tour of duty without fail. There was a high turnover of staff as a result of officers being promoted or moved to a different police station. Many officers joined specialist departments to get experience of other parts of policing.

On one particular day, I was on duty at Pompey Central. This was an early turn shift, starting at 7 o'clock in the morning. The probationer on the shift carried a large thin wooden tray, containing lots of large mugs and the huge metal pot of tea. The pot was packed with multiple tea bags and filled to the brim with steaming hot water.

Sitting around the large rectangular parade table were around 10 officers. Waiting for the sergeant to join us, we all sat down with pocket notebooks open and pens at the ready.

A sergeant walked in and sat down at the head of the table. The light chatter drifted to silence and all eyes looked up, but we remained seated.

Had this been an inspector walking into the room, the standard protocol would have been for everybody of a lesser rank to stand up, and maybe even salute, before being advised to sit back down. This was to show deference and respect to the rank.

This was not our usual patrol sergeant, and I did not recognise him as being an officer from Portsea Island. He was a shortish, portly man in his 30s with a serious look on his face.

He introduced himself by name and then started by saying: 'Good morning. I am your new patrol sergeant, and have been moved to Portsmouth following a PSD investigation.'

PSD stands for the Professional Standards Department, who investigate the police for discipline or criminal matters.

'I was arrested for cottaging, but I am innocent,' the newcomer announced.

An older offer next to me slightly spat out a small spray of tea from his mouth as he gasped, stifling a laugh. Everyone's eyes glanced manically around at each other, not sure if this was a wind-up.

A female police probationer asked innocently, 'What's cottaging?'

One of the 'old sweats' on the shift muttered loudly, with his head down facing the table looking disgusted, 'Men, cruising for sex in public bogs.'

The probationer asked again, 'But how do they get caught?'

It was obvious that she was thinking through the legal and evidential gathering approach to this offence, having recognised the difficulties that a private and personal space, such as a public toilet, would pose.

Another officer spoke up: 'I heard the Vice Squad sit on top of the public toilets looking through the skylights.'

I'm not sure how true this last statement was. In my head, I had an episode of Eastenders coming to a close and was expecting the 'Doof Doofs', which are the drum beats used to signify a cliffhanger at the end of an episode.

Needless to say, I felt a little sorry for our new sergeant, who went on to be one of the best skippers I had worked for. He was very fair, helpful and professional. I don't believe any criminal prosecution was made against him and the offence was NFA'd (No Further Action).

The thing was, at the time, that allegation must have been consuming him. He probably felt that everyone and his dog knew what had happened.

The truth was, hardly anyone knew this sergeant's name, never mind what he was being investigated for by the PSD. In hindsight he had probably done the right thing in telling his shift. It would only be a matter of time, I knew, before these rumours and gossip spread like wildfire.

So, just to recap, what exactly is cottaging? Put simply, cottaging is an informal term for having sex in a public toilet.

Cottaging can apply to both heterosexual and homosexual relations. However, the term is far more closely associated with gay men and transexual men, often labelled as 'cottage queens'. The term 'cottaging' itself goes back to the Victorian era. Male-only bathhouses, often known as cottages, were used for casual sex between men.

I'm not sure what actual offence the sergeant had been investigated for. There is a common law offence of 'outraging public decency' and can be applied to cottaging, dogging and cruising for sex by gay men.

In the UK, under section 71 of the Sexual Offences Act, 2003, cottaging is illegal, as it comes under 'engaging in sexual activity in a public lavatory'. Although not labelled as 'cottaging', the Sexual Offences Act clearly states that a person commits an offence if:

In a lavatory to which the public or a section of the public has or is permitted to have access, whether on payment or otherwise, he intentionally engages in an activity, and the activity is sexual.

Understanding the previous legal framework is crucial before considering the Sexual Offences Act 2003. Prior to this, the Acts of 1956 and 1967 governed offences relevant to 'cottaging'. This was a time in history when many homosexuals were 'criminalised' for their sexuality in the UK.

The 1956 Act, under Section 13, made it an offence for a man to commit an act of gross indecency with another man, whether in public or private. This law, sometimes viewed as a reaction to some public 1950s scandals, was used to prosecute homosexual activity. While the 1967 Act decriminalised homosexual acts between consenting adults over 21, it crucially stipulated this applied only 'in private'. It did not legalise such acts in public settings. This distinction highlighted the ongoing legal complexities surrounding sexuality and public versus private conduct. The relevant sections of both the 1956 and 1967 Acts were superseded by the 2003 legislation.

This type of activity came to the attention of the public a few years later. In 1998, the musician George Michael was arrested in Beverly Hills after being caught soliciting sex by an undercover police officer in a public restroom. This incident resulted in a fine (reportedly $810 USD) and a sentence of 80 hours of community service for Michael, alongside considerable, often negative, attention from tabloid media.

Eight years later, Michael was again the subject of media reports concerning similar activities, allegedly involving sexual conduct with a stranger in a public place. This second event brought further global attention to such activities.

George Michael released a great song called *Outside*, featuring a music video, that was set in a public toilet with disco balls and police officers in the toilets. This was thought to be Michael making a statement that he would not be shamed for his sexuality.

I still have great sympathy for that sergeant.

293

The tragic death of a boy

One warm summer evening I was getting ready to go to work for a night turn. At that time, I was living in Fareham, about 10 miles away from Portsmouth. Dressed in half-blues (my police trousers, short-sleeve blue shirt but without any tie or epaulettes), I jumped into my car and started the drive into work.

I passed through Portchester and reached a junction known as the J&J roundabout. Nowadays there is no roundabout at this junction. It is a confusing mass of lanes that cross into one another with a number of sets of traffic lights. The history of that location refers to the fact that the company Johnson and Johnson once had a large factory positioned close to the roundabout.

My wife, Janet, told me that one of her first jobs was working in that factory. Someone had the job of screwing on the caps to the KY jelly, then Janet would have to pack the tubes into boxes. On occasion she would be counting out plasters to put into boxes. Mind-numbing work, but a good wage for a student job.

I digress. I had turned right into the junction, so I would join the M275 which would take me swiftly into Portsmouth, ready for the 10 o'clock night shift to start. Unfortunately, on this occasion, there was a temporary motorway closure for some repairs and all the traffic was being diverted onto the M27. Back towards Fareham! Shit, I was gonna be late for the shift, I thought.

I drove up the motorway and came off at the Fareham junction, only to find I would have to come back down the A27 again. This was turning into a bit of a nightmare. I reached the Delme roundabout, turned left to join the A27 near Cams Hall estate and headed back towards Portchester. I had only driven 300 or 400 yards up the road when the traffic stopped. Bloody hell, what now?

We've all been there. When everything seems to be conspiring against you to make you late. I was trapped on a section of dual carriageway. All the traffic ahead had stopped. There were only two or three cars in front of me, but I could not quite see why all the traffic was at a standstill.

I noticed in the outside lane that a couple of cars had moved forward, passing what appeared to be some sort of accident that had occurred in the inside lane, just a few yards ahead.
I guess this was telling me that my duty had just started, even if I didn't have a radio with me. I assumed the accident must have just happened. I could see a bicycle lying on the ground and some people crouched down next to it. I manoeuvred my car very slightly towards the centre of the road and turned the hazard lights on to protect the scene and

the people in the road. I got out of my car and walked over to where the accident had happened.

I could see a hatchback-type car stopped in the road with a large dent and damage on the front. On the ground was a pedal cycle, bent and twisted with the wheels buckled. A young boy, aged about 14 or 15 years old, was lying in the road on his back. An elderly man was standing to the side, looking distraught. I assumed that this man was the driver of the vehicle that had collided with the boy on the bicycle. Two women in their 20s were kneeling down next to the boy.

Identifying this was a serious accident, I automatically started to take control, as my training took over. Back then, as you know, we didn't even have mobile phones, so I asked a bystander, who had got out of a car, to go to one of the nearby houses and dial 999, asking for police and an ambulance.

I identified myself as a police officer to the women, who were attempting to provide first aid to the boy. One of the women stated they were both nurses en-route to the hospital to start work. They both looked quite shaken, and they said it was strange to be dealing with this sort of incident outside of a clinical setting. The nurses said they were going to start chest compressions on the boy, as he appeared to have stopped breathing and had no obvious pulse.

I offered to provide the rescue breaths, while we all attempted CPR. This was not going to be straightforward, and a lot different from our training. The boy had a massive chest injury, having been hit by the car. He was unconscious and his eyes were dilated, with blood coming from his mouth and ear. It was obvious he was gravely ill, but all we could do was try to save his life. One of the nurses started chest compressions but, with every compression, bright oxygenated red blood would foam out of the boy's mouth.

Using my fingers, I swept the contents of the boy's mouth out to one side. Taking a deep breath, I made a seal around the boy's mouth and provided two rescue breaths. Blood poured out everywhere. The boy's face was covered in blood. It was on my hands, on my face, in my mouth, on my uniform.

None of this mattered, as we just had to try to keep him alive. The women continued the chest compressions and I kept going with rescue breaths. However, it was becoming futile, with the volume of blood coming up through the boy's mouth, due to his excessive internal injuries.

I had a small resuscitation aid in my pocket. It was a plastic sheet with a small valve. The idea was to help prevent cross-contamination of fluid when providing rescue breaths. I placed this over the boy's mouth but, due to the volume of blood, I couldn't create a seal to breathe air in. The plastic continued to slip.

Adrenaline was coursing through me, and we had been delivering CPR for about 10 minutes. I spotted blue lights coming up the road and was relieved that the cavalry had arrived. A young woman police constable drove up in a panda car and came over to help.

My hopes of the cavalry arriving were dashed as, on the sight that greeted her, with the four of us covered in blood carrying out CPR, the WPC started panicking and appeared struck with shock. She had been overcome with the 'freeze' response, from 'fight', 'flight' or 'freeze', which is the body's natural reaction to a stressful, life-threatening situation. This can sometimes be totally unavoidable as hormones are released by your brain in such situations in an attempt to keep you alive.

I shouted over to her, to direct traffic and maintain a free route for the ambulance that would be arriving soon, hopefully. I also asked her to start grabbing witness details. She snapped out of her paralysis and started directing traffic.

The nurses said they were tiring from the chest compressions, which are often very physical. We agreed to swap positions and I then conducted chest compressions, while the nurses continued with rescue breaths. The boy was not responding and just made a gurgling sound as blood rose up through his mouth and nose.

We continued for another few minutes until we heard sirens. Thank goodness it was the ambulance and the traffic police arriving. The police quickly closed the road off, with the assumption that this could become a fatal accident scene. The paramedics joined us, quickly attaching a number of wires and machines to the boy, to monitor his vital signs.

All the time, we continued with the CPR. The paramedics placed a mask over the boy's face that was able to provide oxygen. After attempting heart compressions, we lifted him carefully onto a stretcher and into the ambulance.

I stepped back with the two nurses and we all took a moment to compose ourselves. Shortly afterwards, I was joined by a traffic sergeant who informed me that the boy had been pronounced dead. I felt numb and emotional with my lip quivering. However, I was relieved that the two nurses and myself had done everything possible to try to save the boy.

The traffic sergeant then said, 'You don't mind travelling with the boy to hospital do you, for continuity? Just until we can get an officer over to you?'

I agreed, and got into the back of the ambulance with the now deceased boy lying on the ambulance bed. I passed my car keys to the traffic police to move the vehicle when they opened up the road. This would now be treated like a crime scene while they investigated the accident.

That trip to the hospital in the back of the ambulance was slow. It was quiet, with no lights or sirens; just the occasional side-to-side rocking as we turned a corner in such a high-sided vehicle. I sat looking at the boy, who was at peace.

I stayed at QA Hospital in Cosham for about an hour before another officer came to take over. I was given a lift home by a traffic officer. I was told to write up my pocket book, but could leave writing a statement about the incident until the following day.

I sat at home adding the details of the incident into my pocket book, when the doorbell rang. It was the duty inspector from Pompey Central. This was a genuine welfare visit for me and was totally unexpected, but greatly appreciated. Only once I had stopped and was writing things up, did the enormity of what had happened hit me.

We had a cuppa and talked about the events of the day. That really helped. The inspector said, taking into account what I had been through, to take the rest of the duty off and come back the following night.

It turned out that the boy had been drinking beer with friends before the accident, and riding with no lights. He was well over the drink drive limit and had been having difficulty keeping upright on his bike, wobbling in the road. He had wobbled straight in front of the car that hit him. The driver had no chance of avoiding him and the boy, unfortunately, had no chance of survival, due to his extensive internal injuries.

It was an awful incident all round, especially as it happened so close to my home. I was reminded of the crash every time I drove past that spot, as the boy's family marked the nearby hedge with memorial flowers.

I was later nominated for an award. That was a lovely gesture, but I like to think most people would try to save a life if placed in that same position.

I highly recommend that people take some basic first aid and CPR training, so that they would feel a little more prepared if faced with a life-threatening incident.

Hopefully, you never will come across a tragic accident like this.

Working in the danger zone

I sometimes get asked, 'Who's the most dangerous person you've dealt with as a police officer?' It's quite a difficult question to answer, because anybody can be dangerous in so many different ways and you always need to have your wits about you.

I once was deployed to a report of a drunk at a pub in Old Portsmouth, causing a disturbance. I was just driving a panda car, single-crewed. If I recall correctly, the venue was the Dolphin in the High Street, Old Portsmouth. This is a wealthy area of the city, and calls like this were quite unusual.

I got out of the police car in full uniform and entered the pub. I was immediately greeted by a barmaid and an elderly gentleman who was standing inside, close to the entrance door. The man was in his early 70's, about 5'8" tall, medium build, dressed in a suit, wearing a long grey woollen trench coat. He was swaying from side to side, as if he was on a naval ship but had obviously had one too many sherbets to drink.

The barmaid quickly explained that the male had been refused service as he appeared drunk. He had become abusive and started swearing. The pensioner was refusing to leave the pub on being asked to do so by the staff. I asked him to step outside the pub. In hindsight, this was probably not the best use of words, as he obviously thought I wanted to have a fight with him outside!

The man did leave the pub at my request. I started to ask him where home was and how he planned to get back.

Without warning, the pensioner, using his right fist, jabbed me hard in the face with a punch. It connected with a loud whack and knocked me back off balance. The man continued towards me, swinging his left fist in an uppercut motion towards my face.

It was apparent this man had some boxing experience behind him, and was putting up a good fight, even though he was pissed. I ducked the punch and he was now off balance.

It felt unfair to punch back, so I wrapped both my arms around him in a bear hug to restrain him, and prevent him punching out again. This worked, but he was muscular and as strong as an ox. We both lost our balance as he pushed me backwards towards large wooden planters either side of the door. The oversized plant pots were made from old wooden beer barrels, cut in half and filled with soil and attractive fresh flowers.

I felt the back of my legs against one of the planters, and my balance was completely lost. We both crashed down with spectacular force on top of the planter. I was still struggling to restrain the drunken man who was swearing and thrashing out as we crashed down on the barrel, completely splitting it open. I found myself rolling on the pavement, covered in soil and daffodils.

Metal hoops from the barrel along with strips of wood lay strewn all over, as I radioed for police assistance that arrived only a few minutes later. The drunk was placed in a police van, and I now looked like Worzel Gummidge. I never in a million years thought he was going to kick off when I first met him!

Obviously, he was not the most dangerous person I had ever met. Even with violent robbers, rapists or murderers, you kind of know what you are dealing with. In the main, you can predict if things are going to escalate. If somebody is holding a knife, you would normally always try to give yourself some distance, creating a space to react to any escalation. In personal safety training, situational awareness is really important.

The **White Zone** can be dangerous. This is autopilot when you are doing tasks automatically and are not aware of your surroundings.

The **Green Zone** is a state of relaxed awareness. You remain calm and go about your routine while quietly observing your surroundings and noting anything unusual – without drawing attention to yourself. Developing this awareness starts with simple actions such as putting your phone away and paying attention to people's body language. You only leave the Green Zone if you notice something that seems out of the ordinary.

The **Amber Zone** is triggered when something doesn't feel right: for example, spotting a suspicious van in an area that's normally quiet. You become more alert, gather more information and start assessing the situation. This is the planning stage, where you consider possible responses. You may choose to avoid the area or take a different route.

Another example may be a suspect reaching into a pocket when speaking to them. Do they have a knife? A needle? Are they trying to discard incriminating evidence? Once the situation no longer seems concerning, you return to the Green Zone. Regularly shifting between Green and Amber is normal and healthy. It's important to relax as easily as you react.

The **Red Zone** is when a clear and immediate threat presents itself, as in someone pointing a weapon or launching an attack. Ideally, if you've moved through the previous zones with awareness, you'll be better prepared to respond appropriately. Those who panic in emergencies are often the ones caught off guard, jumping straight from the White Zone into the Red Zone.

I have always been quite a relaxed type of person. Physical activity, I found, really helped to keep me calm. Exercise helps relieve tension and can interrupt the stress cycle. Activities like walking, cycling and running combine movement with mental focus, promoting relaxation.

Also having a good social support group helped. Police shift nights out were a must, including some memorable house parties! For a couple of years these became legendary parties you had to attend. They were hastily advertised by handwritten posters giving details of the date, time and place.

An honesty box was placed beside the photocopier in the police station, asking for 20p pieces. Then the posters would be distributed around the internal notice boards in all the local Pompey police stations. Everyone was welcome, so long as you brought a bottle. We had some great parties in our rented house. It was a great way to blow off a little steam.

I also continued to keep in touch with lots of my mates from 'up north' and ensured that I had friends outside of policing. Friends from outside of 'The Job' helped keep me grounded and stopped me from being institutionalised. Maintaining relationships with friends, family, and colleagues provides emotional resilience. Strong social connections are believed to buffer the effects of stress and may even contribute to longer life.

For me, the most dangerous of people are those who can be impossible to predict. Persons with serious mental health conditions stand out in this category. As their brain is not working in an expected way, it can be difficult to predict how they will react.

They are also often taking strong prescribed medication for mental health. Some people may have stopped taking medication, making things worse, or possibly taken too much plus a mixture of drink and illegal drugs. This cocktail can be scary in how they react to you. This combination of drugs can numb normal pain responses, so restraining them can prove difficult. They may also have episodes of voices in their heads telling them to 'do things' that they would not normally do.

One such call I attended single-crewed was on a day turn. I was driving a panda car and was sent to a report of a disturbance/concern for welfare of a male in a flat, after 'crashing' sounds could be heard from his accommodation.

I arrived at the house towards the bottom of Green Road in Somerstown, close to the junction of Kings Road. The address was set in a row of traditional Victorian terraced houses, characterised by red brick façades, white-painted window surrounds and bay windows. Each house had a small front garden area bordered by low brick walls. Some of these gardens had hedges or plants, while others were more open. Short paths led from the front doors to the pavement.

The front door of the property was open and this house had been split into multi-occupancy, with two flats downstairs and two upstairs. I entered the building and reached the top of the barren staircase, furnished only with a single dusty light bulb hanging from a length of electrical cable with no shade. I turned to my left and saw the correct flat number attached to the door, and knocked.

'WHAT IS IT?' a male voice shouted back.

'It's the police. I just want to check if you are okay?'

There was no reply. I continued to talk, trying to get the male to engage with me. No more communication. What was I to do? The initial call to police was concerned for the man's safety and welfare. All was quiet now, but I knew someone was in there.

I reasoned to myself. What if there was a second person holding him captive? The occupant may have self-harmed and could be dying, as I waited outside the door.

'I'm going to come in to check if you are all right,' I said softly.

There was still no reply. Cautiously, I placed my hand on the metal door handle and turned it slowly. The door was unlocked and I opened it carefully, peering in to take in the scene before entering. The room, a self-contained bedroom, was nearly empty of furniture.

A wooden chair was placed against the back wall, with a pile of dirty looking clothing in the corner of the room. There was no bed, but on the wooden floorboards I could see a duvet and pillow heaped in a pile. The bay window lit the room with daylight, as the curtains were pulled back and open.

Standing before me was a man in his 30s. White and athletically built, he stood at the back of the room facing me. He was barefoot and wearing only a pair of boxer shorts. His eyes looked like they were on stalks, fixed in a mad stare. His face and chest were covered in a sheen of perspiration, as if he had been running, but his skin had no redness or glow, like you might expect when exercising. His breathing was heavy, but not laboured.

I spoke softly again, 'Are you okay mate? We had a call from someone concerned for you.'

Silence.

'You're not in any trouble, I just want to check you are all right,' I announced to him. 'Is it okay to come in and chat?'

He didn't reply. I glanced around to check he was on his own, which he was. I stepped into the room, but left the door open. I kept a distance of about eight feet between us. I am no medical expert but, from my experience, he appeared to be suffering some type of mental health breakdown. His eyes maintained the look of madness, and he was not even blinking.

My tutor, Nick, had taught me to always watch the hands of people you deal with. This was excellent advice. Often people clench their fists just before striking out, and this can be a great indicator of an imminent assault. Suspects also try to discard or hide evidence such as drugs or weapons, so watching someone's hands can help to predict their next move. I glanced down at the man's hands, but on this occasion there was no clue as to his intentions.

Without any warning, the man touched the back wall of the bedroom with the palm of his hands and pushed off from it. He then ran like a sprinter with great acceleration towards the front of the house, leaping up into the air like a kangaroo. In a split second, the male was now horizontal, heading head first towards the window.

There was an almighty crash as he flew, head first through the glass of the double-glazed window. Shards of broken glass flew off in all directions during the commotion. The male went out of my sight. I moved towards the bay window and looked out through the human-sized hole. I could see him lying motionless on the pavement outside. The force of his jump had caused him to clear the whole of the front garden and low wall.

'Shit,' I thought, and called urgently on my radio for an ambulance. I didn't even know if he was dead at this point. Unlike in the movies, when a human travels through a window wearing just a pair of boxer shorts, they don't just get up and brush themselves down. This guy had cut himself to ribbons. I could see deep lacerations in his skin and muscles which were now leaking bright red blood. He lay face down on the pavement and was not moving or making any noise. Not a good sign.

I ran, jumping two or three steps at a time down the stairs and out to the pavement where the man lay. I could see his chest rising so I knew he was breathing and his heart was pumping, but with every breath the deep cuts opened and closed, leaking blood.

Fortunately, he had not severed any arteries but he still had catastrophic bleeding. I grabbed the first aid kit from the car and started applying lint pads and bandages with direct pressure to stem the blood loss. An ambulance arrived within minutes and the paramedic crew set about their lifesaving work. The man was quickly stabilised and then transported to hospital.

The shift police inspector had attended the scene at this point. Colleagues started to tie the plastic blue and white 'Police – Do not cross' tape to the garden walls and parked cars as they cordoned off the scene.

The inspector asked me what had happened and I explained the entire incident. He looked down at my bloodstained uniform.

He spoke into his radio and talked to the control room. 'We will also need scenes of crime officers down to the scene and to recover the officer's clothing and swab his hands.'

It then suddenly dawned on me that I was being treated as a suspect! Did they really think I had thrown a fully grown man through a window into the street? Then, to be fair, how realistic did my story of a man throwing himself through a window sound in the cold light of day?

I would just have to trust the process. My uniform and boots were seized in large brown evidence bags and sealed with tape.

I provided a statement, but was never arrested or interviewed under caution. The scene revealed that what I had said was true, backed up by witnesses from the house and street outside.

Anyone under investigation, guilty or innocent, is subjected to a certain level of stress. I can vouch for that!

A glimpse of life on the inside

Have you ever been to prison? Hopefully not, but you might have been. We take prisons for granted. A place where society can lock up all the wrong'uns. If they are paedophiles I like to use the term, 'proper wrong 'uns'.

Prisons house all sorts of people: those convicted of crimes that carry a prison sentence, or people who the courts have 'remanded' in custody as they pose a flight risk, or a risk to witnesses or victims prior to a trial.

The prison sentence might be based on the seriousness of the offence, such as murder for example. The prison system is struggling, just like the police, with lack of funding, lack of officers and overcrowding. There are too many offenders to deal with.

Many governments have tried to tackle the issues, but it is an expensive problem to solve. Most UK prisons are from the Victorian era; although feats of engineering at the time, many are no longer fit for purpose.

Most police stations refer to the 'custody suite' or the cell block as 'The Bridewell'. But why? I was never told during my career, and had to do a little research.

The first House of Correction was established in 1553 at Bridewell Palace in London, a former residence of King Henry VIII. Following this, Houses of Correction – and later, jails in general – came to be known as 'Bridewells'. The term 'Bridewell' originated from the nearby holy well associated with St. Bride's Church in London. So that was it: all police cell blocks became known as Bridewells.

I have always wondered what it would feel like to be sentenced in court and then sent to a prison for the first time. Even the toughest of criminals must be somewhat apprehensive when they receive their first jail sentence.

I'm sure that fear is reduced if you come from a criminal family or network and have friends on the inside. But they probably have enemies as well, and everyone must have their wits about them to avoid conflict.

I have visited prisons quite a few times. My first experience of a prison was in 1990 as an onlooker before joining the police. I was just watching events at the jail from the outside. It all started with a rooftop protest that took place at HMP Strangeways in Manchester. The protest became a 25-day riot by inmates.

The trouble started on 1 April when inmates seized control of the prison chapel, sparking unrest that quickly spread across most of the facility. The stand-off concluded on 25 April after the last five inmates were removed from the roof.

During the riot one prisoner lost his life, a prison officer died of a heart attack, while 147 prison officers and 47 inmates were injured. Strangeways was extensively damaged, with repairs costing £55 million at the time. It remains the longest prison riot in British history. As young teenagers Matty, Jon, Brad and I would drive over to the prison to see the events unfolding. We witnessed what the world was watching on live television news.

Enterprising individuals had set up burger stalls and tea stands so that the crowds could grab some roadside refreshments, while standing on the pavement watching inmates throw items off the roof. The prisoners would occasionally try to communicate with the media below, but the police played Barry Manilow songs from loudspeakers in an attempt to drown out the prisoners' demands and messages. Yes, *Copacabana* at full volume! Everything was really exciting for us at the time, not appreciating the severity of the situation.

I have never been on the 'wing' or in a prison as an inmate, but I have visited jails while transporting prisoners. Before the days of civilian private security firms obtaining government contracts to manage the safety of detained persons, the police organised their transport. We were responsible for the journeys between courts and prisons.

We travelled to and from two main prisons, HMP Winchester and HMP Reading, that housed young offenders as well as adults. Hampshire also had other prisons such as

HMP Kingston, in Portsmouth that housed category B/C adult males. A lot of them were 'lifers'.

We had prisons on the Isle of Wight, too. These, being on an island, tended to house some of the most dangerous and notorious criminals and paedophiles the country has ever locked up. The jails were Category A prisons, but later downgraded. HMP Albany, HMP Parkhurst and HMP Camp Hill all ended up catering for category B adult male prisoners. The prisons on the Isle of Wight have now since merged into one 'super prison'.

When I was asked to do prisoner runs back in the 1990s from the magistrate or crown courts at Portsmouth, we mainly attended Winchester or Reading. We only went up to London if we had female prisoners, to take them to HMP Holloway. We would always be double crewed in case a prisoner became difficult.

The first time I did a prisoner run was from Portsmouth Crown Court to HMP Winchester. I was with my tutor, constable 'Nick', who was showing me the ropes. First, we went down to the custody holding area in the crown court. We signed all the paperwork to take custody of the prisoner. If he escaped, it would be my fault and for me to explain what happened.

We took hold of his belongings and placed them in a large clear plastic bag, sealed with a zip lock, that had a unique reference number. We didn't want a prisoner accusing us of theft en-route to prison!

The prisoner transport was normally a large plain van with small individual cells in the back to keep inmates separate.

This was parked in a secure bay inside the crown court. My tutor told me to raise my left wrist in front of me. I complied, only to have my wrist placed in a 'transport' handcuff. These were thicker than normal handcuffs and more comfortable for officers wearing them. Not that my bony wrist thought so!

The door to the court cell was unlocked with a loud metallic clunk. A male prisoner in his 30s, who looked straight out of a Guy Richie film, wearing a dark tracksuit and trainers, stepped forward. I gave him a friendly nod, but he blanked me. I got the impression he didn't really like coppers. He knew the routine and put out his right arm, which was as wide as my leg.

His heavily tattooed arm was placed into the other hoop of the transport cuff. This was locked into place with a key and we were now joined together. We walked to the prison van and climbed into the back. The rear door of the van was closed to prevent any chance of escape. He was placed into one of the individual cells and the handcuff removed. My prisoner was not the chatty type, having shared no conversation with me. However, he was compliant and did not want to 'kick off'. I'm not sure I would have fancied my chances against this fella.

We had another couple of prisoners loaded into the van, then it was time to go. The secure doors to the court opened so that we could drive out. We were off to prison! The journey took only about half an hour. That said, we still had prisoners moaning about being hungry and wanting to buy a McDonalds, needing the toilet and wanting a smoke. All of these requests were declined.

Nick was driving, with me as the passenger. We arrived at the entrance to Winchester Prison, situated next door to Hampshire Police Headquarters on West Hill. At the time of writing, the prison is still there, but the HQ building and grounds have gone, sold to developers to build a housing estate. The front of the prison building had a large Victorian-style door for vehicles, set into a white stone arch. A smaller door for pedestrians was set into the larger main doors.

We stopped outside the main doors for vehicles and announced our arrival to the prison staff. The doors opened and we were waved into a large secure internal holding area for prison transports. A set of similar large doors were positioned in front of us, but closed. The initial set of doors closed behind us and the prison staff checked over the vehicle, while we confirmed our paperwork was all in order and we had the correct prisoners.

I got back into the van with my tutor, and Nick said, 'Best if you put on your helmet.' I thought this request was a little strange, but complied. He said it was for our 'welcome'!

The second set of vehicle doors opened, and Nick slowly drove into a large internal courtyard. He stopped near the middle and pointed to a metal door off to our right, situated up a small staircase. 'That's where we take them, one at a time.'

I noticed Nick was now putting on his helmet. I clambered out of the van and heard an almighty metallic bang.

'Bloody hell, what was that?' I shouted to Nick.

I could hear inmates shouting and cheering above us. He glanced up and shouted, 'batteries'. I looked up and could see prisoners' arms hanging out of partially-opened windows, tossing batteries towards us. Some were thrown by hand, and others by home-made 'slingshots' made out of material. It quickly became apparent that the prisoners saved up their old batteries to lob at the 'Old Bill' when we entered with new prisoners. This was much to the amusement of the other prisoners watching from the overlooking cells, who were cheering with every direct hit.

I was handcuffed to my prisoner again as another AA battery bounced off the side of the van to a rapturous cheer. I said to my prisoner, 'Okay, time to run the gauntlet.'

With the back doors opened and joined by the wrist, we quickly jogged up to the 'new prisoner' reception area, fortunate not to be hit by any missiles. Nick and I got back in the van, once all the prisoners were safely tucked up in prison, and prepared to drive out.

Nick took off his helmet and quipped, 'It could have been worse. It would have been shit coming down if they didn't have batteries!'

Another more glamorous trip to a Bridewell came during an early turn. The sergeant told me on parade that I had to go and collect a prisoner who was wanted on a warrant for failing to appear at court. He had been arrested in Scotland and I needed to fly up to collect him. I set off in KC99, our station police van, and arrived at Southampton Airport. I put a civilian jacket on over my uniform and caught a flight to Edinburgh.

I was greeted by some friendly police officers in Edinburgh and escorted to the airport Bridewell. I was taken to the cell of the prisoner and could not believe how posh it was. It was all nicely painted, with no graffiti or unexplained brown skid marks on the walls. The prisoner was smoking in the cell, but had been given a new foil disposable ashtray to tip his ash in. I suggested that he should make the most of it, as his accommodation in Portsmouth would not be quite the same.

The prisoner was handcuffed to me using escort cuffs, and his jacket was placed over the cuffs to hide them from view. Our return flight was full of passengers, so we got on the plane last, to avoid being noticed and sat near the rear doors. Nearly all the passengers had no idea that a police officer was transporting a prisoner on that flight. We chatted on the flight back and it turned out this prisoner was a bit of a laugh. He also cheekily asked the stewardess for a whisky and coke while airborne. I shook my head to the stewardess who knew I was a police officer, so she was aware not to give him any alcohol.

In January 1995, Operation Wightwash took place in response to the escape of three 'Category A' prisoners: murderer Andrew Roger, bomber Matthew Williams and another murderer, Keith Rose who had all escaped from HMP Parkhurst on the Isle of Wight. This became probably the biggest manhunt the island has ever seen.

I was due to work a normal night shift at 2200, but was called in early. The island was flooded with police officers including dog units, firearms teams, plus specialist search and public order units. I'm sure there was no reported crime on the island for those five days! The force had a massive issue, staffing such a large operation, and so all officers in the constabulary had the next few rest days cancelled.

The escaped prisoners, all considered extremely dangerous, had approximately 150 square miles to play hide and seek with the police. Every outbuilding, derelict structure and shed had to be searched. The police ran the operation out of Jersey Army Camp at Newtown.

I didn't actually travel to the Isle of Wight to search for the prisoners. My job was on the mainland.

There were lots of theories as to how the convicts could avoid capture. One of the prisoners was thought to know how to fly, so the airport at Sandown was monitored with police patrols. They could only hide for so long. It is possible to swim from the Isle of Wight, but I would not recommend it. As it was a cold January, the chances of this being an option were slim.

The island has three vehicle ferry ports to link with the mainland: Portsmouth to Fishbourne near Ryde, Southampton to Cowes and Lymington to Yarmouth. The most obvious route was on a ferry as a 'stowaway' on a vehicle. The FastCat pedestrian ferry and Hovertravel were also closely monitored in the hunt for the fugitives.

For the next few nights, I was posted at the ferry terminal at Portsmouth. As every ferry arrived, we would stop all vehicles and search them. That was easy for a car, but tricky with all the lorries and vans. I would climb up the outside of HGVs, which were often quite dirty and oily, sometimes using ladders to search every little space or hidey hole on the tops and insides. I did wonder what would happen if I came face-to-face with a murderer or bomber standing on top of a lorry!

As I was on a night turn, the ferry only came in once an hour. When all the vehicles had been searched during those cold winter nights, we spent the rest of the duty tucked up nice and warm in the ferry terminal office eating crisps, drinking tea and playing cards.

The escaped convicts never did manage to leave the island, but were spotted after five days by an off-duty prison officer as they tried to cross open ground. Once the police were notified, they were quickly captured.

Peace and quiet returned to the Isle of Wight, while we returned to our normal duties.

My adventures with PC Spoon

Certain offences and crimes that people commit can really make you quite angry, as there seems to be no real rhyme or reason for committing them. It is just downright selfish behaviour.

One such offence is drink driving or drug driving. As anybody who's been in the emergency services knows, whether you are an ambulance crew or in the fire brigade or police, drink and drug driving can absolutely ruin lives. Terrible accidents can occur as a result of people driving while being impaired, causing loss of life which affects friends, family and those at the scene of the accident.

Sometimes there are life-changing injuries and disabilities affecting the people involved. I loved going out, particularly on lates and nights, hunting down drink and drug drivers.

I became acutely aware of small tell-tale signs in the manner of people's driving that would give them away. Not that I was ever keen on wanting to be a traffic officer, because I didn't. I enjoyed fighting crime, and saw things like drink drive and drug drive legislation as being a tool to catch real criminals who were stupid enough to get behind the wheel after being impaired themselves.

As they say, 'there is always more than one way to skin a cat' in bringing these people to justice. With that being said, not all drink drivers are master criminals. On one particular afternoon, one of my shift colleagues who was known as 'Spoon', found that out.

Spoon had stopped a male for drink driving in Winston Churchill Avenue, literally outside the magistrates' court in Portsmouth. It was daytime, and Spoon had called up on the radio for an SL400 (a handheld breathalyser machine) so I attended the scene because I had one in the car.

This machine had a small removable and disposable plastic tube that was attached to the top, and the subject would blow into it. A traffic light system determined whether there was no alcohol, some alcohol, or if they were over the legal limit and would be arrested.

The suspect would then be taken back to the police station and an evidential sample of breath taken. This would be used as evidence in court. The roadside breath test was just a screening device to determine whether the person should be arrested.

When I arrived, I could see Spoon standing next to the male who was sitting on a mobility scooter. This was like an electric motorised seat with handlebars, designed to help people who have trouble walking to get around, whether indoors or outdoors. They're only designed to travel at slow speeds but, like any other mechanically propelled motor vehicle, they are covered by drink-drive legislation.

Simply put, if this fellow was pissed driving the thing, he could be nicked.

The chap was in his 50s, but looked a lot older. He was argumentative, slurring his words and appeared to have been 'on the pop' all day. He was most upset at being stopped. I handed over the breathalyser to Spoon, and the male was tested quickly, providing a positive sample.

He was arrested and, although very close to the police station, a van was called to transport him to custody. He did have difficulty walking, after all. A police van swiftly arrived and the male was carefully placed in the rear, to be taken to custody.

Spoon and another colleague were now standing on the dual carriageway outside the magistrates' courts, looking at this mobility scooter. It was too heavy to lift in the van and was a danger to other traffic, obstructing the highway. It seemed a bit like overkill, asking the control room to send out a recovery lorry from the local garage.

Ever resourceful, Spoon suggested he drive it the short distance back to the nick, which was clearly in sight at the end of the road. He planned to go via the subway, to avoid driving on the road then into the police station car park and the security of the back yard. This seemed like a good idea. I mean, what could possibly go wrong?

In full uniform, wearing his helmet, Spoon sat on the mobility scooter and set off, very slowly, in the latest of the force's fleet of vehicles. This was much to our amusement as we saw him head to the entrance of the concrete subway footpath.

Mobility scooters have a limit of 4 mph on pavements and travel at about 8-12 mph on roads. I think Spoon had secretly wanted to take the scooter for a ride and had a big smile on his face. However, that smile changed to a look of sheer panic once the scooter had entered the down ramp of the subway. The vehicle started to move quickly, doubling or tripling its original speed. Spoon shouted out, 'How the fuck do you stop it?'

The police helmet saved Spoon. The disability scooter crashed head on into the right-angled wall at the bottom of the subway ramp with an almighty metallic crunching sound.

I was paralysed with laughter at the sight, not able to run forward and assist my colleague, just temporarily frozen with mirth.

We did manage to reach him, but there was bad news. Spoon was OK, but the mobility scooter was not. Parts had fallen off and the front was all smashed in. The vehicle would not move backwards or forwards.

The police have strict guidelines and procedures when an accident occurs and an officer is driving a vehicle. It's called a PVI (Police Vehicle Incident) and requires the officer involved to call for the duty sergeant to attend the scene and investigate.

Although this did not involve a police car it was technically a PVI and so Spoon had to make the 'call of shame' to the control room, requiring the duty sergeant to attend the scene. Another member of the shift was allocated to deal with his drink-driving prisoner!

At a later date, the male was prosecuted and found guilty of being over the limit. I'm not sure what happened to the scooter afterwards.

This incident didn't deter Spoon, who went on to fulfil his burning ambition, becoming a traffic officer.

Yes, that's right, an advanced driving expert in the most powerful vehicles operated by the force. From 4mph to well over the ton!

You haven't heard the last of PC Spoon.

Sometimes you wear many hats as a police officer: crimefighter, first aider, social worker, counsellor, plus many more

On this occasion, the city council's CCTV operator called up on the radio, having spotted an elderly woman lying on the ground in Commercial Road, the main pedestrianised shopping street in Portsmouth.

As it was the middle of the day, the street was busy with shoppers who had started to crowd around her. We feared the worst, that the woman might have had a heart attack, so all free officers from the shift raced to the scene. The lady was lying close to the entrance to the Cascades shopping centre. An ambulance had also been called, but would be about 10 minutes; every second counted.

PC Spoon and another officer jumped into the area car and I drove with blue lights and two tones the short distance from the nick to the collapsed woman, parting the traffic as cars pulled over, like Moses and the Red Sea.

I parked up and we dashed over to where she was lying. The woman was elderly and appeared to have been out shopping. Two carrier bags of shopping lay beside her. Officers collected up the spilt items of fruit and veg while I spoke to the lady.

She was, in fact conscious, and very 'with it'. She explained that she had stumbled and tripped, falling over and spilling her shopping. She was more embarrassed by all the commotion than anything else.

She was wearing a large coat, cardigan and knee-length skirt. I could see one of her knees had a nasty cut from the fall and was bleeding down her leg. I had a small first aid kit on my utility belt containing a few latex gloves and bandages, so I was able to patch her up quickly. The finest paramedics from South Central Ambulance service arrived shortly after I had applied the dressing.

As we went to leave, I updated the police control room on my radio. 'Kilo Charlie Five Two, we are resuming from Commercial Road. The woman was being taken to QA Hospital, as she had a very nasty gash that was bleeding. Yes, a nasty gash.'

Spoon and some of the other officers immediately burst out laughing at my em…er…description of the wound, and could not stop as we walked back to the car. What a load of juveniles!

Stakeouts in the dead of night

The smell was overwhelming. An aged blend of nylon and wool with the faintest whisper of mothballs. I was face down on the floor, chest pressed into decades-old carpet, in what I considered a commando pose. In truth, it was less Royal Marines and more ungainly slug, inching forward with the grace of a wardrobe. I was lying in the dark, with my head hovering inches from carpet fibres that had absorbed a lifetime of hoovered-in dust. It was the middle of the night, and I was on a stakeout!

I glanced out at the street, then back to my radio, then back again, like an anxious meerkat. This was the '90s, when certain crimes were very much in fashion. Car crime had become a volume crime In other words, loads of it was happening! Theft from motor vehicles was routine. TWOC (taken without consent) was practically a rite of passage for most tearaway teenagers growing up then.

Car security still had a long way to go, and the thieves neatly split themselves into two camps. Young thrill-seekers who fancied themselves as rally drivers, tearing around the streets on the unofficial 'Council Estate Touring Car' circuit. Then there were the drug addicts, who specialised in harvesting the bounty from glove compartments and parcel shelves. Car stereos, TomTom sat-navs, sunglasses, loose change and anything not bolted down would be stolen.

Many insurance claims would solemnly note the loss of a leather jacket from the back seat. Personally, I never recovered one when arresting many suspects over the years for theft from motor vehicles. I suspect there were fewer leather jackets sacrificed to crime than there were optimistic insurance forms filed.

Then came the ram-raids. Management in the police at Pompey, to their credit, let us off the leash a bit. Proactivity was the buzzword. We'd scour the duty state, a solid ring binder of recent crimes, trying to decipher the next probable hit. Patterns emerged, as vehicles stolen with towbars on the rear were perfect for smash-and-grabs on commercial premises. Offenders would reverse at speed into the shop front. The towbar punched straight through glass, then they grabbed what they could, and were gone in 60 seconds. Once we clocked these crime patterns, we tailored our patrols, watching for those vehicles and their likely haunts, hoping to catch someone mid-burglary…also hoping they wouldn't reverse into us!

Palmerston Road in Southsea became a recurring location. A busy daytime pedestrianised shopping precinct. I noted over the period of about six weeks a string of night-time break-ins. Mostly occurring between 3 to 4am in the morning, that lull when the city goes quiet and most people are in the land of nod. It's an ideal hour for a burglar. No dog walkers or nosey neighbours; only urban foxes and villains prowled the streets with bad ideas at that time of night. According to my calculations, we were due another burglary, hence I had organised the stakeout.

The plan was simple. I would watch Palmerston Road from above, and the area car drivers and the rest of the shift would stay clear unless I called them in. Portsmouth Central and Southsea were briefed. The control room was notified. A detective inspector gave the nod. I spoke to the security team at Knight & Lee, a large department store that has since closed down, who'd suffered their share of smash-and-grabs, and I secured permission to use their store as an 'OP' or Observation Point. I arrived at 10pm at the start of my night turn. A security officer let me in, pointed out the toilets – always important to know, and escorted me up to the first floor.

The display windows were enormous, dressed with mannequins staring blankly down at the precinct below. Between the mannequins were neatly arranged products: handbags, shoes, bits of domestic aspiration posing under gentle lighting that had been switched off. I found a central spot where I could see the whole length of the pedestrianised street. The security guard bid me farewell, running through the instructions for locking up and escaping without setting off every alarm in the store.

I'd come prepared, dressed in black civilian clothing. No uniform tonight. If I'd stood near the window, my height would have turned me into a human exclamation mark among the mannequins, so I opted for a commando crawl position on the floor, as my eyes adjusted to the darkness in the store. I had a small plastic box of sandwiches and a single chocolate biscuit saved for the witching hour. My tartan thermos flask, with a plastic cup screwed onto the top, was filled with hot tea that could scald a confession out of anyone. I'd need it to keep me awake, I thought. This was my second night on this stakeout, having spent the previous one watching the street go about its business with little drama all night.

I kept a notebook, jotting down times, movements, anything vaguely suspicious. Experience taught me that, what seems irrelevant at midnight, can be the linchpin when a crime occurs and you are standing in court faced with a defence barrister. Mostly, the street offered me a view of students drifting home, shoelaces undone, laughter trailing behind them. Mainly, it was revellers walking back from the pubs, the occasional heated argument between a boyfriend and girlfriend, but nothing that would warrant calling a police unit to intervene. A homeless man appeared, pushing a small shopping trolley with his worldly goods, moving at the pace of someone with nowhere to be. He stopped at each bin, rummaging through pizza boxes, searching out the discarded remains of someone else's feast. I felt for him, and was quietly grateful it was summer and not an icy February with the fierce wind cutting him in two.

Shortly after midnight, my enthusiasm began to fray. The carpet dust had started introducing itself personally to my nostrils, and the fibres were beginning to pierce my exposed hands and through the material of my jeans into my knees. My gaze flicked left, right, left again, desperately trying to keep a sharp edge to my focus as the hours blended together. I found myself glancing at the police radio more and more, listening to the fast, exciting calls for the rest of the shift, all blue lights and breathless updates. Meanwhile I lay among mannequins and mothballs, waiting for someone to break into a shop.

Palmerston Road was its own stage that night. The streetlights hummed quietly, casting pools of amber that made the paving look like warm honey. Far off, a fox skipped along the kerb, stopping to sniff at something best not described. A taxi rolled through, down Osborne road, headlights sweeping the shopfronts in a slow crescendo, and faded away. With the windows between me and the world, the city seemed strangely muted, as if someone had turned the volume down on life. I poured a little tea and watched steam curl into the darkness. It tasted good. Tea was an important ingredient in the fight against crime.

There's a peculiar intimacy to stakeouts. You become intimately familiar with the geography of a place. Which bin gets the most traffic, which door lights come on when someone passes, which delivery van appears like clockwork even when the rest of the town is asleep. You learn the timings of the night, when the pubs are closed, when arguments migrate to the taxi rank, when the drunk bravado fades away and people head home. And you wait. Waiting is the real graft. It's easy to think that police work is a sprint to the dramatic moment, but it's miles of quietly paced endurance punctuated by a few seconds of frantic action.

At around 2am, the mannequins began to take on personalities. One, in a silk blouse, looked permanently shocked, as if she'd seen the price of the very blouse she was wearing. Another, a chap in chinos, had the air of a man for whom everything is a life hack. I entertained myself by giving them names and backstories which, I'll admit, is not standard police procedure. "Sandra" fancied herself as a leader among the window people. 'Clive' had questionable taste in leather shoes. This is what happens when you are alone with your own thoughts and a tartan flask.

3am approached, and the city settled into itself. The homeless man reappeared, paused, considered the world through the slant of the sodium light, and rolled on. I jotted the time, the direction, the trolley contents, two bags, a blanket, a mystery box with tape around it. My eyes never stopped moving. Left, right, down the length of the street, up again. Somewhere behind me, the air-conditioning sighed. The carpet gave off its persistent museum smell. And then, as often happens, nothing happened.

I lay there among the plastic people, practising stillness, on guard for a crash of glass that had not come.

Drastic measures were required. I grabbed my chocolate biscuit and began to unwrap it. The sandwich that I'd been treating like a sacred relic had long ago been devoured as I passed the time while watching out of the window.

I raised the chocolate biscuit to my mouth just as something moved in the street below. A male on a pushbike. He stopped at the end of the precinct, looked down the street, then left and right. It was 2:45am in the morning, the hour when the city is quiet enough to hear your own heartbeat and the occasional fox screaming.

Jeans, black top, white Reebok Classic trainers. He was familiar. I then recognised him. We'll call him David. David was a well-known burglar and general villain in the city. Our paths had crossed on many occasions while on duty. I didn't know if this was going to be 'it', but I felt hopeful in that way you do, when your gut knows something your brain hasn't caught up with.

David paused at the pedestrianised part, then cycled towards Osborne Road. He stopped again. Glanced left and right. I picked up my binoculars and tried not to knock my tea onto the floor. It was definitely him, and I felt the thrill start to rise in my chest. Slowly, carefully, I reached for the police radio. "Stand by, stand by," I whispered into the handset, and gave a neat description of David and his pushbike. I asked for units to make a silent approach, to box him in, if he decided to commit a crime. The worst sound in the world to a burglar at three in the morning is a speeding car, or a siren and a loud police radio squawking.

David cycled back to where I'd first seen him, got off his bike, and placed it casually to one side. He didn't look up, as he knew about the council's CCTV cameras. The operators had heard my radio messages and were already tracking, adjusting the angles, but using cameras mounted much further away, staying discreet at a distance to catch on camera whatever was coming. David knelt down, as if to tie a shoelace. Then, like a magician producing a rabbit, he pulled a small tool from his pocket and started working at the manhole cover set into the street. Both hands now under the heavy steel disk, and with a grunt you could practically hear from up where I was, he lifted the cover and carried it towards a shop.

'Stand by, stand by,' I said into the radio again, keeping my voice as steady as I could. "Suspect has removed a manhole cover." I watched as David swung it behind him, set his feet, and hurled the thing like a giant discus. It went through the plate glass shopfront with a crashing noise and all the drama of the start of a James Bond film. Designer clothes behind, glinting under fluorescent light, were suddenly available to the enterprising thief.

He stepped forward, kicked the remaining shards inwards so they wouldn't fall on him, and entered with a confident swagger. That was my signal.

'Strike, strike, strike. Burglary in progress,' I called out on the radio. The alarm began to scream, slicing the night and breaking the silence, joined by a strobing flash from the alarm box. I lay there, heart in mouth, scribbling notes like a frantic court stenographer with a caffeine problem, trusting my colleagues to make the final act.

Within twenty or thirty seconds, the area cars came in hot, blocking both ends of Palmerston Road. The driver and passenger of the nearest unit leapt out and went straight through the broken window after him. I watched David, now draped in reams of clothing and clutching a large bag he'd conjured from somewhere, only to find himself suddenly reintroduced to the laws of gravity. The officers grabbed him, pulled him down to the floor and cuffed him. Caught red-handed didn't begin to cover it. He looked like a walking display rail!

He was probably glad to have been arrested by the area car team, as the 'Land Shark' had also arrived quickly on scene and was now out on the pavement. Officers used this nickname for the police Alsatian dogs. General purpose police dogs that would bite anything (including cops) if given half a chance. Luckily for David, this Land Shark was firmly attached to a lead, as it barked and snarled at the offender.

The management of the shop, Knight & Lee, were delighted and beside themselves with relief when they heard the news the following day. It's funny, you can only prove one burglary on a lad and people think it's nothing, yet when David pleaded guilty to this burglary and went off to prison, the whole series stopped dead. Cause, meet effect.

I'd started thinking stakeouts were boring after a couple of nights. Turned out they were actually an excellent way to experience adrenaline and existential satisfaction at the same time.

On another occasion, my 'stakeout skills' were requested this time by the sergeant. This was not one of my own jobs, just a straightforward, 'Richard, I need you to man an OP tonight.'

He said it after the night shift briefing with all the casual authority of someone asking you to hold their pint. 'You're going to be inside a bank.' I raised an eyebrow. I'm just a lad from Rochdale, and you're trusting me with a bank? was the thought rattling around in my skull.

The bank, situated on Commercial Road, had kindly agreed to let us use their premises. We'd had a run of smash-and-grabs, many targeting Allders, an independent department store at the corner of Arundel Street and Commercial Road. It was suspected there would be another burglary and we wanted to be ready for them. I was shown how to get in and disarm the alarm for part of the bank I'd be using. Not the vault of course, but another first-floor room, tucked away with a decent view of the pedestrianised street below near the fountain. Less mannequin theatre this time, more mortgage posters and jaunty leaflets about loans for cars. Inspirational, but in a different way.

I set up the room with my same ritual of sandwiches, hot drink, notebook and binoculars. This time I recruited a comfy office chair, adjusted to a height where I could see out of the window, without looking like a silhouette in a thriller film. I positioned myself well back in the room, blending into the shadows. Anyone glancing up would see a quiet window and maybe a plant, not me watching the world tick by.

On this occasion, it didn't take long. Two unknown males approached Allders and each lobbed a brick at the large glass pane set into the door. It was simple, but they were quick, brutal and efficient. The window gave in with a further kick by one of the suspects, and they slipped inside through the jagged teeth of broken glass.

I called it in, another 'Strike' request, and the mobile units did the rest. Blue lights strobing, officers piling in through the door almost as soon as the glass settled. The offenders took one look at the scene unfolding and handed themselves in. They did not have time to leave the store and didn't even have the courtesy to feign a chase. Well, there was a small 'Benny Hill' style chase in the store when uniformed police entered, but the offenders quickly realised they were well and truly captured. It was a right result, and it felt like we were finally getting on top of commercial burglaries in the city.

The Murder of Brian Kitching

Some nights, you just knew. You could feel it in the air, a certain electricity that promised a long shift ahead. September 2005 was serving up one of those evenings in Portsmouth. The police radio, our constant, crackling companion, was having a particularly busy time of it. As the acting sergeant I was not out on patrol, but firmly planted back at Portsmouth Central, orchestrating the chaos from afar while every available unit was out chasing its tail across the city.

Then, another call came through. An assault at the Rock Gardens. On the face of it, this was another run of the mill call. The first officers on the scene updated the control room and painted a familiar picture. A man had been punched, a bottle had been smashed over a car, and a group of four youths were suspects. It sounded like a classic case of teenagers, full of cheap cider and bravado, trying to earn their first ASBO. An Anti-Social Behaviour Order was all the rage back then, a sort of unofficial government loyalty card for troublemakers, that local tearaways would wear, like a badge of honour.

But this wasn't that. Not even close. The details that followed began to change the mood to something more sinister. The youths, it transpired, had been drinking heavily and had been taking drugs.

Their next victim on the seafront was a man named Brian Kitching, a 68 year old local chap. This assault wasn't just a minor scuffle. It was a severe, sustained attack that left him with a traumatic brain injury. The group, two lads and two girls, were seen to walk over the pebble beach towards the sea. They then tried to wash his blood from their clothes in the sea afterwards. It was a desperate, foolish attempt to erase what they'd done, but a number of onlookers had already clocked them.

The initial attending officers, working from descriptions given by witnesses, managed to collar two of the suspects nearby. A 27-year old man, of no fixed abode named Paul, and a 19 year old local man called Lewis. They were arrested and brought into Portsmouth Central Bridewell, and the investigation was handed over to CID. The two female suspects, a 20-year-old called Amie and a 17-year-old, Melissa, had vanished into the night.

Back at the station, the custody block was heaving. A queue of the night's clientele snaked into the backyard, each of the many prisoners waiting in the back of police cars or vans for their turn to be booked in. I was standing out on the backdoor step overlooking the rear yard, chatting with a few of my shift. I was enjoying a rare breath of non-custody-suite air, when a ruckus started up at the entrance to the backyard. Two girls, drunk and belligerent, were staggering about, shouting the odds at the waiting police officers. They were complaining their boyfriends had been 'nicked', and they shouted at us to release the boys immediately. It was a performance worthy of the stage, though perhaps not the West End.

A thought sparked. I got on the radio to the control room. 'Can you give us the descriptions of the two outstanding female suspects for that GBH at the Rock Gardens?' I asked, trying to keep the excitement out of my voice. The descriptions came back. They were a perfect match. I gave a subtle nod to the officers standing with me. It's not often your suspects deliver themselves directly to your door, gift wrapped in righteous indignation and cheap booze. They were promptly arrested, ready to join their partners in crime in the cells and explain their part in the evening's tragic events.

The full story that emerged was sickening. Amie, entirely unprovoked, had screamed 'Dirty paedophile' at Mr Kitching before punching him. There was not a shred of evidence to support her claim. He was simply a man, out for a walk on his own down the seafront, who had the profound misfortune of crossing their path.

Brian Kitching never recovered. The attack had left him with a fractured eye socket, a punctured lung and fractured ribs, but it was the brain damage that proved fatal. It robbed him of the ability to even cough. Six months later, in March 2006, he died in a nursing home, having suffocated. It's a truly horrific way to leave this world.

All four were charged with murder. Lewis pleaded guilty, but the other three denied it all, forcing a trial. In May 2007, a jury took just nine hours to find them guilty. The judge, Justice Dobbs, didn't mince her words.

'*Mr Kitching was subject to an unprovoked and brutal attack,*' she said, describing it as a sustained assault by drunken youths on a defenceless man. She noted that Mr Kitching had been curled on the ground, trying to protect his head, while they continued attacking him. '*Nobody did anything to help Mr Kitching when it was obvious he was in a bad way.*'

They were all jailed for life. Another tragic, senseless act. As for the perpetrators? They were just youths. Young, stupid, and now, murderers. It was a stark reminder that some nights, what starts as a run-of-the-mill job, can end in utter devastation.

A hands-on job at Grandma's

One of the best things about being a police officer is the fact that you have no idea what you will be attending next. Every job is different.

One morning I was on independent patrol, driving a Ford Fiesta panda car. I had a call from the control room to say there was a concern for welfare being reported by a grandmother. Her grandson in the Somerstown area had locked himself in in the bathroom.

I drove into Omega Street and onto Omega house, which was relatively close to the nick. The building was a 1960s style block of council flats. I had no idea what to expect. Could it be a domestic argument or a medical emergency? I just didn't know yet. I approached with an open mind.

Having knocked on the door, a concerned grandmother opened it and appeared particularly upset. She explained that her grandson had gone into the bathroom for a bath. He had locked the door and started to run the bath water, but the tub was still filling up an hour later.

She had knocked on the door frantically but was unable to get a response. She was obviously very concerned that something had happened to him. A number of scenarios were running through my head. He may have collapsed, had a medical emergency or committed suicide.

Outside the bathroom door, I looked down at the floor to see if it was wet. Everything appeared to be dry. I knocked loudly, saying I was a police officer. 'Are you OK in there?'

No response. The water was still running, quite loudly. I asked the grandmother to step back, as I had decided I needed to force the door open. A swift boot to the door, near the handle from my size 14 Doc Martens boots, caused the flimsy lock on the interior of the door to splinter and crack.

The grandmother was eager to get past me to check on her grandson. I explained it would be best if she waited in the living room, as I feared the worst. I slowly pushed the door open enough to be able to poke my head through the gap.

To be honest, it wasn't quite what I had expected. On the floor was a naked torso of the grandson lying motionless. This, I had somewhat expected; the rest of the scene I had not.
The whole floor was covered with pornographic magazines. Each one was opened to show a picture of a naked lady in an intimate pose. The side panel of the bath had been removed and was ajar. I suspect that this was the place where he kept his stash of pornographic mags, squirrelled away, out of sight of his grandmother.

The bath was running, but the plug was not inserted, so the water was going straight down the plughole. I slipped into the room via the gap in the door and was able to shake the grandson's shoulder to see if he was responsive. To my relief, his skin felt warm and very much alive.

The grandson was probably about 20 years old. Motionless, he was still clutching his meat and two veg in one hand. I could hear the voice of the grandmother behind us, asking, 'Will he be OK, constable?'

The dilemma I had in that split second was, should I tell her the truth?

I explained that we just needed to give him some room and he would be fine. I missed out the other details to save everyone's embarrassment. The grandson started to come round. He looked up, saw a policeman standing over him, and appeared really embarrassed. I threw him a towel, which was hanging on the side, and suggested that he get himself dressed and clean up the bathroom.

Once decent, the grandson joined us in the living room. I asked him if he was all right and what had happened.

'I just passed out in the bathroom,' he said meekly. 'That's all there was to it.'

What else was he going to say in front of his grandmother? I confirmed that he hadn't been injured with me kicking the door in. He said he was going to put the incident down to experience.

His grandmother was particularly pleased that he was none the worse for his ordeal. I must say I did have a little chuckle to myself as I left the premises. At the end of each job, it is normal practice to provide an update and result to the control room.

I did this, saying to the effect: 'Kilo Charlie Seven Five to Control. I just want to give a result to that last job I've been to. The male appears to have masturbated himself unconscious, but is now back in the land of the living. No need for an ambulance.'

A stifled laugh came back from the control room. I assumed that bathtime at grandma's would be a much quieter, straightforward affair in future.

It wasn't long before I was back in Somerstown…

More serious domestic incidents are, quite frankly, a bread-and-butter job of the police service nowadays. Back in the '90s, following lots of research and with the help of academia that looked at domestic murders, it was decided the police needed a more robust approach when it came to domestic incidents. Previously, officers may have been sent to a report of a 'domestic' to see if there was a 'breach of the peace'. If everything was quiet and no obvious offenses had been committed, the police would then carry on to the next incident.

To be fair, it didn't take a rocket scientist to work out that many vulnerable partners (men and women, although mainly women) were being left vulnerable and at extreme risk by this approach. Many ended up being injured or murdered at the hands of their abuser. So, quite rightly, the approach changed as to how domestic incidents were policed. In simple terms, if it was felt there was a risk of violence or an assault may have taken place, or possibly further issues, at least one of the parties would be arrested or removed from the address.

On a September afternoon in 2001, I was at a 'domestic' on my own, single-crewed. We often didn't have enough staff to double-crew every vehicle, but I wasn't too bothered. Yes, it made the job more hazardous, but I enjoyed working independently and it meant I would be getting any arrest, and not my crewmate!

I arrived at Tipton House, Warwick Crescent in Somerstown. Another council block of flats that towered 18 floors above Portsmouth. I pressed the lift button on the ground floor.

As I waited I smiled, thinking about the time I had been dealing with a sudden death at the same block of flats. I had helped the undertakers remove the body that had been placed in a black 'body bag' on a metal stretcher. There had been nothing suspicious about the death; it just had not been expected. After all the necessary procedures and paperwork had been completed, the body was placed upright in the centre of the lift to get the deceased downstairs to the undertaker's van. The two undertakers stood either side at the back, holding the deceased upright, still strapped to the metal stretcher.

I was standing by the lift doors, and as the lift went down it unfortunately kept stopping at various floors as residents tried to enter the lift. I held up my hand, gesturing, 'Best you wait for the next lift.'

You can imagine the reaction of the people, reeling at the sight of a dead person standing behind me. It looked like a scene from a horror movie. They stepped back, totally confused as the lift carried on its journey downwards!

On this occasion the lift was out of order…again! I failed to enjoy the smell of stale urine and cigarettes that filled my nostrils as I walked up the staircase. Luckily, I only had to reach about the 10th floor on this occasion.

On arrival at the flat, I could hear shouting and figured that my arrest count might be about to climb even higher. I knocked on the door and was invited in by one of the occupants.

A male and female in their 30s were shouting at each other. It was the usual swearing and nasty aggressive behaviour, but both parties seemed to be giving as good as they got. I stood between them to separate the pair and prevent any assault taking place.

The living room had a tiled floor that was chipped and dirty, with empty beer cans on a filthy, scratched wooden coffee table in the centre of the room. Blue cigarette smoke hung heavily in the air and an overflowing ashtray had a roll-up perched on the side, smoking away.

The brown sofa on one side was threadbare with a discarded copy of 'The Portsmouth News' strewn over it, and pages falling out. I was happy to keep them in the living room and out of any kitchen, as it's always a bad idea to introduce knives into a domestic argument! I was having difficulty in calming both sides down.

I can't even recall what the argument was about but, as I tried to piece together each side's grievances and record the details in my pocket notebook, something caught my eye. To be fair, it wasn't hard to miss: a large plasma TV. Not that my wages would stretch to purchase such an expensive piece of electrical equipment. I had somewhat become used to entering flats and houses where the occupiers had no job and were supported by benefits, but could still afford such luxuries.

On this occasion it wasn't the actual TV that I noticed, but what was on it that had caught my attention. At first I thought I was looking at a film, but the sequence of images and video continued to repeat and it became obvious this was a breaking news story. As I stood in a tower block dealing with this domestic incident, I watched in amazement as I witnessed a large passenger plane crashing into the side of a large tower block. I recognised the World Trade Centre, one of the Twin Towers. The same Twin Towers I'd stood on top of 11 years beforehand.

I told the couple to 'shut up'. I told the man to find the remote control so we could adjust the volume and listen to the news report. The September 11 attacks, now commonly known as 9/11, were four coordinated Islamist terrorist suicide attacks by al-Qaeda against the United States. Terrorists had hijacked four commercial airliners, crashing the first two into the Twin Towers of the World Trade Center in New York City and the third into the Pentagon building, Virginia. The fourth plane crashed in a rural Pennsylvania field following a passenger revolt. The attacks killed 2,977 people, making it the deadliest terrorist attack in history.

It was a sobering experience, and the living room fell silent apart from the sound of the news reporter detailing what was known at that time. The couple had stopped arguing. What we were witnessing put everything into perspective. What had seemed so important to the couple 20 minutes earlier had now paled into insignificance.

I left with the male, who agreed to go as everything had calmed down. No evidence of any assaults had taken place with no other offences disclosed. He said he would stay with a mate for the night. I warned him that he would be arrested if he returned later that day.

I returned to the nick, to find the SDO (Station Duty Officer), who was a lovely civilian lady called Roz, watching events unfold on a small 12" telly in the front office.

'Have you seen the news, Foz?'

I nodded. I could now see from the coverage on the small screen that both towers had collapsed and my mind was drifting to all the occupants and emergency workers who must have perished.

Everyone at work, from officers to offenders, appeared to be 'paused' for the rest of that duty, as we took in the magnitude of global events.

It's one of those occasions where you remember where you were and what you were doing. How extraordinary that I witnessed the events in that flat in the middle of a domestic incident, when everyone seemed to bond in watching the tragic events unfold.

My own beat

I had a look around the nick at the beat officers. Many of them appeared to be old lags who were seeing out their last days before retirement. They had no enthusiasm or get up and go; these weren't the 'thief takers' that I was aspiring to become. I had been on leave for two weeks. On my return, the Inspector had told me I was now a 'Beat Officer' with my own patch to patrol….on foot. It was a disciplined service and, quite frankly, I couldn't say 'no' to my job as a beat officer.

I would now be known as Kilo Charlie One Alpha, my call sign as a beat officer for the area covering Portsea and Old Portsmouth.

These areas were totally different. Portsea was mainly a mix of Her Majesty's Naval Base, the tourist attractions at the dockyard, The Hard Interchange with the train station and the Isle of Wight ferries, and a large council estate. This was a relatively deprived mix of housing, suffering from a lack of resources and infrastructure.

The people on the estate lived in maisonette buildings and a couple of large tower blocks, plus terraced housing, all controlled by the council or housing associations. To many officers, this was known as 'bandit country'.

There was a fierce community spirit in Portsea which you don't see so much nowadays. I kind of liked that; there was a siege mentality, but a large percentage were nice members of the public, just trying to get by on the little money they had. They were often in low-paid jobs, trying to earn an honest crust.

Unfortunately, a small percentage of people on that estate were career criminals; many generations of the same family followed that path. It was an area plagued with drug dealing and, in particular, car crime.

Many thefts from vehicles occurred in Portsea, often with tourists turning up at the historic dockyard. There were camper vans with foreign number plates. Locals knew there would be rich pickings from a variety of vehicles parked in the side streets.

We would often walk around, advising people not to park in certain areas, or at least to leave their vehicles in secure car parks. These warnings often went unheeded. It was easy for the kids to spot the cars pulling up, knowing they had a number of hours to steal as much as they could.

They would often use a life hammer, used for breaking windows in an emergency, to get inside the vehicle. The youths would quickly dive inside, pulling out cases and dragging them away. If they were lucky, they could steal some cash or small electrical items such as CD and Sony Walkman music players. On occasion items such as passports would go missing, causing all sorts of problems for those victims of crime.

I quickly identified the MO of these people committing the thefts. I could see that, whenever a search was carried out, many of the cases and property from the thefts were found in large stainless steel industrial wheelie bins in bin stores. These were near the communal areas of the blocks of flats. Everything could be hidden from view while the thieves rummaged through the cases, identified items of value and dumped the rest inside the bins.

This led to a change in our tactics. When we had reports of a car being broken into, we didn't go straight to the vehicle. We would head for the communal bin areas where we would often catch the offenders red-handed, going through their booty. In Portsea, many people were distrusting and looked upon you with suspicion.

My other area was Old Portsmouth. This was a beautiful gentrified area with some of the most expensive housing stock in the city, overlooking the waterfront. I remember lovely historic pubs and a large grammar school. What a change in fortunes for the area. Back in Nelson's Day, the streets of Old Portsmouth were full of drunks and prostitutes. In those days, this was the worst area in the city for crime.

There were issues with the two neighbourhoods being so close together. Criminals would cross into Old Portsmouth for rich pickings from burglaries and car crime.

I decided to take on the role of beat officer with gusto, getting things done and making the most of it. If I was going to do this job, it would be on my terms. I went about trying to improve community relations by visiting local shopkeepers, Salvation Army, military establishments, housing associations, schools, pubs, churches and the main transport hub.

I made myself known, explaining that I was trying to improve the lives of the locals. To be fair, I was welcomed with open arms by most of those people. Nowhere, as far as I was concerned, was a no-go area.

A rite of passage for many new officers was passing a cycling proficiency test in the police station back yard, so they could be authorised to use a pedal cycle on patrol. I'm not talking about mountain bikes with officers wearing all the tactical gear, official helmets, special cycling trousers and all that. This cycling proficiency test was, of course not actually required and was just a wind-up for new recruits. Officers would be asked to cycle around *no waiting* cones, cycle one handed or even attempt to cross a small makeshift wooden seesaw! This was done much to the amusement of other officers watching on from the first-floor windows.

The station bike was known as an 'old tredder'. This steel Apollo or Raleigh pedal cycle carried officers in full uniform and custodian helmet with some bicycle clips for your trousers legs. I did my best to avoid going on patrol on two wheels.

I must point out that many police officers might refer to the 'station bike' as something else, but that's another story altogether!

A drugs bust that almost backfired!

I've always had a great interest in fighting against the drugs culture. From watching episodes of *Miami Vice* and other American cop shows, this stirred excitement in me.

One of the great things about being a beat man, walking your own small area of the city, was that you had time and opportunity to speak with locals.

A regular friendly face visiting and taking an interest meant that a lot of people would, intentionally or inadvertently, provide you with excellent intelligence as to what was going on in the local area concerning criminal activity.

Any intelligence you gathered would be submitted into the main intelligence system. Back in the '90s it was all done on paper on a form called C67. This pink-coloured paper was vital for intelligence-led policing to be successful and would be classified and documented by the local intelligence officers (LIO), who were also known as 'collators'.

These god-like officers had a memory that would put people appearing on Mastermind to shame. They had a great memory for faces, names, MOs and everything else. If you ever wanted to know what was going on in your local area or who was doing what, you would speak with the LIO.

Those intelligence forms were a good indicator of a productive, proactive, busy officer soaking up intelligence and information. From those small pieces of info, often large investigations could be solved.

I was tipped off about a criminal who was cultivating cannabis and had a large and successful cultivation in a residential property down in Portsea. It was really good intelligence and I spoke with the drugs intelligence officer, as well as the LIO, to find out as much corroborating information as I could about the suspect.

It was all looking good. A male in his 20s was well known in the local area and had a long criminal record including drugs warning markers.

This was my opportunity to put together a 'drugs bust' on my patch! So following my intelligence gathering phase I spoke with the detective inspector from CID, who agreed I should go ahead and prepare a search warrant.

I gathered some local officers who would be free in a couple of days to assist in the execution of the warrant. I attended the magistrates' court and swore out a warrant in front of them, filling out all the various forms required and showing what intelligence had been considered.

I also had to show my considerations for risk, not only to the officers entering the premises, but the occupants of the flat involved and surrounding neighbours. I had to consider the possibility of children and pets in the building and the impact caused by the execution of any warrant.

The magistrate seemed very approving and authorised the warrant for the day I had chosen to work with the other officers.

I went back to the nick and created a briefing. You've always got to think about health and safety in this job! We would, after all, be using the 'big red key'…the large heavy metal battering ram. We would have to make sure we had an exhibits officer to document any items found, and that I had a plan for how we would search each room. I needed details of occupants as well as any potential hazards and warning markers concerning individuals.

There are a number of ways to smash the door open. Police want to gain entry quickly to avoid suspects flushing drugs and other incriminating evidence down the toilet.

Stealth and speed are definitely your friends on these kinds of jobs. Doors can be just kicked in with a pair of size 14 boots, but if it's a pre-planned operation you would normally use some kind of hydraulic tool, or the big red key, to break the door frame. You also need to know if the door opens inwards or outwards.

So, being keen as mustard, I went down to the address to do a physical recce (reconnaissance), so I could check out the lay of the land. We didn't want to get caught out by any surprises on the day of the warrant!

I walked down to the address, looking as if I was on normal beat duty. It was a council block of flats in a maisonette style. I pressed the 'trades' button on the stainless-steel intercom entrance system. The external door buzzed and I pushed it open.

I quietly tiptoed up the tiled staircase to the first floor. The floor had approximately four or five flats on that level. I checked the flat in question and could see the door opened inwards. I lightly pressed against the door to see if there were any extra locks or deadbolts behind it that could slow us down. The wooden door gave a little bit towards the top and bottom, suggesting there was just the one lock. Bingo! The trap was set and the following day would be D-Day.

I continued my duty for the day. When I returned to the nick I finalised plans, ready for the briefing the following day. I went home excited, keen to get an early night.

My alarm clock sounded at 4:00 in the morning. I jumped out of bed, showered, put on my uniform and set off to work. It was too early to eat and I would grab a cup of tea at the police station.

I glanced up at the clock in the parade room which showed 04.55 hours. There was a quiet buzz of anticipation from the six local police officers who had joined me nice and early for the briefing.

I went through all my briefing notes and addressed the room, delegating tasks and roles to various officers, providing updated intelligence about the suspect and what our methods of entry would be. Everybody knew what their role was.

We jumped into a large Mercedes Sprinter police van and drove down to the premises, parking nearby. The time was now 05.45 hours, and we walked the last 300 metres quietly, so as not to wake the suspects.

I pressed the trades button on the external door and the door buzzed. We tiptoed up the stairs, carrying all of our equipment in large holdalls. We stood to the side of the door. We were concerned that, if the suspect was looking through the spy hole, he might see police activity in the hall and dispose of evidence.

Using hand signals, I instructed the door entry officer to force entry. This officer was dressed in dark blue overalls, wearing a NATO riot helmet with the visor down, large gauntlet gloves and plastic protective knee and elbow pads. He swung back the 'big red key' and, using his whole bodyweight, smashed the battering ram into the door just next to the handle.

The silence was broken in spectacular fashion! The front door of the flat slammed open, splintering the wood around the lock. The door bounced back slightly on the hinges with the force that had been used. The door entry officer stepped back to allow everybody else to rush into the flat, securing each of the rooms.

All the officers were shouting at the tops of their voices ,'Police! Stay where you are!' The occasional cry of 'Clear!' could be heard as officers secured each room in the flat. This was a 'shock and awe' effect, to surprise and disorientate the suspect. I had the typed and signed warrant in my hand and was called into the master bedroom where the occupants were still in bed. It was normal procedure to provide a copy of the warrant to the occupant, and explain what would happen next and how the search would be conducted.

I strode confidently into the bedroom and my heart sank. I was confused as there was no sign of a suspect aged about 20 years old. Instead, an elderly man and woman were sitting upright in bed in their pyjamas and nightgown. They had more of a look of surprise than me!

I asked them for their names, as this was obviously not what I was expecting. Maybe it was the suspect's parents or grandparents? After providing a name and date of birth, it was obviously apparent that something had gone drastically wrong. The names didn't match and this couple had no knowledge of the suspect I was talking about. This never happens on *Miami Vice*, I thought to myself.

I started to double check and triple check everything with the occupants. I checked the names and the addresses on the warrant.

The elderly lady said, 'Oh I think you've got the wrong address, officer. You want Cumberland House in Cumberland Street. This is Privett House in Cumberland Street.'

How could I have been so f****** stupid. I had forced entry into the wrong address! After all, I was the beat man for the area, and should have known. In my defence, not a strong defence, the two blocks of flats looked very similar and were nearly next to each other.

Yes, I'd messed up, but I wasn't going to dwell on that. I had to rectify the situation as quickly as possible. I apologised profusely to be elderly couple who took the early morning wake-up call surprisingly well. Luckily for me, they were supportive of the police and the activity we were conducting to prevent drug supply in the local area.

I told the couple I would get the door fixed as soon as possible. They could expect to see me again after the warrant had been properly executed. They seemed happy with this.

I updated my bemused search team and we all headed on foot to the correct address, a short walk away. We arrived at the flat and forced the door again with the big red key. The door smashed open as expected; after all we were now highly experienced in breaking in doors in the local neighbourhood. The suspect was on the premises, as well as a massive cannabis crop, with a number of rooms set aside to grow the plants.

Electricity cables snaked across the floor and large lights with metal reflectors hung from the ceiling powering the 'hydroponic grow'. It turned out to be an excellent job in the end, and I arrested the suspect for cultivation of cannabis and possession with intent to supply controlled drugs. All the necessary evidence was seized and he was 'banged to rights', having been asleep at the premises.

Unbelievable that he was still there, considering the amount of noise that we were making in Portsea in the early hours.

I quickly arranged over my police radio, to get the door at the first flat repaired. I also updated the duty inspector on the day's events. Mistakes do happen and the most important thing is to fess up and admit them. No good ever comes from trying to cover something up!

The inspector was surprisingly calm about what had happened and pleased at the successful outcome of the actual search warrant.

I purchased a large bunch of flowers for the elderly couple, returned to their flat and updated them on the successful operation. They were very pleased with the flowers and the fact they were able to help the police. As you would expect, my colleague took the piss out of me for weeks after this event. I only had myself to blame.

As for the suspect, he pleaded guilty at court to cultivation of cannabis. I got there in the end!

Humour, Pranks, and the Paranormal

You learn a lot of things quickly when you join the police. The one thing they don't teach you at training school, is that a sense of humour is as important as your handcuffs. Sometimes, it's the only thing that'll get you through a shift.

While on patrol as a beat man down in Portsea, slowly walking the streets with a WPC called Louise, we ventured into one of the housing estates. I'd grown quite fond of the locals in Portsea. It was a place with a certain reputation, home to a few well-established crime families, but I always found that if you were firm but fair, especially with the kids, you got along just fine. Most of the time. On this particular day, however, the local youths were on what could only be described as a bit of a rampage. Even I, with my policy of taking no nonsense, was struggling to keep a lid on things.

Then the call came through from the control room. A report of disorder in a nearby street. We headed straight there, only to discover it was a planned ambush. The moment we turned the corner, the air filled with stones, half-bricks, and splintered bits of wood. We were properly under fire, and any one of those missiles would have caused a serious injury. We did what any sensible person would do under the circumstances. We ran.

Ducking behind a sturdy brick wall, we radioed for reinforcements. Now, I have a strong northern accent, which has been known to cause a bit of confusion south of Watford. I grabbed the radio, my voice probably a few octaves higher than usual, and explained the situation. 'We're under fire,' I yelled, 'We've gone behind a wall to take cover!'

There was a brief pause. The control room operator, clearly not sensing the panic in my voice, or perhaps just mishearing my vowels, chirped back, 'Right you are. While you're getting a Walls, could you pick me up a Cornetto?'

Walls, of course, is a brand of ice cream in the United Kingdom.

For a second, Louise and I just stared at each other, the sound of bricks thudding against our hiding place, punctuating the silence. Then we started laughing. Properly laughing, tears rolling down our faces, while still crouched and trying to avoid a hail of projectiles. The absurdity of it was just perfect. Thankfully, the incident was short-lived; the kids scarpered as soon as the first back-up unit screamed around the corner. But the image of us risking life and limb while a colleague put in an ice cream order has never left me.

When I was a young officer, you'd hear stories that bordered on urban myths - tales from the late eighties and early nineties of policing methods that would make a modern-day sergeant's hair turn white. One of my favourites was the 'scenic route' method for dealing with drunks at kicking-out time. Rather than bog everyone down with paperwork and processing a prisoner at the Bridewell, if no serious crime had been committed, officers would often scoop up the rowdiest individuals, arrest them for being drunk and disorderly, and pop them in the back of the van.

They'd then be treated to a little drive just outside the Portsmouth city limits. After a few minutes of kicking and punching the cage, the fight would usually go out of them. Once they'd calmed down, the officers would simply stop the van, open the cage, and de-arrest them. It was surprisingly effective. The long walk back into the city gave them plenty of time to sober up and reflect on their life choices. Of course, it was a practice that had to stop. Rightly so, the police have a duty of care. Abandoning a drunk person in the middle of nowhere, however therapeutic the walk might be, wasn't exactly textbook procedure.

Then there was the tale of the phantom doctor. A certain habitual drug user was getting arrested on an almost daily basis for petty thefts. He'd quickly learned that if he complained of heroin withdrawal symptoms, the police surgeon would be called. This meant a prescription for something like methadone, a legal and medically prescribed substitute for the heroin he claimed to be craving. The Bridewell staff, having had quite enough of his antics, decided it was time for a bit of amateur dramatics.

The next time he was brought in, drunk and already moaning about needing a visit from the police surgeon, a plan was hatched. An officer was dispatched to the medical room, where he donned a white doctor's coat. Looking the part, he strode down to the cell block. The detainee immediately launched into his usual performance, complaining of terrible heroin withdrawals.

Our 'doctor' gave an Oscar-winning performance of his own, conducting a very brief assessment before delivering his diagnosis. He declared the patient was simply drunk, that it was impossible for him to be suffering withdrawals in that timescale, and that under no circumstances would any drugs be administered. The detainee's face was a picture of thunderous disappointment. He accepted the verdict, and from that day forward, he never asked to see the doctor again. His rate of being arrested for petty crime also dropped off a cliff!

The nineties were a different world in other ways, too. Our wage packets were a paper affair, arriving in a long, sealed envelope. Inside, a carbonated payslip detailed your hours, earnings, and the taxman's considerable share. It didn't take long for some bright spark to discover that you could write on the outside of the sealed envelope with the back of a pen, and the pressure would leave a secret message on the carbon copy inside.

One colleague of mine had been given a rather unfortunate nickname by his teammates: 'Spunkbubble'. Every month, on the fifteenth, he'd open his payslip to find this term of endearment lovingly inscribed on his official earnings record. It was all fun and games until he and his girlfriend decided to buy a house. The bank, quite reasonably, required several months' worth of payslips to approve their mortgage. He proudly produced the documents, only for his girlfriend to see 'Spunkbubble' written across every single one. She was not amused. The banking staff, however, apparently had a hard time keeping a straight face.

But not all the strange things we encountered could be explained away by pranks or misunderstandings. One late turn, my crewmate Simon and I were on patrol in the area car, when we were called to a road traffic collision very close to the nick on Isambard Brunel Road. On arrival we got out the official accident form called a T1, a cardboard document for sketching the scene and recording driver details, witnesses and generally everything that happened. We also had one of the latest gadgets in the car boot: a Polaroid camera, for capturing immediate evidence.

We took three or four photos of the crash scene, and since they were slow to develop, we just tossed them onto the back seat of our BMW. By the time we got back to the station, the images had appeared. Three of them were perfectly normal. The fourth was not. It showed Isambard Brunel Road, clear as day, but crossing the street was a ghostly, translucent figure. It was a woman, all in white, wearing what looked like a Victorian dress. You could see straight through her to the road behind.

Simon and I were stunned. Neither of us had seen anyone like that at the scene. We'll never know if it was a bizarre fault with the instant film, a trick of the light, or something altogether spookier. All I know is that somewhere in a dusty old police file, there's a photograph of a car crash that looks for all the world like it was photobombed by a ghost!

Danger at the top of the tower

Portsmouth is understandably proud of its rich naval heritage. Portsea Island itself has a number of military establishments. When I joined the police in the 1990s walking 'Kilo Charlie One Alpha,' which was Portsea and Old Portsmouth, I would often speak with the security and Naval Provost while visiting the various military establishments.

One was called HMS Vernon, between Old Portsmouth and Portsea. It was interesting to watch the military helicopters flying in and out. Well in 1998 HMS Vernon finally closed and was being converted into a major retail, commercial and residential location on the waterfront. Most people know it today as Gunwharf Quays, which was finally completed in 2001.

Between 1998 and 2005, an iconic landmark was also built on the old HMS Vernon site, to become known as the Spinnaker Tower. It is a 170-metre-high tower, with two observation decks, a glass floor to look down to the sea, offering stunning views of the Solent and beyond. It is designed to look like the 'spinnaker' sail on a yacht. It is an amazing building which really helps to promote Portsmouth as a tourist destination.

In the early hours of the morning, one summer's night in 2004, an urgent call was broadcast on the police radio in the area car that I was driving.

'Can you respond to a report of intruders spotted breaking into the Spinnaker Tower site?'

I quickly confirmed that I was on the way with my crewmate. We switched on the blue lights and started to 'make' at speed across Southsea towards the Gunwharf Quays building site.

We didn't turn on the sirens, as there was no point in giving a burglar a 'heads up' that we were on the way to arrest them. As we raced across the city, we discussed possible motivations and options as to why a criminal would break into such a place.

The iconic site would have been a perfect location for a politically motivated or terrorist organisation to cause a scene and create maximum publicity. Another option, and the most likely, was the threat of base jumpers.

These are daredevils who jump from tall buildings or high cliffs, wearing just a parachute which they open immediately after jumping. There is a high level of kudos for people to jump from brand new buildings, being the first to have ever done it, basically giving them bragging rights. The final assumption was a good old-fashioned burglary, to steal construction equipment which can be very expensive.

Due to the time of day, we arrived quickly and were met by a security guard who was in radio communication with the control room on the building site. The young guard excitedly told us that two males had been seen climbing over a large 10-foot wooden fence to gain access to the site, and had been seen on CCTV heading towards the Spinnaker Tower. He was out of breath, but explained that the CCTV operator had lost sight of the intruders.

Having updated the police control room, I went to the back of the area car and removed the Dragon light. This was a powerful rechargeable torch that produced 200,000 candlepower. It practically made night become day, A great piece of kit.

We walked on over to the tower itself, which was nearing completion. I switched on the Dragon light and made large sweeping arcs with the beam. I searched the building site on the ground level, but saw no movement. I waved the beam skywards up the tower, which was reminiscent of a scene from 1939, and the large anti-aircraft searchlights looking for the Luftwaffe! Still nothing.

We entered the Spinnaker Tower, illuminated by emergency lighting as the full electrics had not yet been fitted. Everything was dusty and I looked over at a set of concrete steps leading up the tower. The security guard said, 'Don't worry, the internal lift works.'

We stepped inside the lift and the security guard pressed the button for the top floor.

The lift made a pinging sound on reaching the top and we walked out onto one of the two observation decks. I was hit initially with a strong cold breeze, then the eerie whistling sound of the wind.

The whole level facing out towards the water was open and exposed to the elements. There were no protective glass windows, sealing us safely inside. There was just scaffolding as a barrier to prevent people falling off the edge!

The tower was swaying slightly as it flexed in the wind. I waved the Dragon light around and could see dust particles blowing through the room in the strong beam.

As a hobby I love going rock climbing in the mountains, and enjoy extreme exposure but only if I have ropes on, plus all the other safety precautions. I'm not sure my police helmet would have cut the mustard if I fell from this height. A quick search of this level proved negative in finding the offenders, and I made sure not to go too near the edge. We headed down one level to the next observation deck.

I shone the Dragon light across the room and could immediately see two sets of eyes reflecting back towards me. We had found the two intruders who were huddled on the floor. Both wearing dark jeans and T-shirts, they were breathing heavily and sweating profusely. They were only 10 feet away, but I shouted across so they would hear me over the sound of the wind, as this level was also exposed to the elements.

'Police. Stay where you are!'

One of them responded to the effect of, 'I'm not goin' anywhere, mush. We're fucked!'

My colleague and I approached slowly and placed the two men in handcuffs, arresting them on suspicion of burglary. They both smelt very heavily of drink and at this stage could only just about stand up.

On speaking with them, it turned out they had been enjoying a night 'on the pop'. Their pub crawl had ended at 'Fifth Avenue' nightclub on the seafront.

On the walk home they had decided that it would be a 'bit of a laugh' to climb to the top of the tower, so they had broken in and made the climb upwards. They hadn't realised there was a lift that was working, so instead had climbed all 560 steps of the emergency staircase!

Now they were completely knackered and worn out. They spent the night in the cells at Pompey Central to sober up. Remorseful and apologetic, they received a caution and released with a warning never to try that again. Luckily, they were just a couple of drunk idiots on the way home; it could have been a lot worse.

As for me, I did return a number of years later with my lovely wife to enjoy an afternoon cream tea on one of the observation decks. It was delightful taking in the views, with the tower properly finished.

There were no intruders, it was a lot less windy and all safety precautions were in place!

A wedding present from the night manager

During one night shift, probably about 2am, I was on patrol in the area car with my crew mate Simon. We were slowly cruising around the streets, and we would often have the windows slightly down. Travelling at maybe 10 miles an hour. This assisted us in hearing what may be going on, listening for the sounds of shouts or breaking glass to identify offences that may be occurring.

We drifted slightly over into Southsea's Patch, when the faintest smell of smoke touched our nostrils. It wasn't a familiar coal or wood fire scent, more a strange acrid waft that makes the back of your throat prick. I tilted my head and watched the sky, clear, star-studded, no obvious plume rising from anywhere. No glowing windows, no shouting, no orange flicker. Nothing to see, but something to smell. We kept going, a slow rolling search, and turned left as we continued to trace the seat of any fire. Off to my left, there it was: the feeble, irregular chirp of a smoke detector. If you've ever heard a cheap one, you'll know the sound – like a nervous budgie. That made it easy; we just had to follow the chirps of the alarm.

Simon steered us closer until we pulled up outside a posh cake shop: the sort with wedding displays in the window so immaculate you half expect a choir to kick in. Grand layers, ribboned tiers, fondant swans making eyes at each other. A whole romance in sugar. The shop had a large glass front window with a glass door. I jumped out the police car and headed over towards where I could hear the sound of the internal smoke detector bleeping. Through the glass, you could see it: a grey gauze of smoke hugging the ceiling, thickening in that ominous way that says "this will get worse before it gets better".

We called it in at once, hoping the squirters would arrive before the situation developed quickly. Meanwhile, we banged on the glass door, window, anything to raise the alarm, just in case anyone was inside and in danger. We started to assess nearby buildings, as to whether there was anybody there that needed to be evacuated, as fire can travel very quickly. Within minutes: that glorious sound of salvation, the siren of the fire engine drawing in. Our control room had reached the key holder who was mercifully close. They arrived almost simultaneously, fumbling the keys with hands that were awake but not yet coordinated. The door swung open and the fire crew stepped into the sugar-scented haze.

The culprit made itself known immediately: an oven left on, contents charred to a crisp, the kind of small, contained fire that's more show than substance. No flames licking the walls, no dramatic hose action required. The keyholder was invited in with ourselves to turn off the ovens. A weary twist of a dial, a blast of ventilation, and the crisis dissolved quickly. No lives lost, nothing ruined, property secure. Job done.

And then the cat crept in. Black and white, with that effortless disdain particular to felines who suspect you're about to interrupt their evening plans. It stared at us with the regal indifference of a duchess at a bus stop. Cats are their own bosses, and this one had clearly promoted itself to night manager.

I was already thinking that a cat padding about in a cake shop wasn't a triumph of hygiene, but my inner food safety inspector had only just started tutting when we noticed it. On the gleaming worktop, where cakes were prepared, where fondant dreams began: a large, freshly minted offering. Six inches of steaming chocolate log that nobody had ordered.

Standing in a smoke-hazed bakery at two in the morning, breathing in the mingled scents of singed fruit cake and feline audacity, the cat obviously wanted to congratulate the happy couple getting married, in its own little way.

We ushered the furry night manager off the surfaces as we could tell the keyholder had absolutely no appetite for turning a minor incident into a public relations catastrophe. The fire crew were professionals about it. Pretend you don't see the thing on the counter, restore oxygen to the room and be careful to avoid knocking over any fondant swans.

As we backed out and handed the scene over to the grateful key holder, I looked again at those perfect wedding cakes in the window. I can tell you this much: I never bought a cake from there.

Some off-beat moments

By now, you will be convinced that everything seems to happen to me. If there is an accident waiting to happen, I'm your man.

On the lighter side, the same outcomes apply. Most of these unfortunate situations caused me great embarrassment at the time, but now I can look back with you and smile. Of course, other participants in my story have had calamitous moments, too.

Remember that I am six feet and six inches tall; anything at a certain height in my path faces a severe risk.

I was on patrol, walking around an area known as 'The Hard' in Portsmouth. It's close to the dockyard gate where the tourists go in and out.

I strode confidently along, approaching the pub on the corner. All seemed perfectly fine on a perfectly normal day. No sign of any trouble; plenty of exuberance coming from dozens of foreign tourists, keen to explore Portsmouth's rich naval history.

I walked outside the pub, quite unperturbed, and then… *CLANG*. My helmet collided with the pub sign, sending my headgear plummeting to the ground. I bent down to pick it up, only to hear the clapping and cheering from about 100 tourists on the other side of the road. They enjoyed every moment. I nodded to them, slightly embarrassed of course, and continued on my way!

Now, in the police, we were always playing tricks on each other. We all liked a bit of a laugh. But one thing you never messed with was another officer's food. Their meals were sacrosanct. Lockers could be moved to another part of the nick, turned the wrong way round and so on. Occasionally, they ended up being moved to another nick altogether. Harmless stuff. Some pranks, of course, did backfire.

We were always doing daft little things, often just to keep morale high. There was a lot of camaraderie, really. So it was all part of that. The ranks above us knew stuff was going on, not really about the specific incidents, but they turned a blind eye as long as things didn't get of hand.

One prank, which could have had much more serious consequences, involved a WPC who fell asleep in the police station canteen. We learned a lesson there about taking things too far.

For anybody who has worked shifts you will know how difficult it is to stay awake in the early hours of the morning. This is especially true after you've just had your meal. Feeling sleepy with a warm stomach your eyes start to doze, and many police officers have been known to fall asleep in the canteen.

One of the shift, a WPC called Mandy, would often succumb to the power of sleep in the early hours after eating. One night, at about 3am, my crewmate Tommy and I walked through the locker room and could hear this almighty noise. It sounded like a hippopotamus having difficulty breathing whilst underwater. As we got closer, we could see it was Mandy snoring.

She was sitting on a blue plastic chair alone in the canteen on her meal break, fast asleep. Tommy quickly hatched a plan, giving me a knowing look. He went to his locker, and returned a few minutes later holding a banger firework. He picked up an old empty biscuit tin off the draining board and placed it underneath Mandy's chair.

Tommy pulled out his lighter and lit the fuse to the firework, placing it carefully into the empty tin. The firework fizzed and sparks erupted from the end as we ran back into the locker room.

BANG! The biscuit tin amplified the sound, creating an almighty din. Mandy screamed and got to her feet quickly, having been woken so suddenly from her slumber. We returned to the room, laughing. Mandy also had a smile on her face, realising it was just a prank and the police station was not under attack.

However, we shouldn't have been so quick to laugh. Moments later a large mushroom cloud of smoke from the firework hit the ceiling of the police station, including the smoke alarm sensor! Now there was a real commotion as the fire alarm bell sounded throughout the whole of the police station.

Being a public building, the fire alarm was linked directly to the fire station, and they would now be responding. We had to think quickly as to what to do next.

Do we contact the police control room and let them know the alarm has been set off in error? Or do we rush to the Bridewell and let the custody sergeant know? He would have to consider whether to evacuate prisoners from the cells as a result of a suspected fire in the police station.

This was obviously a warning to both of us, because these pranks can escalate with unfortunate consequences. Tommy called up on his radio to inform the control room, while I ran to the Bridewell to update the custody staff that the alarm had been set off in error. Disaster was averted and no prisoners had the chance to escape.

However, 'Trumpton' did arrive at the police station with their hoses. After confirming everything was okay and giving us a dressing down, they also laughed at what had happened.

We explained to the 'squirters' that we were having a bit of a mess around, and it wouldn't happen again. They took it in good nature…although not an incident to be repeated!

Jokes and pranks were a daily occurrence. These jokes would range from sneaking in song titles to the custody sergeant, summing up the arrest, to much more elaborate pranks.

All police officers in uniform have a collar number, so they can be identified. Traditionally collar numbers were polished metal numbers worn on each shoulder of a tunic. As uniforms changed, fabric epaulettes were worn on the shoulders of shirts, jumpers and waterproof jackets.

Most police forces moved away from metal numbers to embroidery, as they were cheaper and safer. We had a dark blue or black epaulette with white numbers that slid over a plain, permanent one.

We would often turn over the epaulettes on officers' outer jackets when left unattended in the nick. Using correction fluid and a hand as steady as a sign writer, we would paint on the numbers of other officers for a laugh. Special constable collar numbers always started with a number 9, so this addition was given to many regular cops. You quickly became aware of this and regularly checked your epaulette for tampering!

The same went for pocket notebooks. These were your personal record of evidence when you attended an incident. Everything was recorded in your PNB which, at a later date, you would rely on in court.

There are strict rules as to how to fill out your PNB. It is the most embarrassing and humbling experience when using your PNB in court, only to find a childish 'cock and balls' drawn in pen in the middle of your evidence! If the defence asked to see a copy of your PNB, you unfortunately had to look very unprofessional, explaining to a court the reason for the cartoon image.

I did not agree with this practice of writing in other officers' PNBs, but once you had been subjected to it, you never, ever, left your PNB unattended!

One summer's night, we carefully crafted a prank. My shift was on a late turn. At 10pm the night turn had just started, taking over all the response calls on the radio. My shift was finishing up jobs the day shift had been involved in. They were returning to the police station to write up their paperwork.

One of the PCs, called Mark, was driving the panda car: a Ford Escort, call sign Kilo Charlie Seven Five. Mark was taking a statement from a witness at the student halls of residence, Bateson Hall in The Mary Rose Street. This is literally behind Portsmouth Central police station.

Mark had driven around and parked outside the halls of residence, so we hatched a plan. We drove to Greetham Street, close by, the scene of a theft from motor vehicle earlier that day. Using the broom from the back of the police car, I swept up the small pieces of broken glass left on the ground. I scooped them up with a plastic snow shovel and returned to the police station.

It was prudent to make the night shift sergeant and rest of the shift aware of the prank, so nobody would go racing to the scene at speed, causing an accident. I also phoned the police control room, so they would be ready, should Mark call up on his police radio asking for assistance.

I took my equipment and the broken glass from the police car and handed over the keys to the night shift. I then removed the spare set of keys for the panda car from the safe and walked over to where Mark had parked it. I poured the broken glass into the gutter where the police car was parked. Using the spare key I then drove it back to the police station and handed the vehicle over for the night shift to use.

Sure enough, after Mark had finished taking the statement, he prepared to return back to the nick. To his horror, all he could see was a pile of broken glass on the ground. He immediately assumed the worst, that one of the local car thieves had stolen the panda car! He immediately called up on the radio with panic in his voice, saying his police car had been stolen.

The control room took the details, while we all laughed back at the police station as the prank unfolded. Lots of other units joined in over the air, reporting that they would attend the scene, with others stating they had started an area search for the car, none of which was true. This was in the days before trackers were routinely fitted, so quickly locating the car could be difficult. Mark was told to return to the police station on foot to explain himself to the sergeant.

He walked back into the rear yard of the nick, to a round of applause from officers who had gathered and were standing by the 'stolen' car. He was initially confused, but then saw the funny side and had look of relief all over his face, when he realised it had all just been a prank. I returned to the pile of glass to clean everything up before heading off home. From that day onwards, Mark never let the panda car out of his sight!

We used to do seven nights in a row, using the Ottawa shift system. We also got six days off, following a set of nights. But a week of nights meant you had to be on your guard for pranks. Sly things did go on in the middle of the night, with a tit-for-tat series of events. The following story is a typical example…

Officer A finished his shift in Portsmouth and couldn't see his locker. After searching around the police station, he found it in the ladies' loo. He suspected officer B. The perfect opportunity arose when a dead rat was sprawled out across the entrance to the back yard. It had been squashed by a police car going out of the gate. This rodent was horrible, about a foot long with maggots oozing out of its mangled body.

So, Officer A picked up the dead rat and lobbed it onto the windscreen of Officer B's personal car at the front of the police station. In the morning, Officer B was horrified to see this disgusting specimen adorning the windscreen of his Porsche. It was a Porsche 944, not a high-end model, but our man's pride and joy.

Time, then, for Officer B to strike back.

The following evening, a pigeon managed to find its way into the police station through a high-level open window. What an opportunity. Officer B captured the bird, went and got the spare key for Officer A's locker and put the pigeon inside. It was in there for a couple of hours, safe and sound with the ventilation holes, but obviously keen to get out.

So, Officer A finished his shift and opened up his locker. The pigeon flew off in a flurry of feathers and poo; it had sprayed the white stuff everywhere. Officer A's pocket books were covered, along with his uniform when the bird flew off around the room.

The relieved bird was guided to an open door and flew away, happy to be free. Eventually, a truce was declared between the two officers and that was that.

Often the police have to call on the assistance of the media when a case is difficult to solve. During my career, some officers shy away from this, leaving the help of the press to the big cases.

On one particular occasion, I had been called by a member of the public to a street in Southsea where a large wheelie bin had been seen. When opened up, it was full of Jaffa Cakes, all in sealed packets.

As the available uniformed PC, I was sent down to investigate. There was no documentation on the outside of the bin and no paperwork on the inside. There was nothing at all to suggest where these tasty treats had come from.

In my head, I thought this could be a lorry jacking, a theft from a motor vehicle, or a commercial burglary. There were far too many cakes in the bin for just one person to consume.

Had a shop or a delivery van been broken into? I needed to get to the bottom of the mystery. Scenes of crime officers weren't too interested as they were run off their feet at the time with various cases. I was told it would be a very slow response, fingerprinting the packages.

Instead, I decided to ask for help from the media in a similar vein to the TV series, *Crimewatch*, at the time. I phoned up the local newspaper, the Portsmouth News, who were excited about the story and instantly sent a reporter and photographer to the scene.

I gave all the details to the reporter, in the hope that readers might be able to help. The photographer asked if I could pose for a few pictures. I was young and naïve and agreed.

I was asked to lie down on the grass, with my helmet full of Jaffa Cakes.

'Maybe you could put one in your mouth?' the photographer asked, hopefully.

I did as he asked and, when I bought paper the next day, received non-stop ribbing from my colleagues.

Even though the article generated a lot of publicity, no one came forward as a victim. I wondered what to do about the cakes. They were nearing their 'best before' date.

When they reached that date, they could no longer be sold and ended up in the police canteen, to be devoured by eager officers.

I always wondered where they came from in the first place. Were they stolen Jaffa Cakes, or fake ones planted to poison the local constabulary?!

I love Portsmouth when the sea fog rolls in. The whole city takes on a new persona, especially in the historic areas such as Old Portsmouth and the Hot Walls. That name came from heating cannon balls to make them more deadly when fired at wooden ships!

You can hear the lapping of the sea against the shingle, although it's nearly impossible to see the water or ships passing by. Everything is quiet and still. You can see the moisture in the air as the fog slowly rolls in.

One of Portsmouth's most famous residents was the iconic writer, Charles Dickens. He was born in a house on Mile End Terrace, very close to the end of the M275 motorway as you drive into the city.

As far as I am concerned, that makes him a 'Buckland Boy'. Famously he used the setting of fog in *'A Christmas Carol'* to create a sense of gloom and mystery. That's exactly how I would describe Portsmouth when the sea mist and fog rolls in. I very much doubt whether Charles Dickens ever actually saw the fog in Pompey, as he only lived in the city for a few years as a baby, having been born here.

In more modern times when the fog rolls in, it is when some criminals use this to their advantage. They commit crimes such as burglary or theft from motor vehicles, using the cover of the fog to avoid detection.

On one such foggy evening, I was on duty and darkness had fallen. The fog was a real 'pea souper' and visibility was limited, even with street lights and a torch. My radio lit up and I heard the control room say 'Kilo Double Nine from Charlie One. Can you attend the Rock Gardens for a report of screaming?'

I responded, 'Kilo Charlie Double Nine, answer yes, en-route.'

It sounded like a spooky deployment! I was driving the Ford Transit police van, and I switched on the blue lights to make progress quickly. I was blinded by the pulsing blue lights reflecting back from the fog and could hardly see a thing. I switched them off and drove with a dipped beam. It was going to be slow, but at least I would arrive safely.

I finally arrived at the Pyramids Centre, a glass pyramid on the seafront housing an indoor leisure centre, swimming pools and live music venue.

I updated the control room of my arrival.

The Pyramids Centre was next door to the Rock Gardens, an outside space with various plants and small water features. Benches are hidden away in alcoves and, in the daytime, it is a lovely place to relax for a short break, while walking the length of the esplanade seafront.

However, in the '90s at night-time, it could be an area where teenagers hung out, drinking cans of beer or smoking a spliff. It was also known as an area for gay men to meet up.

With a torch in my hand, I walked past the wine bar, known as the 'Frog on the Front', which was part of the Pyramids, and I headed into the Rock Gardens. I could only see about 10 feet in front of me. I could hear the water lapping against the sea wall and the sound of a low-pitched foghorn, periodically and rhythmically breaking the silence. Another foghorn from a passing ship sounded, but this was slightly higher-pitched than the other one.

The seafront was dimly lit by the yellow street lighting and the glow from the glass Pyramids Centre. My torch was like a fat laser beam, but fairly useless in the conditions. The beam did not improve what I could see in the thick fog. I walked on slowly into the gardens, down a set of sunken paved steps. The air was cold and damp, and it felt like someone was going to jump out on me. This better not be some of the shift playing a practical joke, I thought to myself…

I stopped suddenly and the hairs on the back of my neck sprang up with urgency. The silence was once again broken. My head twisted quickly, eyes squinting through the fog, trying to make out what or who had created this noise. This sound was different, a blood-curdling scream. It was like a wild animal howling in pain, having been caught in a trap or stabbed with a spear. The sound was off towards my right-hand side. I updated the control room that I had also heard screaming and was conducting an area search.

I slowly tiptoed to give myself the element of surprise against whatever was making this terrifying noise. Slowly, one step at a time, I moved closer and closer towards where I had heard the noise. Unfortunately the sunken footpath was not a direct route towards the noise, but I had to follow this to avoid the small ponds and low walls.

My eyes darted to the left on hearing another harrowing scream. This was shorter in length, but with a sense of urgency. These haunting noises troubled me, alone in the dark, hidden from sight. My mind began to race as to what was causing this terrifying sound… and would I be safe?

It now seemed to be higher up, out of the Rock Gardens towards the East Battery, next to Southsea Castle, overlooking Castle Fields. Walking behind the Pyramids

Centre, I was now on the flat, wide promenade. The sound of the sea was noisier here.

I headed up the thin path towards the top of the East Battery with a sense of renewed urgency. The screams had stopped and I feared the worst. I braced myself mentally to find a body on top of this large hill, that in clear conditions gives great views over the Solent.

Now higher up, I was more exposed and the wind was stronger. The cold, damp, fog was blowing over me, making me shiver. I continued searching and came across a bench that had something on it. I switched on my Maglite torch and illuminated the Victorian-style wooden bench.

I could see crimson red blood on the wooden seat and what appeared to be blood smudged on one side of the metal arm rest, like an injured person had been struggling. A white piece of tissue was tucked into the slats of the bench and also appeared to have blood on it.

Further along the bench I saw a tube of KY Jelly, often used as a lubricant for sex. By the sound of the noises being made, I think they needed to apply some more!

I searched the length of the East Battery and Castle Field, as I returned to the police van. Nobody contacted the police to report a crime at that location. I pressed the transmit button on my police radio, 'Kilo Charlie double nine. Area search, no trace.'

There was also no more screaming, so hopefully the delicate situation on the bench had come to a satisfactory conclusion!

The start of cyber crime

Hampshire Terrace and Landport Terrace in Portsmouth are positioned within walking distance of the courts and Portsmouth Central police station. Therefore, it's the perfect place for many of the city's solicitors to be situated.

It would have been about 1994 or 1995, when I was called to a report of the sound of breaking glass. All I knew was, the noise came from the rear of the Terraces.

On foot patrol in full uniform, I walked stealthily down the rear access road to the row of buildings. Being a Sunday morning, all was quiet and I listened for the sound of anybody moving around. I glanced over to my right and noticed a ground floor window broken. This was an office at the rear of a firm of local solicitors.

The buildings were brick-built with offices on the ground floor and more offices upstairs as well as residential accommodation. Many had steps on metal fire escapes, twisting up the back of the buildings to the floors above.

Most of the wooden window frames had metal bars covering them on the ground floor, but this window was unprotected. The window was still locked but there was a human-sized hole in the pane of glass. I approached and looked in, listening all the time. Nothing.

I assumed the building was empty and the offenders were long gone. I notified the control room and then proceeded to enter the offices, searching for any intruders.

As I suspected, unfortunately for my arrest statistics, the offenders had left – but not before making a real mess. It was as if the burglars had decided to ransack and smash the place up. I was a little puzzled, trying to work out what the offenders had been after. There was a small amount of cash in a tea-fund pot, which had been left undisturbed. Some A4 plastic filing trays and folders of case papers were scattered across the floor, having been moved off the thick walnut desks.

My next thought was: could it be a criminal trying to sabotage the evidence in a criminal case, or trying to identify witnesses? None of this really made sense. Two large desktop computers along with monitors had been smashed on the floor. The side of the computer had been ripped open and the circuit boards exposed. I could see obvious spaces on the circuit boards.

It looked like the burglars had been after computer chips. I love chips. but normally with salt and vinegar on them! This was a first for me. Many burglars are drug addicts who are trying to fund their habit. Desperate to buy their next fix of heroin or crack cocaine, they will normally steal cash, jewellery or other high value items that can easily be converted into cash. I'd never been to a burglary where they wanted the computer chips; I guessed the computer itself was too big and heavy to carry away unseen.

I called out a Scenes of Crime officer to look for any clues such as fingerprints and take samples of the broken glass. I was really grateful for the work they did, as any forensic evidence massively helps when a case goes to court. Nowadays, they have a much more glamorous name as a result of the TV series, CSI. Crime Scene Investigator would be the term used nowadays.

Back in the '90s, all house burglaries were always investigated by a CID officer. It was only minor commercial burglaries that 'uniform' would investigate. This job was mine, so I set about some house-to-house enquiries and checking for CCTV.

I spoke with the Scenes of Crime officer, who told me about this new type of crime wave; office buildings and tech firms became prime targets for a modern breed of burglar. The officer had noticed a rise in this type of break-in.

The loot? Not cash, jewellery, or high-end stereo systems. No, what these lads were after was something smaller, quieter, and increasingly valuable: computer memory chips.

At the time, RAM (random access memory) was fast becoming the new gold dust. Computers were popping up on every office desk, and Microsoft had just released Windows 95, which demanded more memory than its predecessors.

Suddenly, having 4 megabytes wasn't enough; 8MB, even 16MB, became the new norm. Each of those tiny chips could fetch a decent price, and with businesses keen to upgrade on the cheap, a thriving black market emerged. In 1994 insurance companies paid out in the region of £175-£200 million in claims for physical computer-related theft.

We weren't dealing with your average smash-and-grab burglar, either. These were smart operators. Some were genuine computer enthusiasts with a solid understanding of tech. They knew how to strip a PC of its memory without leaving a mark. Often, businesses wouldn't even realise they'd been hit until they booted up on Monday morning and the machines refused to play ball. My burglar was not so skilled and a little blunter in his method of entry.

A major operation run by the Met Police, Operation Eastside, was one of the first large-scale crackdowns on tech-related theft. After a six-month investigation, police raided 44 addresses across London, Leicester and Swindon in July of '95. Twenty-nine people were arrested. The scale of it was staggering, as one suspect alone had turned over £500,000 in stolen memory chips in just 16 months.

The frustrating bit? Despite the scope and effort, getting convictions was another story. Memory theft didn't have its own crime statistic category back then; it all came under general burglary. And, while burglary carried a maximum sentence of 18 years, the reality was usually far lighter.

Community service, suspended sentences and other soft penalties didn't reflect the damage done or the scale of the problem. Many of the people being arrested didn't even get charged, as it was difficult to link the persons holding the chips to the original crime scene.

Often suspects just claimed they had bought the chips in good faith. The tricky part? The chips all looked pretty much the same. The 4, 8, and 16MB SIMMs each had 72 pins, so unless you knew exactly what you were looking at – or had the kit to test them – you couldn't tell the difference just by eye. That made sorting and selling the gear a job for someone who really knew their way around computer hardware.

An Intel chip was about six inches long and an inch wide. It had a street value four times that of heroin and cocaine. The smaller chips, those old memory modules, only held about 1MB each, so they weren't worth much on their own.

The real value was in the larger modules. A 4MB chip might fetch around £50 on the black market. An 8MB could go for double that, but the real prize was the 16MB modules. They were rare and in high demand, often selling for upwards of £400 each. So, a 16MB SIMM worth £400 back in 1994 would be the equivalent of nearly £900 today (at the time of writing), taking into account inflation. Not bad for a piece of silicon the size of a chewing gum stick.

Some of us police officers on the ground felt the courts didn't yet grasp the seriousness of these tech crimes. It wasn't violent, and there were no victims in hospital beds, so the crime didn't raise alarms. But in reality, it was organised, profitable, and increasingly sophisticated. And, unlike drugs or firearms, there was very little risk.

In reality, chip thefts were probably funding the supply of drugs into the country and all the violence that is associated with organised and serious crime.

Looking back now, it was one of the first signs of how crime would evolve in the digital age. The criminals were ahead of the curve, and we were just starting to catch up. Stealing chips evolved over the decades to the theft of data.

Like those bigger operations in the Met, I was never able to charge any suspects for this burglary. I had some intelligence and a suspect, but not enough evidence. The offenders would soon be 'at it' again, though.

Later that same year, I attended a training course back at Netley. As I left the main entrance at Victoria House to walk back to the accommodation blocks, I noticed a large lorry. It was parked near the main car park, and emblazoned down the side with the BT (British Telecom) logo. A man was standing at the rear by a set of steps and called out to me. Curious, I walked over to see what was going on.

'What are you doing?' I asked with a smile.

The man, dressed in a BT polo shirt, said: 'We're showing people the internet. Do you want to have a go?'

I had read about the internet, but never seen it before. I even had a home PC but it was not connected to a network. I climbed the steps and into the lorry. The inside was like a mobile office, with counter tops on either side and large CRT box-shaped monitors screwed down onto the desk space. A number of desktop computers hummed away under the counters. A wired keyboard and mouse completed the set-up and I sat down on one of the stools.

The BT representative briefly explained what the internet was. I was well impressed.

'Want to see what it can do?' the rep said, enthusiastically.

'Sure.'

He continued: 'Think of anything. Anything you want, and type it in that box on the screen. Let's see if you can find a picture of it?'

At this point I could have been childish, but instead typed in 'Black Toyota MR2'. This was a cool-looking sports car from the period and I had been interested in buying one, second-hand.

As if my magic, rows of pixels built upon each other. Then an image started to form. After only 30 seconds or so, I was looking at a photo of my dream car. Having seen the internet in the back of a lorry, I was sold. This was going to be the future! It was probably only a year later that I purchased a dial-up internet connection to get online at home.

I guess I was in the 'right place at the right time', with regards to cyber crime. New technology was coming at everyone: computers, phones, the internet. The trouble was, the police did not have the ability to investigate effectively in the beginning. Rules of collecting evidence were all about seizing physical evidence, not digital evidence. We had to adapt quickly. Some officers did not want to embrace new ideas and ways of working. I did, and wanted to help lead the way.

Social media then arrived shortly after the internet, connecting everyone in the digital world. The likes of Facebook, MySpace and Twitter ruled social media. Online chat rooms and online multiplayer games using email, bulletin boards and blogs, all became the norm.

If you were interested in technology, it was an exciting time to be growing up. It felt like we were all online digital pioneers. This new wave of technology brought with it a new wave of digital crimes. Police forces around the world struggled to cope and deal with minor and serious bullying, and sharing of inappropriate content and images: frauds and impersonation enabled by computers and the internet.

The police did not know how to deal with it all. Do we seize the computer? How do we capture the evidence while trying to remain proportional?

It was really tough. Some officers took a low-key approach, dismissing complaints of online bullying. It was only when the effects of this offending were recognised, such as children taking their own lives, that a new approach was needed. The problem of dealing with these nasty crimes, having limited resources, is not a new one. It is a balancing act that aims to protect as many people as possible. I like to think that online bullying is taken much more seriously now.

An even darker side to computer crime then appeared.

My interest in cyber crime and computers did not go unnoticed, and soon I was investigating paedophiles online. I was understanding the workings of TOR (The Onion Router) software to access the dark web. With my new found self-taught computer skills, I became involved in helping to investigate child sexual abuse and the sharing of IIOC (indecent images of children) and CSAM (child sexual abuse material).

Before the internet arrived, it was difficult for child sex offenders to network and meet each other. It's not the kind of thing people talk about down at the pub, unless they are looking to get their teeth kicked in. The internet made it much easier to network and share this horrific material. Many turned to new technologies like P2P (peer to peer) to share images. For each image or video created and shared, a real victim was being abused.

This was dreadful work, but equally very rewarding, knowing you were helping to safeguard children from abuse. We always aimed to catch the hands-on abusers or offenders involved in the distribution of CSAM. But we also dealt with the people downloading this material, as we recognised that they would possibly become the abusers of the future. They were generating the supply and demand problem, causing more children to be abused. I don't plan to go into detail of how we investigated these offenders, technically or otherwise, as these people don't need any help in trying to avoid the attention of law enforcement.

Online fraud really started to take off after the launch of eBay in the UK during 1999. Online shopping is a great service that we all take for granted now. Like any new service or business, criminals will look to abuse it. Scammers took advantage of returns policies or would send empty boxes via the postal service after advertising an expensive item like a laptop or iPod.

eBay helped to solve this issue by introducing 'feedback' for sellers and buyers. This worked well in creating trust between both parties. In those early days, buyers would send cheques, postal orders or even money in the post. It sounds ridiculous. The only other option was inputting your credit card details on a website. This made people nervous, mainly because credit card fraud was the most common form of online payment scam. Most criminals involved were using stolen or compromised credit card details to make unauthorised purchases.

This was followed by the launch of PayPal in 2003. Originally owned by eBay, PayPal provided a service to send money electronically or to buy items on websites with limited risk to the consumer. Great, a solution to the problem? No, it wasn't.

Scammers abused the PayPal service and, although consumers were 'protected', the company was not. So the company simply 'froze' suspect accounts. Criminals were losing money, and the problem of trust in online financial transactions was still missing.

A digital currency was needed.

Bitcoin was invented in 2008 when an unknown entity published a white paper explaining how it worked under the pseudonym of Satoshi Nakamoto. Use of Bitcoin as a currency began in 2009, with the release of its open-source software. In its most simple form, traditional banking is based on a centralised system of ledgers and trust in the bank looking after your money.

Bitcoin is different. This is a digital currency, or 'cryptocurrency' that operates independently of a central bank or single administrator. Imagine it like digital cash you can send over the internet. Instead of physical coins or notes, Bitcoin exists as entries on a public ledger called a 'blockchain'. This is like a massive, shared, and constantly updated record book distributed across thousands of computers worldwide.

When someone sends Bitcoin, that transaction is broadcast to the network, verified by powerful computers called 'miners', and then added as a new 'block' to this ever-growing chain. This process ensures the security and integrity of transactions, preventing fraud and double-spending, because every participant on the network has a copy of the ledger and can verify its authenticity.

Unlike fiat money, that a government can create more of if required, Bitcoin is limited to 21 million. This scarcity helps create value. A benefit of Bitcoin is your account cannot be frozen as it is decentralised. Also, the large percentage of people around the globe who do not have a bank account can now transact with others online.

I was self-learning about cryptocurrency and could see the benefits and the negative uses, especially when used by criminals. I bought small amounts to understand how the system worked, and how people would buy and trade. I wanted to understand everything about Bitcoin.

A chance discussion with a colleague, who was a police negotiator, raised some questions in my mind. In extortion and kidnap situations, law enforcement around the world have a playbook as to how they deal with any ransom money.

Everything was geared up for dealing with fiat money, cash, bank notes, call it what you want, but cryptocurrency changed all that. Criminals committing digital crimes now had a way to extort money from victims over the internet.

But what about real-world crimes such as kidnap, where lives were at risk and the criminals wanted or asked for cryptocurrency? Hostages could die if law enforcement got it wrong and I could visualise some nightmare scenarios.

I was asked to provide a training session on cryptocurrency and surrounding issues for negotiators to a group of regional police negotiators from the south-east region.

The training was a great success and warmly welcomed, although I suspect some of the 'non geeks' maybe didn't understand it fully. That didn't really matter, so long as they understood the key messages that would hopefully help prevent a hostage being hurt or killed.

As things turned out, I was the one facing imminent danger...

The day my life changed forever

I woke up early on 18 July 2020 with a real spring in my step. It was a lovely warm summer's day. Little did I know what the day had in store for me. I had a shower and got dressed into a pair of jeans and a shirt. I was no longer in uniform, but now working in the world of serious and organised crime investigations.

I made a cup of tea for Janet to drink in bed. I then checked on the kids who were both still asleep; there was no rush for them to get up. School was closed due to Covid-19, and both of them were already in the groove with remote home schooling. That said, the wife and I kept a regular routine for the kids and their school work, much to their disappointment.

Being a 'Key Worker', I was still lucky enough to be able to go to work and leave the house during lockdown. Well, I say lucky. When I looked at my friends on social media, enjoying the extra time off from work, I was not so sure. That said, I still loved my job and I had the privilege of not being as restricted in my movements during Covid. I was working mainly from home on a laptop. Obviously I couldn't 'just' work from home, as I still had to go to police stations, attend meetings and engage with members of the public.

Janet was now up and awake having her breakfast. I had arranged to go to police premises and collect some equipment. I gave Janet a kiss as I was leaving the house, explaining that I would be just going out to work for about an hour.

I said, 'Don't worry, I won't be long. I'll be back in time to make you and the kids lunch.'

I slung a rucksack of paperwork over my shoulder and left the house. I slipped into the driver's seat of the unmarked police car and turned the ignition. I switched on the car radio that was tuned into my usual station, belting out those classic tracks from the '80s and '90s. I set off driving down the main road close to my home. It was dead, really quiet and eerily spooky, as there was nobody on the road at all. No cars or pedestrians. This lockdown did have some advantages, after all.

As I drove to an upbeat Michael Jackson song on the radio, my mind drifted. It nearly felt like I was back in America, on some long empty highway, with the warm sun beating down on my face. I glanced at my watch which said 08:45 hours. I was definitely going to make it in good time for the 09:00 collection I had arranged.

With nearly no traffic at all on the roads, I was making great progress, driving along a country lane. Ahead, off to the left on the verge, I spotted approximately six full large white plastic sacks. A small handwritten sign in front of them said,

'Free horse manure'. Brilliant I thought, just what I needed for the garden.

I had to make a split-second decision whether to stop, there and then, placing the bags into the boot of the car, or collect them when coming home.

'Sod it', I thought, I'll get them on the way back, as I would have to stop really suddenly and was already going to miss the driveway.

I drove the remaining short distance to the police building and parked my car. I removed my warrant card from my back pocket and swiped the access control panel to gain access to the building. Walking past the canteen, I considered making a brew, but I didn't really have time for a cup of tea yet. I collected the envelope that I needed from a colleague, then headed back towards the canteen to make myself a cuppa.

As I walked down the sterile corridor, I bumped into a colleague called Chris, coming out from an adjoining door. He said, 'All right, Foz?'

'Yeah, all good mate. I'm glad I bumped into you as it happens. I need to have a quick word with you if you're free for five minutes.'

At that time, I was in the process of planning a large regional policing operation, and I was hoping his department would want to be part of it. I already had the backing of a number of police forces.

'Yes, sure, if it's gonna be a quick five minutes,' he replied.

'Great', I said as he pushed opened a door to a large modern meeting room. The room was dominated by a large table surrounded by chairs. A couple of computer terminals sat in the corners and we took our seats opposite. The room lighting was soft, as it was controlled by a dimmer switch on the wall. The wall leading to the corridor had large floor-to-ceiling glass panels with privacy venetian blinds pulled down.

Chris and I had known each other for years, working together on many occasions within the police. Chris was not just a work colleague; I would describe him as a friend. As he had no real time to spare, we got straight down to business. I was doing the talking and he was listening, as I delivered my elevator pitch for the policing operation, hoping he would want to come on board.

I was about three minutes into the pitch when I started to feel uncomfortable. My forehead and cheeks felt flushed as if I'd been exercising. I felt a slight sweat crossing my brow. Strange, I thought, as I was just sitting down. Suddenly, I had what I can only describe as a thunderclap headache at the front of my head. I'm not one to have headaches, to be fair. I'm not one to really have any illness, having only taken about two weeks off sick during my whole three decades of service.

I would just shrug off a normal headache, often not even taking a painkiller. This headache wasn't one of those annoying dull thuds, like you might have from a hangover. It wasn't like the kind of pain you get with straining your eyes all day, looking at a computer screen. No, this was the most intense pain I have ever felt. It was as if the front of my head had just exploded.

The pain then washed over me. It felt like I could literally feel the pain travelling through my head, over the crown of my skull towards the back. My body felt like it was burning up and I had what seemed like a raging temperature. The sensation had only lasted for maybe a minute at the most, but Chris noticed my demeanour had changed.

Trying to be 'ever the professional', I carried on with the pitch, but Chris stopped me and asked, 'You okay Foz? You don't look too well?'

I explained that I felt hot and had a headache. He offered to go and get a glass of water for me, which I accepted. Chris filled a plastic cup from the water cooler and put it down in front of me on the table. I reached out over the table pick it up, but I missed the cup with my hand by about three inches. I was a little confused at this point, not sure what was going on.

I focused with my eyes carefully on the plastic cup and realised that I was seeing double. It was the strangest sensation, seeing an exact copy of the object in front of me. I gazed around the room and could see multiple copies of everything.

I moved my hand to clasp the cup and brought it to my lips, feeling the cold water run down my throat; that was so soothing. I was now sweating like never before.

Chris glanced at his watch and apologised. He said he had to go to another meeting. He was going to be late, but that he would call me later on the phone. He was keen on the proposal and wanted to discuss it further.

'Cheers mate, I'm gonna go for a piss and a sit-down outside in the car to cool down,' I told him.

We shook hands, then Chris rose up from the table and left the room. I stood up and started to walk towards the door. My large frame crashed into the partition wall and then the glass panels. I reached out with both hands to prevent myself falling fully, keeping upright. For some reason I was unable to balance and it felt like the end of a stag do, with my arms and legs unable to be controlled in a coordinated manner.

The room was spinning around me and I was lucky I did not crash through the glass. I paused for a second to regain my composure. It's bizarre that I didn't think anything serious was up at the time, but I was conscious that I urgently needed to use the urinal. Luckily, the gents' toilet was just the other side of the corridor from the meeting room. I crashed through the toilet door and stumbled towards the urinals.

There was nobody else in the toilets and I managed to empty my bladder in time. I was holding myself up against the tiled wall in front of me with one arm, swaying as if drunk. I managed to make my way to the sink and wash my hands, looking into the large wall mirror.

I looked and felt totally dreadful. The thunderclap headache was still raging at the back of my head. It was the worst headache I'd ever felt. It was also compounded with this raging heat I felt within my body, and I was still sweating profusely. As I mentioned earlier it seems strange that, as a police officer, I was trained in advanced emergency first aid and did not realise something more serious was happening to me.

I had to cool down quickly. I managed to leave the toilet. Using both hands against the corridor walls, I was supporting myself as I stumbled towards the exit to the building. Pressing my warrant card against the access control system, I heard the door click as it unlocked and I pulled the front doors open. My car was just outside the main entrance and I pressed the remote control fob.

The indicators blinked as the car unlocked and I sat down in the front seat. I started the engine with the key and switched on the air conditioning to full. The rush of ice-cold air blowing over my hot skin felt amazing. I sat there for a few seconds, just enjoying the cool breeze. I felt tired and exhausted, so I closed my eyes for a brief second, capturing some short relief from the intense headache at the back of my head and the dull pulsing pain in my eyes. I was still straining to see anything clearly.

I reclined the car seat back to a more horizontal position. Lying back with my eyes closed felt good for another 30 seconds until I felt a tightness in the pit of my stomach. A wave of nausea washed over me. It was like that moment, when you are drunk and your body decides to tell you you've had too much to drink, and I was going to be sick.

I managed to open the car door but I had barely enough strength to move my head out of the vehicle. With my head now close to the gutter, I vomited violently for about a minute. Retching up what appeared to be my breakfast and a mug of tea, the discoloured liquid and bile was now running towards the drain.

I wiped my mouth with the sleeve of my shirt. I pulled the door closed, feeling the sweet relief of the cold air running across my skin. Again, I closed my eyes and started to drift off to sleep, not realising I was dying and would probably never wake up.

I was woken suddenly by a loud knocking on the window. Startled and disorientated, I opened my eyes. How long had I been asleep for?

Looking out of the car window I could see a woman. Although she was blurred, I recognized her as a colleague called Charlie. She appeared to be speaking as her lips were moving, but the sound was dull and I could not hear her. She pulled on the handle and opened the door.

'You okay, Foz?' she asked, calmly and softly.

'Yeah, I'm fine. Just got a headache …and I've been sick', I thought I replied. It turns out those words didn't come out. My speech had now become extremely slurred.

Although I was trying to communicate and say how I was feeling, the words coming out of my mouth were totally different. To be fair, some people say I talk a lot of s***, and others might have difficulty understanding my northern accent. But this was truly different.

'Let's get you inside, you don't look so well,' she said, reaching into the car and helping to support me into an upright position.

As I got out of the car, I was taken back into the reception area and sat down in the chair near the door. I became aware of a number of other officers being present; some that I knew and others that I didn't recognise. At this point, my symptoms consisted of the severe headache at the back of my head, the double vision, an inability to balance, an extreme temperature across my body, slurred speech and a feeling of nausea.

'I'm gonna be sick,' I muttered, pulling a waste paper bin towards me. I was violently sick, as I emptied the remaining contents of my stomach into the small metal bin. I attempted to say sorry, but my words were totally slurred.

Unbeknown to me at this time, I was critically ill. I was not 100% sure what was taking place as I sat there. I was aware of people making phone calls and Chris had returned to see me. From what I've been told afterwards, there had been a long discussion between officers, to try to establish what was wrong with me. They had to rule out that I was drunk and drove to work which, if correct, would have resulted in an arrest.

My supervisor, this time a male colleague called Charlie, was spoken to on the phone. Although not present, he quickly recognised that this was a medical emergency and told them to call an ambulance immediately. There was no time to lose.

A blue light run to hospital

An ambulance was called. It attended swiftly and two paramedics joined me in the reception area of the building. They quickly triaged my condition, taking my blood pressure, pulse and looked at my vital signs. I recall them asking me questions such as my name, what year it was, and who the current Prime Minister was. Now I've never been one to 'ace an exam', but I felt fairly confident I had smashed this one, answering all the questions correctly.

I'm told, however, that my answers were unintelligible due to my slurred speech. If this had occurred two years later, I would have probably got the Prime Minister question wrong, having had such a quick succession of leaders from Boris Johnson to Liz Truss to Rishi Sunak!

One of the paramedics explained they were going to take me to hospital to get me checked over. I was unable to walk now and was strapped into an ambulance chair. I was laid down on the bed in the ambulance and seatbelts applied across my body.

Other than the paramedics, I was on my own. The ambulance set off. I could see the tops of street lights and trees pass by, out of the top of the window of the ambulance. The siren was on and I assumed it was a blue light run straight to the hospital.

The paramedic spoke calmly to me as if everything was absolutely fine, and I was just getting a ride home. He told me we were going to the Queen Alexandra Hospital just outside Portsmouth.

The trip to hospital only took about 20 minutes. That sense of calm changed on arrival at hospital. My ambulance trolley was rushed through the emergency entrance and we were greeted by a team of eight medics, all dressed in scrubs, wearing surgical masks, and plastic eye visors held in place with headbands. I noticed a doctor who was wearing a brightly coloured tabard. This reception committee was obviously waiting for me. I was drifting in and out of consciousness at this point. I'm not sure if I had been given any drugs or pain relief, but I do recall being told I was going for a CT scan. I blacked out shortly afterwards.

When I awoke, I was being lifted by a number of nurses, to be transferred from a hospital bed to an ambulance trolley. As the ambulance paramedic placed the seat belts across me, she informed me that I was being transferred to the specialist neurological centre at Southampton General Hospital. They suspected that I had had a stroke.

My nostrils filled with the smell of antiseptic cleaning spray as I entered the ambulance with a new crew. The ambulance slowly lurched away from the accident and emergency department and, as it joined the main road, I heard the 'blues and twos' activated. A blue strobing effect reflected into the ambulance. I was lying there, feeling the motion of the ambulance as it turned corners and changed lanes. Just like at work I remained calm, breathing normally. It's not like I could take control of anything. I just had to go with the flow and trust in the care and expert decision-making skills of the NHS staff who were looking after me.

There is a saying, that 'A little bit of knowledge, is a dangerous thing.' As an advanced police driver, I had been deployed on a number of occasions to escort ambulances on blue light runs between hospitals.

Similar to police escorting VIP convoys, they would race ahead to traffic lights and junctions, blocking the way to allow free passage for the ambulance. It was an exciting deployment, driving at high speed on blue lights, knowing that your actions would hopefully help to save a life.

I once even had to drive an ambulance, as both paramedics worked on the patient in the rear. I drove that ambulance to the hospital on blue lights.

Being involved in escorting ambulances, I quickly realised that most patients being transferred between hospitals on a blue light run were critically ill.

I tried to tell this to the paramedic during the drive, but my speech was still slurred, so I'm not sure I was making much sense. I could see the heart rate monitor attached to the wall of the ambulance had increased in speed. This was probably the first time that I had considered I was in a bit of a spot and might not make it.

The ambulance slowed down as it travelled through a long stretch of major roadworks on the M27. I could hear the ambulance driver curse the occasional motorist who had not used their mirrors and failed to move over to allow the ambulance through.

We arrived safely at the hospital in Southampton. The Wessex Neurological Centre is a specialised unit located within Southampton General Hospital, part of University Hospital Southampton NHS Foundation Trust (UHS).

The Wessex Neurological Centre is a significant regional hub for neurological and neurosurgical care, serving a large population across Central Southern England and the Channel Islands.

The building is regarded as a Centre of Excellence for neurological care offering comprehensive, high-quality, and often life-changing care for complex neurological conditions such as strokes and TBIs (traumatic brain injuries). Luckily for me, I was about to be exposed to some of the best specialist neurological nurses, doctors and consultant surgeons in the country.

I was already feeling fortunate as, had the brain haemorrhage occurred 10 or 15 minutes later, I would have been driving down that country road and would most likely have crashed and killed myself as a result.

Also, I hadn't placed the horse manure in the back of the police car, as that vehicle sat for a month afterwards and would have stunk to high heaven!

I arrived in the neurological intensive care unit at Southampton. There was no waiting in queues for me on arrival. I was whisked inside and placed in a very fetching hospital gown and had a surgical face mask placed on my face. We were still in a Covid lockdown and no vaccine had been developed at that time. Everyone in the general population was worried about contracting the virus.

I was transferred from the ambulance bed to a hospital bed. The overhead lights were bright inside the hospital, and I recall finding the brightness a little annoying, like when you drive in sunlight but have forgotten your sunglasses. In fact, this was most likely my eyes and brain adjusting to the haemorrhage and blood that was now building up inside my skull. Everything was out of my control, which felt strange for someone who was used to being very much in control. I was aware that my condition was serious, but maybe not how serious things really were…

Similar to those TV medical drama shows, there was an initial flurry of activity by doctors and nurses at my bedside, following my arrival. Cannulas were inserted into both of my arms to allow the easy administration of fluids and drugs. The headache was still strong and painful, with my brain feeling like it wanted to explode. I was unable to see very well, with double/blurred vision remaining a constant problem. My balance was poor but, as I was lying down in a bed, that was not an immediate concern. I was able to communicate and answer the relentless string of questions about knowing my name, date of birth and everything else.

Unfortunately, my speech was still very much affected by the brain haemorrhage, and my responses were difficult to understand (notwithstanding my northern accent) but I managed as well as can be expected.

The good thing was, I was still conscious and my vital signs were being stabilised. The on-duty neurological consultant, Mr Salima Wahab, came to me to explain what was going to happen next. Standing next to my bed, he said, 'We believe you have had some sort of brain haemorrhage. We now need to fully understand what has happened and what has caused it. We can then look at how best to treat you, but this will take some time.'

He explained I would be shortly going for another scan; this time it was an MRI scan of my head, as I had been for a CT scan in Portsmouth. The MRI scan is an effective imaging tool for detecting brain haemorrhages, often being more sensitive than a CT scan for identifying various stages of bleeding and chronic bleeding, such as microbleeds.

A little while later, I was laid out on a table in a cold room and scanned again. I was feeling really tired and my stomach was moaning. Not because of lack of food; I had the constant urge to be sick. The feeling of nausea was overwhelming at times, but I now understand this can be a common symptom of a brain injury.

I had a light grey moulded paper mâché disposable sick bowl with me at all times in the hospital, normally resting on my chest or just tucked under my arm ready for action. My ever-faithful friend followed me around, ready to catch the contents of my stomach at a moment's notice. I was returned to the neurological ICU where my bed was one of six. The only other patient was an elderly chap wired up to medical machines, sleeping on the other side of the ward, wearing a matching hospital gown and face mask.

Mr Wahab came to see me to give a brief update. He explained I had suffered a bleed on the brain. It was not yet confirmed what had caused the bleed, but I would be kept in the ICU while they stabilised my condition and did more tests to know how to proceed. I thanked him and lay in my bed a little in shock. I was only 49 years old. Surely this kind of stuff only happens to old people? I was relatively young, fit and healthy. I had never suffered with any symptoms such as 'fitting' or issues with my cognitive function. Why me?

I had lost track of time, and glanced at my phone sitting on the bedside table, which appeared to hover on a metal leg with wheels over the side of my bed. The table also contained another sick bowl and a plastic water jug with a well-fitting lid to prevent spillage sat next to a plastic cup. The water remained untouched. The phone showed the time as 16.15 hours and a battery level at 20%.

'Bloody hell,' I thought. 'I'm in the shit now.'

I had told Janet that I would only be gone about 1-2 hours this morning when I set off from home! She would probably be worrying and wondering what had happened to me. I knew I needed to call her and give her some sort of update. The trouble was, if I called, she would hear my slurred voice. I opted for sending a WhatsApp message to break the news. But what do you say to your wife in these circumstances?

The first issue was not being able to see the phone very well. My eyesight was blurred and my eye-hand coordination was not exactly great. I started typing and came up with the following message:

'Sorry to scare you. I m at Southampton now on tyke neuro ict ward. They will be doing tests today and tomorrow. Wyken I see you next can you bring my glasses and phone charger. Thanks love you loads. Kisses to u and the kids xxx'

Reading that back now, I realise it was probably not the greatest of messages I have ever sent, spelling mistakes included! I did not know at the time, but a police officer who I worked with had been to visit Janet at our home address. This was to update her as to what was happening and why I'd not returned home. I'm very grateful to that police officer for delivering that message, as I know it provided a great deal of comfort, if not a little shock at the time.

As my wife was also in the police, she had delivered 'death messages' in person. The sight of a police officer standing at your door with a sombre face is not normally good news. The only problem was, nobody knew what my condition was at that time or if I was even alive. We were in the thick of a global pandemic lockdown, so obtaining information was proving problematic and difficult.

We messaged a little more and Janet explained that she had collected the kids from school and they had been told, but were understandably upset. I responded with the following message,

'Been transferred to s/ton on a blue light run. Confirmed bleed on the brain. Bummer ☺. I'm sure ill be ok. Will be in hospital a couple of days at a guess

while they work out the cause. Love you and the kids. Try not to worry.'

I received a quick response from Janet starting, **'*It's a bit of a ridiculous statement saying 'try not to worry'! I'm worried out of my mind!......'***

I guess I would have been worried too. My little message home helped slightly in reassuring Janet I was alive and okay. But it also opened up a Pandora's box of questions. Would I live? If so, would I be disabled? Would I be paralysed? What would the extent of my disabilities be? Would she be faced with the prospect of wiping my bottom? How long would I be in the hospital? Did my parents need to be told or had I told them? Would I be able to work again and how would we cope for money?

Obviously all those questions didn't come up at once, or even in that order, but there was an overwhelming sense of so many unanswered questions and the recognition that this was not going to just affect me, but also the many other people close to me in my life.

My head hurt so much, as did the pressure in my eyes. My body was crying out for sleep, so after a short flurry of messages, I placed down my phone and closed my eyes. That first night sleep came quickly, but not for long. The nursing staff had to keep waking me on a regular basis so they could give me medication, check on the saline drips attached to me while checking and recording my vital signs such as blood pressure and pulse. More questions.

'Can you state your full name?'
'What is your date of birth?'

'What are you allergic to?'

'Are you in any pain right now?'

'On a scale of 0 to 10, with 0 being no pain and 10 being the worst possible pain, what is your pain level?'

'Can you tell me all the medications you are currently taking?'

'Have you passed urine/had a bowel movement today?'

It was only day one and I was already getting bored of these questions. I gave the pain level as 9.

I thought it best to update Janet as to how I was, because I knew she would continue to worry. I wanted to let her know that I was still alive. I was also aware that my phone was on about 5% battery. I sent another WhatsApp message,

'Morning. Just woke up xx'

I got no immediate response, but about an hour and a half later a message pinged in.

'R u ok? It's just gone 2am?'

What? Had I read that correctly? I glanced at the time and it was indeed the middle of the night. I was totally out of it. A mixture of the bleed on my brain, the drugs and fatigue had caused me to think it was daytime again. Oops! I fell back into a deep sleep. Well, that type of sleep when you get woken up every hour, but you know what I mean!

On waking at breakfast time, I messaged Janet to apologise. I was greeted with the news that she had packed me a bag containing a few clothes, my phone charger and toiletries plus my glasses, as I was not able to wear my contact lenses. This was great news and it really lifted my spirits. She had told a close friend, Sam, what happened to me; Sam was amazing in supporting Janet and helping with the kids. Janet and the children came to the hospital and dropped my bag off.

Mr Wahab came to my bedside on his morning round and asked how I was. I felt so fatigued and tired now; I just gave a feeble nod of my head to acknowledge him. Mr Wahab then explained that I was going to have to have an angiogram. Like a lot of people not used to visiting the inside of a hospital, I had no idea what he was on about! My only real experience was a full fry-up breakfast at St.Mary's hospital canteen in Pompey every Sunday morning on early turn with the rest of the police shift!

Well, an angiogram is a diagnostic procedure that uses X-rays and a special dye to visualise the blood flow inside your blood vessels. In my case, inside my brain. It is essentially a 'roadmap' of your arteries and veins, mainly used to identify blockages, narrowings, aneurysms, or other abnormalities.

He explained the procedure would take about an hour to perform and I would be awake and conscious throughout. 'Cool,' I thought.

He described the procedure and the risks associated with it. A very thin, flexible tube called a catheter was to be inserted into an artery in my groin. The tube would then be threaded into my heart via my arteries and veins. Then it would continue into my brain. I would be placed inside a CT scanner (computed tomography scanner) while a dye was pumped inside my brain, as the medical team took images of what was actually going on inside my head.

The risks included bruising and soreness. He said it was common to have a bruise and feel tender or sore at the insertion site.

A hematoma was possible, which is a collection of clotted blood under the skin at the puncture site. While usually small and harmless, a large or rapidly expanding lump could occur. I hoped that would not happen in my case.

Some people have a mild reaction to the contrast dye such as an itchy rash, hives, or mild nausea, which he stated is usually easy to manage with medication. I am normally not allergic to anything, so I was unconcerned.

He went on to explain the other more 'rare' risks associated with an angiogram: possible kidney damage. The contrast dye is processed and eliminated by the kidneys. In rare cases the dye can temporarily or permanently damage kidney function. I was going to be encouraged to drink extra fluids afterwards to help flush the dye out.

A severe allergic reaction to the contrast dye is rare, but can be life-threatening. Hmmm…not ideal, I thought.

Blood vessel damage was another risk. The catheter can potentially injure, tear, or dissect (create a flap in) the artery wall, which may require immediate emergency surgical repair. This procedure was now starting to sound a little more serious!

More risks included blood clots, heart attack, or a stroke! While the procedure is meant to prevent these, manipulating the catheter can sometimes dislodge fatty deposits from the artery wall. These fragments or blood clots can travel to the heart or brain, potentially causing a heart attack or stroke. At times like these, I started to think I should have skipped that extra sausage or black pudding while getting my breakfast at St. Mary's hospital!

Infection is always a risk with any operation. Any procedure that breaks the skin carries a small risk of infection at the insertion site, which may require antibiotics. Another 'slight' risk is something called arrhythmia. Passing the catheter near the heart can occasionally irritate the heart muscle and cause irregular rhythms, which are usually temporary but may cause a heart attack.

The final risk is **Death!** The risk of death is extremely low (estimated to be less than 1 in 1,000 for a diagnostic angiogram), but it is a potential complication of any invasive procedure, especially in critically ill patients.

Now to me, 1 in 1,000 seems too close for comfort. I have since done a bit of internet research to give that some context, and this is what I found. The odds of being struck by lightning in the UK are very low, estimated to be around one in 33 million per year. You have a one in 14 million chance of winning the National Lottery with a single ticket. Keeping to a policing theme, the odds of being burgled in the UK in 2022 were approximately one in 100 per year. However, the odds of having more than 10 toes in the UK are approximately 1 in 2,000 births.

The reality for me: I was critically ill and didn't really have any other options. It all seemed safe enough and I fully trusted these complete strangers to keep me alive, so I told them to 'crack on' with the procedure, formally giving my consent. What was going to happen next?

Mr Foster, you must not move at all!

While in the intensive care department, I was being constantly monitored for blood pressure, heart rate etc. I was strapped to various machines with a spider's web of wires and tubes. A short time later, I was told I was being transferred to the hospital theatre for the procedure. As my bed was pushed by porters, I looked up at the ceiling tiles and lights flashing past me as we travelled along the corridors. We arrived in the theatre room, and the nurses asked if I would be able to move across from my bed to the operating table.

Always eager to be helpful I said, 'Yes, no problem.'

I tried to shift my weight, shuffling my bottom over towards the other table. I had now been lying down for a few hours, not realising this would really affect my balance. I had been crashing around heading for the toilet immediately after the haemorrhage in the police building, but now I found it nearly impossible to control or balance my body.

As I shuffled over, my whole torso and legs started to roll in what felt like slow motion, similar to being a child rolling down a grassy hill in the summer. I was, however, heading straight for a sheer one metre drop, off the operating table onto the hard floor below!

With the room spinning over and over and no way to stop myself, the amazing nursing staff raced to the side of the operating table and multiple hands caught me as I rolled off. They lifted me back onto the table and joked at the near miss I had suffered. I was grateful for their quick reactions.

It felt like moments later, my leg and groin were being swabbed and the procedure was due to start. The surgeon clearly stated, 'Let us know if you are in any discomfort or pain. Whatever happens, don't move. You must stay totally still during the procedure, or you may be permanently paralysed.'

It was one of those motivational speeches that resonated with me. No way was I going to move for the next hour! Strangely I did not feel the catheter moving inside my body. I just lay there, totally still.

Have you ever tried to stay totally still for an hour? Very quickly your body decides to start complaining. For me, my body was complaining about my position on the table.

I dared not to move.

A tickly throat quickly developed and was giving me the sensation of needing to cough. For God's sake!

What was that noise? Oh yes, my breathing, of course. Why was I now focused on breathing? Was the rising of my lungs and chest too much? How would I control my breathing? I was becoming more and more anxious.

I knew I still could not move.

The room was filled with the mechanical noise of the CT scanner spinning inside the giant white plastic donut. My head was deep inside the donut hole, and my body was supported on the table protruding out of the machine.

The machine operator was positioned behind a glass window in a control room, looking in at me in the theatre. I could not see her, as I didn't want to move and was looking straight up. But I could hear her. Like a ringmaster controlling the show, she would offer reassuring words of advice and explain each step of the procedure over loudspeakers embedded in the ceiling. I smiled, thinking about being on a fairground ride and the operator shouting over the loud music, 'Scream if you wanna go faster!'

I then felt a warm, flushing sensation as the dye was injected inside my brain. This felt strange but the feeling only lasted a few minutes. The donut finally stopped spinning and I was taken out of the room, without being dropped.

On my return to the intensive care unit, I felt a sense of disappointment. I spotted that my bag had been delivered and an excited nurse told me it had been dropped off today. Unfortunately, nobody was allowed into the hospital due to the Covid rules. I was not going to get my visit. It did not matter that I was still critically ill.

It dawned on me at this moment that, other than the hospital staff, I was on my own. Yes, I knew my family and friends and colleagues would be thinking and supporting me from the outside, sending best wishes, but I was not going to get any visitors during my stay in hospital.

Difficult though this was, I totally understood the reasons why. The virus could not be allowed to spread uncontrolled through a hospital with so many vulnerable people being cared for. Myself included.

After the angiogram, I was exhausted and managed to sleep relatively well. When I woke up, though, my head still felt like a heavy bucket of sand with a bit of water sloshing around. Every time I moved, it felt like my brain was slowly catching up, nothing instantaneous.

There was a heavy, dull pain, and my eyesight was still blurry. The consultant, Mr Wahab, came to update me. The angiogram had diagnosed a ruptured arteriovenous malformation, or AVM. I'd never heard of it before and had no idea what he was talking about.

He had to explain it in layman's terms: a jumbled-up bundle of capillaries, veins, and arteries that had grown malformed. In my case, a weak spot in this network of tubes had ruptured, causing a subarachnoid haemorrhage. He described this as a serious type of stroke, with bleeding in the space between the brain and the skull. All these new terms, and here I was in my forties, surprised this was happening to me!

The AVM was in my cerebellum, known as the 'little brain' at the back, just above where the spinal cord connects to the brain. It regulates muscular activity and coordinates movement. Suddenly, my sudden balance issues and slurred speech made perfect, terrifying sense. This damage was the reason I couldn't walk straight or say words correctly.

I asked what might have caused it, but he explained it's not fully known why they occur. AVMs usually form as developmental errors in the brain before or shortly after birth. They aren't inherited, not really down to genetics. Just one of those things. I was just very unlucky to have one, and even unluckier that it had burst without any prior symptoms. The consultant told me that the brain tissue itself has no pain receptors, which is why neurosurgeons can operate when a patient is awake. It's the nerves in the surrounding blood vessels and muscles that send pain signals. On hearing this my mind was blown, no pun intended.

I was keen to know more and asked about survival rates. The consultant didn't hold back. He said they would do everything they could, but I was stable although still critically ill. He explained that roughly half of people with a brain haemorrhage don't even make it to the hospital alive. Of those who do, a further 25% face severe, permanent disabilities. The final 25% survive with minor or no disabilities. It's estimated 40% of patients die within a month.

I was fortunate to be in Southampton neurological unit, in the hands of some of the best neurosurgeons and nursing staff in the world. He went on to explain the possible treatment options: medication, endovascular embolisation and Gamma Knife radiosurgery. A team of specialists would be holding a case conference to decide the best course of action for me.

The days in the hospital began to roll into one another. I grew accustomed to the daily rhythm of the ward: nurses buzzing around the ICU, the clatter and squeak of the tea trolley. I could drink tea, but keeping food down was still a struggle due to constant nausea. As my sight and balance failed me, other senses became acute, especially my hearing. It's amazing how the body adapts. I managed to continue to stay in touch and message Janet and the kids on WhatsApp, as phone calls were difficult with my slurred speech.

While I was stabilising, I was completely unaware of the ripple effect this had on everyone. My daughters, who were eight and eleven years old at the time, were obviously concerned. Janet was fantastic, being sensitive enough to protect them, but honest enough not to build up false hopes.

The children had so many questions that Janet couldn't answer, so she spoke to the nurses on the neurological unit. They suggested something amazing: the girls could email their questions, and the night staff would reply. It helped them understand what was happening to their father and prepared them for the future. This new initiative was so successful that the unit decided to implement it for other patients. It was a testament to the genuine, caring nature of the hospital staff.

After nearly two weeks, the consultant announced I was going home on 3 August. The plan was for me to return in about a month for neurosurgery to remove the AVM. I was thrilled to be going home, but also nervous about leaving the care of the medical team. On the day of my discharge, a nurse wheeled me in a wheelchair to the main entrance where our close friend, Sam, was waiting.

The drive home felt like a relatively friendly conversation to me, though I was extremely tired and weak. I later learned Sam had told Janet that I seemed 'very odd' and not myself at all, lacking my usual sense of humour and bordering on rude! I feel mortified about that; I was just so ill without truly realising it and how it was affecting me as a person. My youngest daughter had given up her bedroom for me, which was an amazing act of kindness. This allowed me to stay in bed during the day and in the evening as I was still unable to move around freely, without assistance. I was ever so grateful.

Janet and my eldest daughter were equally brilliant in looking after me. Preparing drinks, preparing meals, and helping me with all those things that we take for granted when we are fit, well and healthy.

The plan was to return to Southampton at the end of August for brain surgery. The only fly in the ointment was COVID-19. The hospital needed to ensure my family bubble and I remained virus-free. So, on my birthday, I was driven to a testing site in a large car park, just outside Southampton. A medic in full PPE swabbed my throat and nostrils, while I sat in the car. Thankfully, the result came back negative.

My symptoms continued at home, but the sickness had subsided, and my speech was slowly returning to normal. That evening, we celebrated with a takeaway curry, dropped off by a work colleague, Helen. A small act of kindness that meant so much. I didn't know if it would be my last curry.

On 27 August, the big day had come. Janet woke me early. She packed a bag with clothes, toiletries, and an Android tablet my work colleagues had bought for me. She drove me back to the hospital, but due to COVID restrictions, she couldn't come in. My vision was still affected, but I could now walk, or rather weave my way towards the entrance. I kissed Janet, told her I loved her, and got out of the car.

Tears were running down my face as I walked towards the main doors, and I couldn't bring myself to look back. My head was swimming with questions. Would I live? The statistics were in my favour, but you just don't know. And if I survived, who would I be? Would my personality change? Would I still have my sense of humour? Would I be paralysed? I had a brief, panicked moment wondering if I'd remember my PINs and passwords.

I brushed the tears aside with my sleeve and weaved my way through the entrance. There was no turning back.

The big day had arrived

After shuffling along the surprisingly quiet hospital corridors, I found my way to the neurological unit. I presented my details, was welcomed onto the ward with a reassuring smile and shown to an empty bed that would be my little island for the foreseeable future.

All I had was that small bag. The Android tablet would become a lifeline, my portal to the outside world.

A nurse bustled over, handed me a hospital gown that looked about as dignified as a paper bag, and instructed me to strip naked. With the flimsy curtain pulled around the bed for a sliver of privacy, I did as I was told, emerging moments later clad in the rather fetching, backless ensemble. I sat on the edge of the bed, my feet on the floor, and caught the eye of the chap in the bed opposite. He looked to be in his fifties. I offered a friendly nod; he smiled and nodded back, though his silence suggested his condition prevented him from communicating verbally.

Soon, the relentless ritual of pre-op checks began. Nurses came and went in a blur, taking my blood pressure, temperature, and heart rate with a practised efficiency that was both comforting and slightly unnerving as I thought about what lay ahead for me.

The plan, as it had been explained to me in soothing tones and bullet-pointed leaflets, was simple: arrive, get whisked in, have the pre-planned operation, wake up to a future with fewer risks of my brain exploding and have more tea. I liked the idea of being 'whisked', as it sounded efficient, almost culinary. Unfortunately, the morning had a different flavour.

My consultant surgeon, Mr Diederik Bulters, appeared. He was calm, kind, and very clearly carrying the weight of someone else's crisis, yet still totally focused on me and my needs as a patient. He explained that a patient with a similar AVM to mine had been rushed in during the night after a brain haemorrhage and had gone straight into emergency surgery to save his life. I could see my plan of an early morning operation rapidly fading away. Depending on how long the emergency patient needed in theatre, he said, would depend on when I'd have my turn. He hoped for the afternoon.

'We'll have to wait and see,' he added, which is never quite as reassuring as medical professionals think it is.

Mr Bulters then calmly walked me through the surgical nitty-gritty: the incision across my head, the peeling back of the skin, the drilling of holes into my skull and the use of a small circular saw to remove a large piece of skull. He spoke of dissecting the delicate membranes protecting the brain and, finally, the careful snipping and sealing of any stray veins left behind by the AVM. Once it was out, he assured me, it was unlikely to grow back. My skull would be put back in its rightful place, held together with staples, and I'd wake up a few hours later in an intensive care recovery ward.

His explanation was so matter-of-fact, so devoid of drama, that it had a strangely calming effect. I knew none of this was under my control. My only job was to trust these professionals to do their best work, and in doing so, keep me alive. With any luck, they would preserve the person – the memories, the quirks, the very essence of me – that resided inside the brain they were about to fiddle with. Bizarrely, I was thinking: how many people have their brains exposed to the outside world?

Then came the risks. I'd heard them before, but he repeated them again, just to be sure. The operation could cause a massive stroke, cause disability and in a worst-case scenario, kill me. But, he added with quiet confidence, he considered that a low risk. Frankly, from my perspective, with the odds of another catastrophic bleed increasing every year, it was a no-brainer. Pardon the pun. So, with my eyesight still blurry, I signed my life away on his clipboard.

The operation was likely to last between eight to ten hours. For me, thankfully, it would all happen under a general anaesthetic. I would be blissfully asleep for the whole performance.

He did, however, mention that some of these procedures are done with the patient awake, a nurse casually chatting and asking questions while the surgeon is, for want of a better phrase, rummaging around in their brain. The very thought of it was mind-blowing, and I felt a fresh wave of gratitude that I'd be completely oblivious to my own cranial renovations

Mr Bulters arranged for the anaesthetist to run through a final pre-operation checklist. The whole thing had the feel of a space shuttle launch, a meticulous series of checks and double-checks to ensure nothing was missed and nothing could go wrong. I hadn't been allowed to eat or drink anything all morning, though a kindly nurse did let me have a tiny sip of water to quench a nervous thirst.

I messaged Janet to say there had been a delay. I kept it short and practical, but there's only so much you can squeeze into a text while wearing a hospital gown and thinking about having your skull cut open. It wasn't just me who was nervous that day, so it was important to keep people updated. I knew there were people at home carrying their own versions of the worry, pacing kitchens, refreshing phones, making tea they weren't going to drink. Hospitals have a way of stretching time so it feels both endless and very definitely happening right now.

The waiting was now like its own theatre. There's that antiseptic bite in the air, the soft shuffle of rubber soles, the ripple of paper curtains being pulled in their runners. You become very aware of every sound: the distant rumble of a trolley, the clipped murmur of a nurse, the whisper of your own breath when you've run out of things to think about. I wasn't sure what happened to the emergency patient, and that uncertainty hummed in the background like a fluorescent light. It's odd, feeling your fate braided with a stranger's. There's a solidarity in that, even if it's silent.

But earlier than expected, at 11 o'clock, a nurse popped her head round the curtain and said, with a smile, 'You're going in.'

No grand fanfare, no drumroll. Just those few words, quietly pulling me forward with the help of a porter. Relief arrived like a warm blanket, then took on an edge. Relief meant the part where they try to fix you, and it was about to begin. I sent a quick message to Janet to the effect of 'It's happening' and put the phone away.

Here we go.

I lay back on the bed. With a clunk, the brakes were released, and I was suddenly in motion, being whisked down the corridor, the ceiling lights flashing past above me. My thoughts raced. Would I wake up? Would I ever see my wife and children again? All I could do was put my faith in the people wheeling me towards my fate. I remember the coolness of the corridor air and the bright, officious lighting that makes everything look clean and unforgiving.

The theatre doors opened with that calm certainty hospitals do so well. I think of that other patient sometimes. A ghost companion to my memory of the day. We were strangers who never met and do not know of their fate, but we shared a timetable written in blood and chance. And at 11 o'clock, the clock finally decided I was next. It was my time to be called, grateful, terrified, and quietly aware that somewhere, someone else has made room.

The trolley juddered to a halt, and I realised we were in a lift, which groaned its way to the theatre floor. I was taken into a room that looked like a set from a TV medical drama – a vast array of bright lights on overhead gimbals and a smattering of equipment. This, they explained, was just the pre-op room; the main event was through the adjoining double doors. The space shuttle checklist continued: name, date of birth, my understanding of the operation. More vital signs were taken. Everything was going to plan.

Then, a machine on a trolley, designed to administer intravenous drugs, started making a disgruntled beeping noise. It clearly wasn't happy. The staff fiddled with it, but it just kept beeping back at them in disgust. I found myself wondering if this sort of thing happened at Cape Canaveral. Now was probably not the best time for me to suggest, 'Have you tried turning it on and off? A restart?'

'It's no good, it's not working,' one of them finally declared, explaining that the machine was rather vital and they couldn't proceed without a functioning one. It turns out that, just like at NASA, operating theatres have a back-up for everything. They simply swapped it for a spare, and we were back in business.

The preparations continued. Cannulas were inserted into my arms, ready for the cocktail of drugs. The anaesthetist leaned in and told me he was going to put me to sleep now, and that I should start counting to 10.

But this was my Cape Canaveral, my very own space launch. Counting up felt all wrong. So, I decided to count down. Ready for blast-off.

'Ten… nine… eight… seven… six… five… four…'

I never made it to blast-off. I drifted happily away into the land of nod before I even got to zero. And funnily enough, I don't recall a single thing about the operation. Which is probably just as well.

I woke up roughly eight or nine hours later. Night had settled like a blanket over the hospital, and I seemed to be parked on a ward, softly lit and wonderfully hushed. The nursing station glowed off to the side, a warm little island in the gloom. I wasn't wearing my glasses or contact lenses, so everything was gloriously blurry. Still, I smiled to myself. I was alive.

Blast off!

A nurse noticed that my head had wobbled and my eyes had opened and she drifted over from the nursing station. She spoke in that gentle, honeyed tone that nurses must learn from years of experience in caring for patients, and welcomed me to intensive care within the neurological department.

I found it incredibly difficult to move my head from side to side, left or right, as my neck and spine were probably still quite swollen as a result of the surgery. As far as seeing who else was on the ward, I could only manage a squint at shapes that could have been people or could have been trolleys, and there was no real way to tell.

The thing I did notice immediately, was the sensation before the operation of my brain inside my skull, like sand in a bucket of water, always taking time to catch up, had gone. It felt amazing. I smiled to myself, knowing that part of the operation had gone well.

Machines murmured unseen around me, the steady rhythmic bleeping like a metronome for life. The nurse explained it was night, I should try to sleep, and I would feel better by morning. She took the opportunity to check my vital signs yet again: blood pressure, oxygen, pulse. Little beeps answered back as if everything was ticking along nicely. I felt exhausted, despite having done absolutely nothing beyond lying perfectly still and attempting not to pop a stitch with enthusiasm.

I was still obviously well medicated, but I could feel a slight headache and my bottom lip hurt. Closing my mouth and putting my lips together, I could feel my bottom lip was very swollen and I could taste the blood in my mouth, which I had not expected.

It emerged that, during the procedure, the medical team had struggled to insert an airway tube into my mouth and throat. The tube itself is rigid and is designed to create a clear passage for air between the front of the teeth and the base of the tongue. It's inserted upside down and then rotated into position once the tip has passed the tongue. I'd actually been trained to use them during advanced first aid courses in the police.

In my case, the airway tube proved stubborn and became stuck. The theatre staff had to apply a bit of force to persuade it into place, and in doing so managed to split my lip, leaving me looking as though I'd just stepped out of a boxing ring.

Then an idea struck. It's not every day you have brain surgery, and I had to capture the occasion. I asked the nurse if she'd do me a favour: could she take a photo of my head using my phone so I could see what I looked like? She happily agreed. I passed her the phone, feeling faintly ridiculous and faintly brilliant.

I was a little underwhelmed, but thought, oh my God, what have they done to me?

She held the phone in front of my face, displaying the photographic evidence. What I saw can only be described as a reverse Mohican, which felt perfectly accurate in its wrongness. The back of my head had been shaved in one thick strip, like a runway for a tiny plane. Everywhere else, I still had hair left untouched and somehow mocking me. The surgical area alone was bald and stern.

Note to self: if I ever have to sign up for brain surgery again, shave the whole of my head first.

They'd covered the wound with a dressing I can only describe as a giant sanitary towel, now firmly stuck to the back of my head from the top of my spine reaching up towards the crown. It looked ridiculous. I'd been secretly hoping for a hero's scar – something cinematic, evidence I could show off, a souvenir of survival. This was definitely not it. The nurse smiled, and I could tell she meant well, but I also knew the photo would not see the light of day, never mind social media. I looked ridiculous. Terribly, magnificently ridiculous.

And yet, lying there with the soft beeping keeping time and the antiseptic air pricking my nose, I felt a flicker of relief. There I was, awake enough to recognise myself, even through my blurry vision and cunning disguise with a sanitary towel on my head. Not the scar shot I'd hoped for, perhaps, but indisputably me. Alive, and that was a better souvenir.

I was only in intensive care recovery for a few hours, barely time to acquaint myself with the bed controls, before the nurses announced I was fit to be moved to the neurological ward. It felt wonderfully encouraging, like being upgraded from 'vital concern' to 'mildly worrying'.

On arrival, I managed to send a few WhatsApp messages to Janet to update her, saying all appeared to have gone well. She could then update the immediate family that I was fine. Look, I could do basic tasks. I could talk with a slur and I could type. I could even locate the emoji with the sunglasses.

I put some music on my tablet, pressed my earbuds in and let myself drift off to a carefully curated selection of '80s classics. There's a particular comfort in synth lines and drum machines when you're trying to drift off to sleep. I woke after an hour or so, still in pain, my ear hating the indignity of being tangled up with a wire. The earbuds had to go. Back to the full orchestral score of hospital life.

Sleep, though, had other ideas. I had a friendly chap in the next bed along – a large Asian gentleman with a cheerfulness and jolly demeanour. He reminded me of the 'Raj' corner shop character from the David Walliams books: wonderfully jolly, endlessly polite, and now very clearly frightened about his own health. Whatever confidence he'd had, it seemed to be trying to escape.

He was obviously nervous about his current medical condition and just wanted to chat. Every hour. All night. Gentle questions, small observations, a stream of conversation that flowed through the dark, like tea through a strainer. He was very nice, genuinely kind, but my goodness, I wanted to sleep. The ward lights dimmed, the machines hummed their lullaby, and he kept talking, a one-man radio show with me as the captive audience.

The tea lady appeared in the morning, pushing her trolley. Things were looking up, I thought. The nurses, however, had marked my bed 'nil by mouth' and swooped in, both apologetic and efficient, to offer me a small drink and see how I managed. I would have sold a minor heirloom for a biscuit, but there's only so much rebellion you can stage with a dry mouth and a cannula.

By mid-morning, with the tea lady's trolley rattling past and my neighbour rehearsing another round of midnight musings in daylight, I realised that recovery isn't a straight line. It was going to take time.

I felt the call of nature as I lay in my bed and sunlight started to fill the ward. I was unable to walk. It would be a few days before I could even sit in a chair next to the bed. A small wave of panic came over me as I needed to have a wee, and started looking for the button to press for the nurse. I looked under the sheet and spotted a clear catheter tube, snaking off to the side of the bed.

I could see what I can only describe as a large transparent plastic briefcase with a handle, attached to the bed in a cradle. It was already half full of urine. When the hell did they put that in? I was having silly thoughts. This would have been done for the operation as well as the recovery.

I lay there for a second, praying that when I released my contracted muscles, I wouldn't wet the bed. Of course, it all worked exactly as it should. However, in my search for the button to call the nurse, I found another button that looked like a detonator switch a suicide bomber might use, attached to a long lead on my left-hand side. I pressed the button on the bed for the nurse and awaited her arrival and inquired what this second remote button was for.

She explained it was linked to a machine next to me that could administer painkilling drugs at my request. It was specially designed to prevent any chance of overdose and would only dispense a certain amount of drugs over a period of time, but it was for me to decide when to administer it. She explained it was strong morphine, but if I felt pain to give it a try. My head was pounding, so I pressed the button.

Boom!

I felt a warm sensation through my whole body and suddenly became more relaxed. The pain just melted away.

I drifted off to sleep again.

When I next swam up into consciousness, the world temporarily still felt like it was moving through treacle. It took a sluggish moment to place myself: white sheets, rhythmic beeping, the faint, antiseptic smell of the hospital ward. My gaze drifted around the ward and I noticed a conspicuous absence. The friendly little machine that had been diligently administering morphine into my arm on request was gone. I had only a chance to use it once, I thought!

'Excuse me,' I said to the first nurse who bustled past, trying to keep the panic out of my voice. 'My… er… my little magic box seems to have vanished.'

She gave me a brisk, cheerful smile. 'Oh, that's just for straight after the operation. Not to worry, you'll be on paracetamol from now on.'

Paracetamol. For brain surgery. I must have looked aghast, because she patted my arm reassuringly before sweeping off to her next patient. I was left to ponder this new development. paracetamol. You'd get more sympathy for a stubbed toe.

The highlight of my otherwise monotonous schedule was, without a doubt, mealtime. My senses, seemingly rebooted by the surgical rummaging in my head, were on high alert. I could smell lunch long before it arrived – a scent I've come to associate with institutional catering everywhere: boiled cabbage.

A plastic tray was placed before me, bearing a plate shrouded by a little plastic stackable cloche, a tub of ice cream, and a plastic beaker of orange squash. I fumbled with the buttons on the side of the bed, raising myself into a sitting position, determined to eat without redecorating my pyjamas. Across the way, my fellow inmates – Raj still beside me, another chap opposite – were all leaning forward with the same eager anticipation. It's funny how a plate of warm food can become the most exciting event of your day.

I managed a few mouthfuls, savouring the change from a liquid diet, when a sudden, volcanic heat surged through me. A wave of nausea crashed over my body. My eyes darted around, frantically searching for the cardboard sick bowl I'd seen earlier. Shoving my tray aside, I grabbed it just in time to unceremoniously empty the contents of my stomach with a series of loud, deeply embarrassing retches.

A nurse appeared at my side in a flash, all calm efficiency.

'Perfectly normal after brain surgery,' she said, wiping my face as if I were a toddler. 'Quite common. We'll get some anti-sickness medication prescribed for you.'

For the next few days, my diet consisted of sugary tea and the odd spoonful of ice cream; I could just coax those past my rebellious stomach. My poor wardmates, who only wanted to enjoy their cabbage in peace, were treated to the soundtrack of my retching at every meal. It was horrendous.

With visitors still banned, my only connection to the outside world was my electronic tablet. Thank God for NHS Wi-Fi. Cut off from my family, I found solace in the Police Anti-Corruption Unit, AC-12. I'd never had the time to get into the TV series *Line of Duty* before, what with work and kids and the general chaos of life. Now, I had nothing but time. I binged the whole thing, spending my days utterly engrossed in the hunt for 'H'. It was the perfect distraction from the fact I couldn't keep a sandwich down.

The following morning, the usual gaggle of doctors and their student entourage descended on my bed. I was quite happy to be a living exhibit, answering their questions about my experience.

'Did you have many fits before the bleed?' one bright-eyed student asked.

'None at all,' I replied. 'No symptoms whatsoever.'

He looked genuinely shocked, a little flicker of textbook theory colliding with real-world messiness. I now know some patients suffer with epileptic-style fits as a result of having an AVM in the brain. Roughly between 20% and 45% of cerebral arteriovenous malformations (AVMs) present with seizures or epilepsy of varying types.

One of the more unusual symptoms I suffered was an itchy scalp. I mentioned this to the doctors and was informed that this was quite common. The sensation is caused by the increased blood flow to the scalp, helping to heal the surgery site from the inside. Interesting for me, but also irritating. I was, however, pleased that my speech had returned back to normal. Well, I say normal; I was noticing that, on occasions, I would say a word that had the opposite meaning. What could possibly go wrong? My brain was still glitching after the operation.

The consultant then delivered the next piece of news. 'As standard procedure,' he explained gently, 'you'll have to notify the DVLA. You won't be able to drive for at least six months, until we're certain there's no risk of post-operative seizures.'

For a man who'd been an advanced police driver and genuinely loved being behind the wheel, this should have been a blow. But honestly, at that moment, driving was the last thing on my mind. Just getting to the loo felt like an expedition to the North Pole.

Ah, the loo. My time in the police, particularly investigating drug offences, had made me uncomfortably aware of the side effects of opioids. Heroin, for instance, is notorious for causing constipation. And after my brief but glorious affair with morphine, I was feeling distinctly…bunged up.

It brought to mind a chap I'd arrested for TFMV (theft from motor vehicles) in Portsmouth. He was a well-known heroin user, who had smashed a quarter light window to remove a TomTom sat-nav and the loose change from the interior of the car. Unfortunately for him, I had caught him only one street away after several calls from members of the public.

He'd started his usual performance at the custody desk, complaining of stomach ache, hoping to fast-track his way out of a cell. This was often a ruse to get to a toilet and flush whatever evidence they'd secreted about their person. The custody sergeant, a man who'd seen it all, told him he could go to the loo once he'd been searched and booked in.

At this, the man turned white as a sheet. 'Too late!' he wailed as he fell to the floor. Then, to the horror of everyone in the charge room, he pulled down his tracksuit bottoms, with his knees bent into his chest he exposed his backside, and unleashed what I can only describe as a liquid fountain of diarrhoea all over the floor. The stench was biblical. We all recoiled, witnessing the spectacular, explosive end of opioid-induced constipation. It wasn't pretty. Luckily I did not get the job of cleaning things up.

I digress. My own journey to the toilet, I'm pleased to report, was considerably less dramatic. Aided by a nurse on each arm, I made the slow, shuffling pilgrimage from my bed. These little walks became a daily ritual. Small steps, literally. Just moving from the bed to the adjacent chair was a victory. Soon, I was managing a few steps down the ward. I couldn't walk in a straight line to save my life, but I was walking.

Then came the day I was introduced to the neurological physiotherapist. She arrived at my bedside with a determined look in her eye.

'Right,' she announced. 'For us to discharge you, you need to prove you can walk down the corridor and get up and down a flight of stairs.'

I was keen, but also terrified.

'Okay,' I agreed, picturing a day or two of mental and physical preparation.

'Excellent,' she beamed. 'Let's go then.'

'Now?'

'No time like the present!'

There was just one small, rather personal snag. 'My catheter,' I said, pointing to the plastic briefcase-like bag hanging from the side of my bed.

'Don't you worry about that,' she said, breezily unhooking it. 'I'll carry it.'

And with that, she started walking away from the bed at a brisk pace, my catheter case in one hand, essentially towing me along by my most sensitive anatomy. I can tell you, if you're ever looking for a way to motivate someone to walk, having a stranger march off with their urine case is startlingly effective. In my time investigating sexual offences and working with the vice squad, I'd become aware that people paid good money for experiences not dissimilar to this.

'Could you…slow down a bit?' I half-joked, half-pleaded, shuffling frantically to keep up.

She finally stopped at a staircase.

'I'll walk behind you on the way up,' she said.

'And I'll keep hold of this,' lifting my plastic case of urine, obviously concerned about my balance.

Tentatively, I placed a foot on the first step, my hand gripping the rail for dear life. Slowly, shakily, I pulled myself up. One step. Then another. Before I knew it, I was at the top. I felt like Rocky Balboa on the steps of the Philadelphia Museum of Art. I was elated. I was going home.

'Right,' the physio said, bringing me crashing back to earth. 'Now down again.'

So I turned and began the slow, painstaking descent. Every single step was a triumph. I'd done it. The physio was pleased, and I was just relieved the ordeal was over. What I realised during that test, and have noticed ever since, is how much your brain does automatically. It uses your eyes, ears, and sense of balance to know exactly where you are in space.

My brain had lost that knack. I needed the handrail to give me a reference point, to tell me where the floor was. It's amazing how you adapt, though. Once I was out of the hospital, I found myself subtly running a knuckle or the end of my finger along the wall as I went downstairs, just to give my confused brain that little bit of extra data. I still do it now, almost without thinking.

Being mobile on the ward gave me a new perspective. I could see the other patients more clearly, and I realised in an instant just how lucky I was. Some had lost their speech, others their sight. Some faced a future of total dependency. Seeing their struggles was all the incentive I needed to push myself harder. Everyone's journey after a brain injury is unique, and I was determined to make the most of mine.

A few days later, I was being wheeled towards the hospital exit, smelling faintly musty from weeks of living in a bed unable to shower fully. Janet was waiting for me; my beautiful, caring wife.

As I got into the car, I saw the concern cloud her face. It wasn't just the smell. She told me later my eyes seemed vacant, staring into the distance. In that moment, she was terrified that the man she knew was gone for good. I was going to do my best to not let that happen.

Back home, my youngest daughter had once again surrendered her bedroom so I could have a quiet space to recover.

The house was calm, the world outside was still, and for the first time in what felt like an eternity, I wasn't just a patient in a bed.

I was home.

Recovering at home and a brainstorm

My recovery at home took nearly a year, and it was a slow, stubborn climb. Bit by bit, my strength returned. My vision, which had been knocked askew, was ultimately fixable with a change to my glasses prescription, a small mercy that felt like a minor miracle. Six months in, the DVLA wrote to say I could drive again. That single sheet of paper did wonders for morale. Not just mine, mind you, I could hear Janet's sigh of relief when she realised she was not the permanent family taxi service. I was keen to get back behind the wheel, determined to prove, if only to myself, that I could still do ordinary things in an ordinary way.

The walking came next. Every day, I practised: first a slow shuffle round the house, then down the street, and eventually far enough to walk my daughter to school and back. This became one of the loveliest parts of a difficult time. She'd hold my hand, not just in a dutiful way, but with a sort of conspiratorial tenderness, the two of us moving together that felt both protective and hopeful.

One of the side effects I suffered was a strange kind of vertigo. While walking, my body sometimes veered off as if I'd been drinking; an unhelpful impression at school pick-up, where you're surrounded by other parents judging you. The faster I went, oddly, the straighter I stayed. If I picked up into a jog, things aligned, as if momentum bullied my balance back into place.

Still, I was determined to walk unaided. My mother-in-law, Ann, asked me more than once whether I'd consider using a stick. She meant well, she had a few to hand, and there was something gentle, almost ceremonial, about the offer. But I was insistent. I would walk without one and 'do my own thing'. Stubbornness is a daft kind of strength, and yet it has its uses.

I'd been back home a week or so when the dressing finally came off, revealing the scar in all its grandeur. The surgeons had stapled the whole thing shut, and there it was: roughly eight inches of candy cane-shaped scar running up the back of my head, the sort of feature that would have been more at home in a Frankenstein reboot. My hair still hadn't grown back at the site, so I had the look of a man cutting his own hair during the Covid lockdown. Even I had to admit it continued to look ridiculous, but rather impressively ridiculous.

Another week passed, and it was time to visit the local doctor's surgery to have the staples removed. There's a special tool for it, apparently. Something that sounds more professional than 'giant staple remover', but fundamentally achieves the same effect. It's a peculiar sensation, hearing little metallic clicks while your head feels oddly lighter. The nurse nodded approvingly at the scar's neatness and told me it had healed well. I took the compliment as if I'd done the surgery myself.

With medical approval in hand and the hardware removed, the next stop was dignity. Specifically, a haircut. Even if I was sporting a landing strip of missing hair, the rest was a long, scraggy mess. So off I went to the local Turkish barber's, hoping that clever angles and brisk confidence might disguise the architectural deficit.

I sat on the bench, waiting my turn, trying not to think about the inevitable reveal. When the barber finally called me up, I settled into the chair, and caught his face in the mirror at the exact moment he glanced down and saw the scar. He physically recoiled, only slightly, like a man surprised by a pigeon, but then, to his huge credit, recovered instantly. He didn't say a word. Not a comment, not a question, not even a politely concerned eyebrow.

He just did what barbers do best: asked, 'Number two on the sides?' and got on with it.

There's a strange intimacy in letting someone you've never met cut your hair while both pretending everything is perfectly ordinary. The buzz of the clippers hummed against my scalp, the smell of Turkish aftershave and hair products hung in the air, and he kept up the usual patter: football scores, holidays, the weather, a faintly universal complaint about parking, all while carefully navigating around the back of my head like it was a cordoned-off police crime scene.

It made me ponder, as my hair fell in cautious little snowdrifts across the cape, how hairdressers must deal with this sort of thing all the time. Scars, birthmarks, odd bumps, the occasional surprise tattoo. They see stories on skulls long before we do, because they look, and then they carry on, kindly, professionally, as if normality were a service they provided along with the hot towel and neck powder.

I stepped out with a fresh cut and that peculiar levity you get when your head feels tidier and your reflection less alarming. The scar was still there, of course, my candy cane calling card, but now it seemed somehow less monstrous and more just part of the scenery. An inconvenience transformed by a good neat haircut.

Strangely at times, I did feel old before my time. My brain and body needed rest. Post surgery, I would normally go for a 2-3 hour sleep during the day, like some old man nodding off in the chair in front of the TV. Even now, I become fatigued much quicker than most people. This, unfortunately, is a common side effect of brain surgery, only having your internal energy battery charged to 70%. The important thing was I recognised this and made allowances to cater for it. Other symptoms included headaches I never previously suffered with and continued balance issues. My hearing was also more acute.

Visitors came regularly: police colleagues and supervisors, checking in to see how I was getting on. Some were required welfare visits, but most were my colleagues genuinely looking out for me. They were kind, and openly keen to have me back in the fold. I wanted that too, or at least I wanted the option of wanting it.

On one occasion, my skipper Al and a colleague called Reg, came to visit. While chatting, I found myself breaking down in tears. I am not normally one to cry at anything, and it surprised me, more than them, I think. After brain surgery, individuals may experience a range of emotional changes, including anxiety, irritability, and mood swings. These changes can often be linked to the brain's altered functioning and may improve with appropriate treatment and support. It can also be linked to post traumatic stress. For me, I feel it was a blip. But also my brain was getting used to understanding the enormity of what I had been through.

A few months in, I booked a two-week stay at Flint House, a rehabilitation facility for serving and retired police officers down in southern England. It's a charity many officers pay into throughout their careers, offering support for physical and mental health issues to officers and their families. And thank heavens it exists, because while there are plenty of physiotherapists around, very few specialise in neurological physiotherapy – the kind I needed – rather than the more common musculoskeletal sort. At Flint House, I was lucky enough to get exactly the right help.

Daily physio made a remarkable difference. In those two weeks, the progress was visible, almost measurable. I'd always loved running, and I wanted to know I could still do it. That was my goal. The team there built a programme to help me get back on track, literally and figuratively. I left buoyed by optimism. Possibly too buoyed.

A few days later, I took my two daughters down to the local running track. A wide-open sports ground felt like a safe place to test things. I still couldn't guarantee a perfectly straight walk on a pavement, and the last thing I wanted was to step into the road by mistake. On the track, I figured, the worst that could happen was I'd embarrass myself in front of my children, which is more or less a father's job description.

We lined up for a 100-metre dash: 'On your marks, get set…go!'

Off we burst, all youthful energy and misplaced confidence, some of us more youthful than others. Within seconds, everything went into that odd slow motion I'd come to recognise. My centre of gravity tipped forward, the ground pulled at me, and I couldn't correct it. I fell headlong, shoulder and arms absorbing the impact before I rolled over like a sack of uncoordinated potatoes.

My daughters ran to me, worried. I assured them I was fine, only the pride had taken a knock. And once they knew I was physically okay, they did what daughters do best: lovingly took the mickey. Gentle ribbing delivered with merciful precision. It was a minor setback, nothing more, and we laughed about it, which still felt like progress.

I returned to the neurological unit in Southampton a few months later for another angiogram procedure. Post operation, I was lying in my hospital bed. I noticed some activity by a patient's bed in the corner by the window. A male in his 40s was with two doctors and a male in a suit on a laptop, which I thought was unusual, all sitting by the side of his bed.

The patient had extreme tremors that appeared to be totally uncontrollable as his body shook, like he had run into an electric fence. Suddenly this male started crying, and the man controlling the laptop apologised, explaining the settings, if not correct, can cause pain. A smile grew over the patient's face and he explained these were tears of joy, as the probes that had been placed into his brain had managed to temporarily stop the tremors for the first time in 30 years. He was overcome with emotion. Myself and some other patients clapped quietly in celebration at the man's achievement. I was, again, acutely aware of the marvels of medical science. Also, how fortunate I was.

I was later elated to hear that the result of my own procedure was good news and the whole of the AVM had been successfully removed. The NHS had saved my life.

As time went on and my recovery improved, the bigger decisions loomed. Two years left before retirement at 30 years' service. Could I return to policing? Not in the role I'd been doing, that much was clear. So I did something I'd been quietly planning for years. I stepped away.

I resigned with gratitude, thanking the police and my colleagues for everything they'd done for me. And then, in the manner of someone who finds themselves reborn at an inconveniently middle-aged moment, I signed up with a handful of 'extras' agencies. 'Supporting actors', darling, as they call it in the trade. The people you see on screen in the background, holding coffee cups and walking purposefully down corridors, pretending not to notice the famous person having a crisis.

I thought it would be a giggle, and it was. I have met all sorts of people on many TV and film sets. I even found myself in a Bollywood film at one point. Who'd have thought it? A lad from Rochdale in Bollywood. I can't tell you which one, thanks to an assortment of non-disclosure agreements, but rest assured it was as gloriously surreal as you might imagine.

Parallel to that, I began building the thing I'd always imagined I'd do after policing: my own business. I've long had an interest in computers, and I'd picked up a range of skills in the force that felt immediately transferable to the private sector, cyber security in particular.

Open-source intelligence gathering, Ransomware investigations. Ransomware negotiation (yes, that's a thing) and my favourite, physical penetration testing. Using social engineering techniques to con my way inside buildings, to gain access to premises, offices, compounds and computer networks. It's like being a detective, only you're the person they're trying to keep out.

I still needed a company name. Hours of scribbling, cups of tea, and an unhelpfully enthusiastic thesaurus later, I landed on Brainstorm Security. In my last policing role, we held brainstorming sessions to work out how best to dismantle serious and organised crime networks. No idea was too stupid, no source too unlikely; everything on the table. I loved that – an open door for ingenuity. And after brain surgery, the name felt apt enough to be irresistible. Brainstorm it was.

One winter's evening, I registered the business and stepped into a new world of marketing, sales, finance, proposals, invoices, contracts, the whole merry-go-round. Then the client work itself, which I thoroughly enjoy.

I have always loved being a lifelong learner. I have definitely been exercising my brain since leaving the hospital. It turns out that recovering from a life-threatening incident teaches you a peculiar kind of confidence. Not the swaggering sort, but the steady, quiet kind. The belief that you can try something new and survive it, even if you fall headlong on the first go!

These days, I still drift and meander when walking, especially if I'm tired, and my children still remind me of the great 100-metre face-plant whenever they want a laugh. But I walk unaided, I work to my own rhythm, and I choose to do the things that make sense to me.

Life is short. Tomorrow isn't guaranteed. And if you're lucky, you get to pick your race, stumble gloriously on the first step, and still cross the line grinning.

Spead the word

If you enjoyed this book, please consider leaving an honest rating/review. It helps me as an independent author to be found by readers among the millions of other books for sale, and I personally read every review!

Reviews on Amazon and Goodreads.com really help, but sharing a picture of the book and what you thought of it on a social media post, means your friends also get to know about the book too!

Scan the QR code to leave a review on Amazon.

https://bit.ly/stoppolice

Thankyou

Richard

Acknowledgements

My deepest thanks go to my award-winning editor, **David Meikle of Clever Writing, located in Winchester, https://www.cleverwriting.co.uk**. From our very first meeting in a café at a train station, you understood exactly what I was trying to achieve with this book. You supported and guided my writing with patience, insight and skill, helping me tell the stories of my life with clarity and purpose. Your expertise in English, grammar and developmental editing strengthened every chapter, and your encouragement kept me writing when the road felt long. I am truly grateful.

To **Angela Forsyth**, for your attention to detail and keen eye. Helping me proofread this book was not a quick task and I am ever so grateful for all your assistance, and constructive comments.

To my small team of **ARC readers**, who had opportunity to 'test drive' the book before anybody else. You are all stars and I am grateful for your comments.

To **Steve Woodward**, for his help and assistance in obtaining images of police vehicles from that era. His own book., **Kilo Sierra Five One: Policing Portsmouth in the 1980s**, is a great read that details policing Southsea and Portsmouth a decade before. I can highly recommend it.

To **my parents** — thank you for your love, support, and for raising me with strong morals and a solid work ethic. When I was younger, I did some stupid stuff, but my sense of right and wrong made sense of it all in the end. Those foundations have carried me through every chapter of my life.

To my wife, **Janet** — your love, humour, support, and love of the outdoors keep me grounded and remind me what really matters. I truly was very lucky to have met you and fallen in love with you when I first moved down south. You stood by me through the 'in sickness and in health' bit, when others might have walked away. You nursed me, cared for me, and helped me back to health, and I will be forever grateful. I love you.

To **Anna and Ellie**, my two beautiful daughters — I love you both dearly and could not be prouder of the kind, caring, ambitious young women you are becoming. Just remember: the dishwasher does not load or unload itself.

To my siblings — **Geoff, Sue and Tim** — thank you for being the best brothers and sister anyone could ask for, and for everything you taught me growing up. And to the wider Foster family — too many to name, but you know who you are — I treasure every family gathering, every drink shared, every story told.

To **Chris Stone** for all your support over the years and creative assistance as a graphic designer, making my book cover ideas come to life. I could not be happier with the results, a big thank you! **https://stone-creative.com/**. I also thank **Giff** for welcoming me into the family, and not letting the cat out of the bag, the day you saw me buying an engagement ring to propose to your sister!

To **The Boyz** — Brad, H, Matty and Jon — friends since the age of five. Your friendship has been a constant through every stage of my life. We still meet up, still take the piss out of each other, still laugh until it hurts. We did some stupid, crazy teenage things together, and I wouldn't change a single moment.

To my **wider circle of friends** — in Rochdale, Portsmouth, and across the world — there are far too many of you to list, but if your name isn't here, it's not because I've forgotten you. I love you all.

My heartfelt thanks go to the **NHS staff** at the QA Hospital in Portsmouth and at Southampton University Hospital. Saving lives and caring for people takes an entire team — from porters and catering staff to nurses, doctors and surgeons. Public services are often criticised, yet they continue to work under immense pressure, fuelled by professionalism and goodwill. You are all heroes.

A special thank you to the **Neurology Department at Southampton General Hospital**. Your compassion, skill and humanity know no bounds. You not only saved my life — you helped me rebuild it. The tub of Celebrations I brought in after my discharge will never feel like enough.

I owe particular gratitude to the specialist consultant neurosurgeon **Mr Salima Wahab**, who first stabilised my condition and diagnosed the haemorrhage caused by the AVM at the back of my brain. And to **Professor Diederik Bulters**, who carried out the long and complex surgery that removed the AVM — thank you. Your skill kept me alive and preserved everything that makes me who I am: my humour, my memories, my personality, my love of life. Facing an operation like that is terrifying, yet you reassured me and my family with honesty and confidence. No one could promise a perfect outcome, but I am living proof of your extraordinary ability. You're a legend — feel free to quote that on your GMC profile. Just remember: keep your feet on the ground. It's only brain surgery!

I know you lead a major research team working to improve treatment for vascular disorders of the brain and spine. I wish you every success in helping others in the future. If any very wealthy readers feel moved to support a worthy cause, I encourage you to look up Professor Bulters and the research programmes he leads.

My thanks also go to the **Scouting movement in the UK** and the **Boy Scouts of America**. Both gave me confidence, opportunity, and experiences I would never otherwise have had. To everyone — staff and scouts — who ever spent time at Parker Mountain Scout Reservation, thank you. That place will stay with me forever. 'Be Prepared'.

Thanks to my other family — my **policing family**. 'The Job' is hard, demanding and sometimes dangerous. Policing, rooted in the Peelian principles of 1829, is built on trust, consent, public cooperation and the belief that *the police are the public and the public are the police*. I have been privileged to serve for nearly three decades, meeting people from every walk of life — from those with nothing to those who rule nations.

Most encounters were in moments of crisis, and I could never have done this work without the support, care, humour and guidance of my fellow officers and staff.

To everyone I have stood beside — Constables, Sergeants, Inspectors, Chief Constables, and all the support staff who keep the wheels turning — thank you. The media may not always show it, but the vast majority of officers are good people doing their best for the public. Tutoring new cops, helping them find their feet on the streets — **Caroline** and **George** come to mind immediately — has been one of the great privileges of my career.

It was an amazing job, and I loved it.

And finally, **to you, the reader** — thank you for investing your time, your attention, and your money into learning about my life. You didn't have to pick up this book, but you did, and that means more to me than you might realise. I hope my story has informed you, moved you, made you laugh, made you think, or simply kept you company for a while. Your willingness to walk alongside me through these pages is something I deeply appreciate.

A collection of photographs and memories from me growing up and working in Rochdale, travelling in America, joining the police and maybe even a few brain surgery scars can be found at **https://www.richard-foster.net** for those of you interested or fancy a jog down memory lane.

www.ingramcontent.com/pod-product-compliance
Lightning Source LLC
Chambersburg PA
CBHW021219060726
47590CB00005B/1565